GENDER-CLASS
EQUALITY IN POLITICAL
ECONOMIES

Gender-Class Equality in Political Economies offers an in-depth analysis across six countries to reveal why gender-class equality in paid and unpaid work remains elusive, and what more policy might do to achieve better social and economic outcomes. This book is the first to meld cross-time with cross-country comparisons, link macro structures to micro behavior, and connect class with gender dynamics to yield fresh insights into where we are on the road to gender equality, why it varies across industrialized countries, and the barriers to further progress.

Lynn Prince Cooke is a professor of sociology at the University of Surrey, UK. Her research, exploring policy effects on group outcomes, has appeared in *American Journal of Sociology, European Sociological Review,* and *Journal of Marriage and Family,* for which she co-authored the 2010 decade review essay on cross-national research.

Perspectives on Gender

Edited by Myra Marx Ferree, University of Wisconsin–Madison

Black Feminist Thought
Patricia Hill Collins

Black Women and White Women in the Professions
Natalie J. Sokoloff

Community Activism and Feminist Politics
Edited by Nancy Naples

Complex Inequality
Leslie McCall

Disposable Women and Other Myths of Global Capitalism
Melissa W. Wright

Feminism and the Women's Movement
Barbara Ryan

Fixing Families
Jennifer A. Reich

For Richer, for Poorer
Demie Kurz

Gender Consciousness and Politics
Sue Tolleson Rinehart

Global Gender Research
Christine E. Bose and Minejeong Kim

Grassroots Warriors
Nancy A. Naples

Home-Grown Hate
Edited by Abby L. Ferber

Integrative Feminisms
Angela Miles

Laboring On
Wendy Simonds, Barbara Katz Rothman and Bari Meltzer Norman

Maid in the U.S.A.
Mary Romero

Mothering
*Edited by Evelyn Nakano Glenn,
Grace Chang and
Linda Rennie Forcey*

Rape Work
Patricia Yancey Martin

Regulating Sex
*Edited by Elizabeth Bernstein and
Laurie Schaffner*

Rock-a-by Baby
Verta Taylor

School-smart and Mother-wise
Wendy Luttrell

Stepping Out of Line
Cheryl Hercus

The Social Economy of Single
Motherhood
Margaret Nelson

Understanding Sexual
Violence
Diana Scully

When Sex Became Gender
Shira Tarrant

Making Transnational
Feminism
Millie Thayer

Gender and Judging
Sally Kenney

GENDER-CLASS EQUALITY IN POLITICAL ECONOMIES

Lynn Prince Cooke

University of Surrey, UK

Routledge
Taylor & Francis Group

NEW YORK AND LONDON

First published 2011
by Routledge
270 Madison Avenue, New York, NY 10016

Simultaneously published in the UK
by Routledge
2 Park Square, Milton Park, Abingdon, Oxon OX14 4RN

Routledge is an imprint of the Taylor & Francis Group, an informa business

© 2011 Taylor & Francis

The right of Lynn Prince Cooke to be identified as author of this work has been asserted by her in accordance with sections 77 and 78 of the Copyright, Designs and Patents Act 1988.

Typeset in Adobe Caslon by RefineCatch Limited, Bungay, Suffolk
Printed and bound in the United States of America on acid-free paper by Walsworth Publishing Company, Marceline, MO

All rights reserved. No part of this book may be reprinted or reproduced or utilized in any form or by any electronic, mechanical, or other means, now known or hereafter invented, including photocopying and recording, or in any information storage or retrieval system, without permission in writing from the publishers.

Trademark Notice: Product or corporate names may be trademarks or registered trademarks, and are used only for identification and explanation without intent to infringe.

Library of Congress Cataloging in Publication Data
Cooke, Lynn P.
Gender-class equality in political economies / Lynn Prince Cooke.
p. cm. — (Perspectives on gender)
Includes bibliographical references and index.
1. Sexual division of labor. 2. Pay equity. 3. Women—Employment—Government policy. 4. Women—Economic conditions. 5. Minorities—Employment—Government policy. 6. Minorities—Economic conditions. 7. Labor policy—Social aspects. 8. Income distribution—Social aspects. 9. Equality. I. Title.
HD6060.6.C66 2011
331.4—dc22

2010052904

ISBN13: 978–0–415–99441–5 (hbk)
ISBN13: 978–0–415–99442–2 (pbk)
ISBN13: 978–0–203–89062–2 (ebk)

SUSTAINABLE
FORESTRY
INITIATIVE

Certified Sourcing
www.sfiprogram.org

The SFI label applies to the text stock.

Contents

LIST OF ILLUSTRATIONS   XI
SERIES FOREWORD   XV
PREFACE   XXI
ACKNOWLEDGEMENTS   XXV

CHAPTER 1 GENDER-CLASS EQUALITY OVER TIME   1
  Introduction   1
  The State and Institutional Equality Frames   5
  The Country Cases: Policy Effects on Class v.
    Gender Equality   7
  The Resilience of Inequality Within Its Institutional Frame 11
  Book Overview   13

CHAPTER 2 PAID AND UNPAID WORK IN CONTEXT   21
  Introduction   21
  Gender Differences in Labor Supply and Demand   22
  The State and the Labor Market   27
  The State and a Gendered Division of Household Labor   31
  So What Happened to the Gender Revolution?   35
  Gender-Class Equality in Post-Industrial Economies   36
  Summary: Policy Paths and Gender-Class Equality   42

CHAPTER 3 POPULATION POLICIES AND GROUP DIVIDES   45
  Introduction   45
  Nineteenth-Century Expansion and Women's Bodies   48

Nineteenth-Century Immigration Policies   52
Post-War Family Policies   55
Immigration Policies in the Post-War Economic Recovery   59
Reproduction in the "New" Global Economy   61
Immigration in the "New" Global Economy   67
Summary: New World, Old Social Order   69

CHAPTER 4 EDUCATIONAL FOUNDATIONS OF EQUALITY   71
Education and the Institutional Equality Frame   71
Group Differences in Educational Foundations   73
Post-War Expansion of Pre-Primary Provision   80
More Secondary Education for All   87
Expanding Educational Attainment   95
Educational Structures and Relative Group Equality   100

CHAPTER 5 POLICY FOUNDATIONS OF GENDER-CLASS
           EMPLOYMENT EQUALITY   103
Introduction   103
Australian Versus US Nineteenth-Century
     Worker Mobilization   106
European Post-War Employment Policies   109
Australian Versus US Post-War Equality Initiatives   114
The European Union and Gender Equality   117
Work-Family Reconciliation Policies and
     Gender Equality   121
Gender-Class Employment Equality in the
     Twenty-First Century   127

CHAPTER 6 CURRENT GENDER-CLASS EMPLOYMENT
           EQUALITY   131
Introduction   131
The Institutional Equality Frame and
     Employment Status   132
Individual Characteristics and Employment in Context   134
Weekly Work Hours of Employed Individuals in Context   142
Gender-Class Wage Inequalities in Context   149

Summary: Employment Equality in Its Institutional
   Equality Frame   157
Technical Appendix   160

CHAPTER 7 GENDER-CLASS EQUALITY IN PAID AND
            UNPAID WORK   167
   Introduction   167
   Housework Over Time and Across Countries   169
   Who Does Any Housework in Context?   173
   Predicting Individual Housework Hours in Context   176
   Couple Time in Paid and Unpaid Work in Context   180
   Equality Exchanges in Their Institutional Frames   186
   Technical Appendix   190

CHAPTER 8 SUSTAINABLE POLICY FOR GREATER EQUALITY   195
   The Resilience of Complex Inequality   195
   The Inefficiency of Market Inequalities   202
   Social Investment Strategies   208
   Policy and Sustainable Unpaid Time   212

NOTES   217
BIBLIOGRAPHY   229
INDEX   259

ILLUSTRATIONS

Tables

3.1	Crude Birth Rates 1870, 1900, 1935–39	52
3.2	Summary of Initial Post-War Family Allowances	56
3.3	Post-War Crude Birth Rates, 1950–54, 1960–64	58
3.4	Abortions/1,000 Women Aged 15–44 in 1986, 1996, 2003	64
3.5	Foreign-Born Population 2005	68
4.1	Percentage of Secondary Students in Private and Public Schools, circa 2004	90
5.1	National Social Expenditures and Percent of Children under 17 Living in Poverty, circa 2000	122
5.2	Relative Class and Gender Equality in Paid and Unpaid Work in the Case Countries, circa 2000	129
6.1	Marginal Effects of Individual Characteristics on Likelihood of Being Employed, circa 2000	137
6.2	Unadjusted Mean Hourly Wages and 90/10 Ratio, Employed Men and Women circa 2000, $US equivalents	151
6A.1	Coefficients from Pooled OLS Regression Predicting Weekly Employment Hours, circa 2000	161
6A.2	Predicting Log of Hourly Wages Controlling for Selection into Employment, circa 2000	163
6A.3	Predicted Log Hourly Wages from Two-Stage Model (Table 6A.2)	164

7.1   Marginal Effects of Individual Characteristics on
       Likelihood of Performing any Housework, Men and
       Women Aged 20–54 in 2002   174
7A.1   Coefficients from Pooled OLS Regression Predicting
       Weekly Housework Hours 2002   192
7A.2   Partnered Women and Men's Predicted Weekly Hours
       in Paid and Unpaid Work by Educational Attainment,
       circa 2001   193
8.1   Relative Class and Gender Equality, circa 2000   201

Figures

1.1   Relative Gender-Class Equality in Australia, East and
       West Germany, Spain, the United Kingdom, and the
       United States   8
2.1   Policy Effects on Household Production   34
3.1   Number of Marriages/1,000 Population, 1970 v. 2007   65
3.2   Nonmarital Births as Percent All Births, 1970 v. 2007   66
4.1   Percentage of Age Group Enrolled in Public or Private
       Child Care, circa 2004   86
4.2   Secondary Education Gross Enrollment Ratios, 1955,
       1970, 2000   88
4.3   Average Country PISA Scores by Father's Educational
       Attainment, 15-Year-Olds in 2003   91
4.4   Rural-Urban Difference in Average PISA Scores,
       15-Year-Olds in 2003, 2006   92
4.5   Between-Group Equality: Immigrant and Gender
       Differences in Average PISA Scores, 15-Year-Olds
       in 2003   93
4.6   Educational Attainment as of 2005, 25- to 64-Year-Olds   99
6.1   Usual Weekly Employment, Men and Women
       Age 20–54, circa 2000   135
6.2   Main and Country Effects of Individual Predictors of
       Weekly Employment Hours by Gender, circa 2000   144
6.3   Women's and Men's Wage Returns to a University
       Degree Across the Wage Distribution, circa 2000   153

6.4   Adjusted Gender Wage Gap Across the Wage
      Distribution, circa 2000   156
7.1   Main and Country Predictors of Men's and Women's
      Weekly Housework Hours Among Those Performing
      Any Housework, 2002   177
7.2   Partnered Women and Men's Predicted Weekly
      Household Hours in Employment and Housework by
      Educational Attainment, circa 2001   182

SERIES FOREWORD

From the time that the Perspectives on Gender series began in the 1980s, it was dedicated to presenting feminist research on gender that was oriented to change. Its enduring commitment has been to highlight the specificity and dynamism that characterize the social relations of gender, and to do so with special attention to the interactions of race, class and gender in a way that has since come to be called intersectional.

Many of the early books in the series focused on the United States alone and explicitly drew out the dynamics of race and gender, such as Natalie Sokoloff's *Black and White Women in the Professions*, Patricia Hill Collins' *Black Feminist Thought*, Mary Romero's *Maid in America*, and Evelyn Nakano Glenn, Grace Chang and Lynne Forcey's *Mothering*. Others, such as Wendy Luttrell's *School-smart and Mother-wise*, Nancy Naples' *Grassroots Warriors* and Peggy Nelson's *Working Hard and Making Do*, foregrounded the experiences of working-class women and the particular challenges facing them because of the combination of their limited economic resources and the pervasive social devaluation of their knowledge, labor and identities.

However, the series has always understood gender relations as dynamic, and not just changing over time of their own accord but as a result of struggles for greater social justice. Thus books in this series took up issues of transformations in gender relations across multiple dimensions and sites. Studies that focused on the US in analyzing change included those considering the relation between feminist identity and political parties (Sue Tolleson Rinehart's *Gender Consciousness and Politics*) and the roots of 1970s feminist consciousness in women's research and gender theories of the 1950s (Shira Tarrant's *When Sex Became Gender*) as well as studies of the activists and their allies in movements around women's health (Verta Taylor's *Rock-a-bye Baby*) and violence against women (Patricia Yancey Martin's *Rape Work*).

Although understanding gender relations in the US is important, it has been the aim of this series also to make clear that understanding the challenges of feminist transformation and applying an intersectional analysis demands looking beyond the boundaries of the US. One of the earliest scholarly books to engage with feminism as a transnational movement was Angela Miles' *Integrative Feminisms: Building Global Visions*. Miles brought her perspective as a Canadian engaged in transnational women's movements to set the tone for considering how feminist politics develops and travels across national borders, while focusing on the "two-thirds world" that is neither affluent nor Western. More recently, Christine Bose and Minjeong Kim, in *Global Gender Research*, take up the challenge of understanding the particular international contexts for the issues with which feminists engage both as activists and as scholars. Bose and Kim's wonderful collection of regionally situated essays illuminates the similarities as well as differences in problems facing women in specific parts of the world, and stresses activist research done by feminists in these countries to explain and transform gender relations accordingly. The global perspective of the series has also been evident in case studies of feminist mobilization in Australia (Cheryl Hercus' *Stepping out of Line*) as well as Millie Thayer's innovative recent study of intersectional issues and international funding as gender relations theory and intersectional practice comes to women's mobilization in Brazil (*Making Transnational Feminism*).

The series has also been methodologically inclusive, highlighting excellent quantitative work as well as ethnographic studies. One such brilliant quantitative study, Leslie McCall's *Complex Inequality*, broke new ground in intersectional feminist analysis of social stratification by offering a grounded account of gender, race, and class inequalities as interacting with particular local economies in the US. Like Sokoloff's earlier analysis of gender and race interactions, McCall's study used complex quantitative data to make her theoretical points but made her analysis accessible through well-organized tables and charts and highly readable prose.

Lynn Prince Cooke's current book follows in this tradition of presenting a complex argument simply and effectively, as well as offering a truly integrated account of social policy origins and outcomes across class and country. Cooke manages to use qualitative, comparative historical process-tracing models of policy development to ground a quantitative analysis comparing the economic effects of such national policies on individuals with different personal choices and histories within each different system. The book follows McCall's injunction to place gender inequality in a context that is shaped by the intersections of multiple inequalities and the particularities of the place itself. But while the variation that McCall explored was between the economies of the Rust Belt and Sun Belt in the US, Cooke tackles a more ambitious agenda in comparing the forms that gender and class inequality take in relation to each other across six complex and historically shifting political economies: Germany (East and West), Spain, Australia, the UK and the US. Moreover, Cooke takes on the further challenge of addressing these policy systems as equally shaped by state concerns about reproduction as they are by the more classically studied politics of production.

This volume thus picks up the challenge that Bose and Kim set for feminist scholarship: to locate the specificity of gender relations in their appropriate local contexts, and to understand contemporary transformations shaped by both the problems and opportunities produced in the past. While Bose and Kim present the diversity of regions in a set of local cases, Cooke integrates the case studies of policy histories with a grounded comparative analysis of women's and men's economic outcomes as shaped by the particularities of national reproductive politics and economic development in advanced industrial democracies. This is a uniquely powerful tool for unpacking the processes underlying the outcomes, and there are many fascinating correspondences that Cooke unearths. For example, her analysis of the structures of educational systems and their effects on class and gender inequalities points to the

XVIII   GENDER-CLASS EQUALITY IN POLITICAL ECONOMIES

similar problems facing Australia and the US in delivering state-funded education to a far-flung, sometimes sparse, and racially stratified population, compared to the different challenges faced by Germany and the UK in educating their dense but highly class-stratified populations.

Cooke does a splendid job here in combining the structures that have developed historically with the contemporary choices facing women and men as individual actors attempting to make it in these systems. But in addition to the balance between structure and agency that her analytic strategy achieves, her understanding of the relevant policy structures is feminist in its integration of systems of reproduction (population policies and education as systems of institutionalizing nations and group differences within them) and systems of production (with education, employment and wage-setting systems in the center of these stratification processes). By taking this approach, Cooke no longer "adds gender and stirs" it into the customary male-centered story of stratification, but rethinks the fundamental processes of inequality as being simultaneously about production and reproduction. The challenge of intersectionality to feminist theory has long been to go beyond additive models, such as the classic "dual systems" theories of the 1980s, to understand the mutual co-construction of inequalities. Cooke succeeds so well in placing reproduction—as both a policy structure and an individual choice of childbearing and a household division of unpaid labor and of time—in an integrated and important position in the overall story of stratification that one might wonder how the old-style production-only accounts ever seemed plausible. The opportunities and lack thereof for women and men are far more understandable when time and money, work and family are part of the story of how states shape fates.

Finally, Cooke's account is feminist also in considering her purpose not merely to describe inequalities but to end them. Because education figures centrally in the systems of both reproduction and production, and education policy plays a key role in the particular constellations of both family and employment opportunities, it is appropriate that her conclusion emphasizes ways that education systems might be transformed to create more fairness for men and women at all class levels.

The critical first five years of a child's life has implications for the opportunities for equality for the parents as well as for the children, and the way that education connects—or fails to—with the labor force is similarly powerful for shaping class and gender inequalities for each cohort coming to adulthood. While also emphasizing that individuals in each national system are making choices, Cooke presents clearly how those choices are enabled and constrained by the systems that make particular options attractive or difficult, and that everything is connected to everything else when it comes to having, raising, educating and supporting children. But as policy-makers are increasingly coming to realize, there is no future without children to carry it on. By focusing many of her conclusions on the role of educational systems as such, Cooke offers a constructive way to think about this future that challenges both the nationalistic pronatalist and economistic human capital approaches. Although placing social justice in the center, her vision of the opportunities for gender-class equality is solidly grounded in the actual systems she so carefully and thoroughly examines throughout the book. I hope that future authors in this series will take up her challenge to expand and deepen this type of intersectional feminist analysis of inequalities, as she has taken up the gauntlet thrown down by previous authors we have had the pleasure of publishing.

Myra Marx Ferree
Series Editor

PREFACE

The academic world reveres the people who drill deeper and deeper into a narrowly defined topic. I am a woman prone to saying, "yeah, but . . .," and asking where specific research findings fit in the big picture. I cannot even stay within the confines of a single discipline. Where does sociology of gender fit with class analysis? How do these mesh with comparative politics? How does history inform modern social relations? Can the parsimonious models of labor economics be contextualized to offer more accurate pictures of divisions of labor in the home and across countries? These are the questions I ask my colleagues when they present their research at conferences. These are the questions I ask my students after summarizing what an eminent scholar has to say on a topic.

This book reflects my own search for answers to some of these questions, a search that has taken me across careers and continents, as well as academic disciplines. The search began in a nonprofit organization in the Pacific Northwest, where I worked in the early 1990s with community leaders to research and develop programs in school-to-work, work-based training, and other policies that affected what the politicians called "workforce capacity." In our search for policy possibilities, a group of area business, labor, non-profit, and education leaders took a study tour of Denmark, Germany, and Sweden. This was my first exposure to how other countries organized their divisions of labor in society and it would profoundly shape my subsequent personal and professional life. In homage to lifelong learning, I returned for a doctorate in midlife to compare German and US policy effects on employment across the life course. A four-month stay in Florence as a guest researcher of the European University Institute sparked my interest in Mediterranean countries. I transferred from my US university to Nuffield College, Oxford University, to be in the middle of my European comparisons. In the midst of the Nuffield focus on British class stratification, I became fascinated by gender and family as sources of stratification. Eighteen months on, a postdoctoral fellowship in Brisbane, Australia, revealed just how different the Anglophone countries were from one another.

Living and learning in so many places has given me a distinctive appreciation of how our lives are embedded in our social categories within different countries. This book offers a synthesis of this knowledge, presented so that the story can unfold for a variety of readers. The book format lends itself very well to teaching, since it builds up a model of how gender-class inequality is constructed over time and then shows how it works today. Instructors can assign individual chapters for specific areas of sociology, such as sociology of education (Chapter 4), sociology of work (Chapters 5 and 6), or sociology of gender (Chapters 3 and 7). Chapters 3 through 5 could be used in labor economics, political science, or sociology courses that use historical comparisons. The book as a whole presents an excellent primary reading in any foundation course on gender or comparative social policy.

For undergraduates, the story is how important the social context is to their experience of daily life, and how their todays are the sum of yesterdays that started long before Twitter. For graduate students, the synthesis of cross-national literature and comparative evidence highlights the many holes in our knowledge to be filled by future scholars. The book also drills down to make its own contribution to our knowledge of the gendered divisions of paid and unpaid work in context. Gender researchers in the 1980s concluded that the gender revolution in paid and unpaid work had stalled. Most explanations focused on women's and men's individual choices, either as rational strategies or as a way of "doing" gender to fit with conventions. This book offers a structural examination of these conventions. I demonstrate how state policies and the institutions they support reinforce gender differences in conjunction with class differences across the life course. The book offers insights into these intersectional effects through a distinctive multi-method approach: historical policy comparisons of six countries are coupled with rigorous multivariate comparisons of current gender-class inequality in paid work hours, wages, and housework. The book thus uniquely offers both breadth and depth to understanding gender-class equality, intersectionally and in context.

ACKNOWLEDGEMENTS

It takes a virtual village to write a book. This particular book would not have emerged from the writing process without the unwavering, if at times exasperated support of Myra Marx Ferree. Many thanks are also owed to Heike Trappe, who clarified endless details on East and West Germany. Invaluable advice at critical junctures was given by Michaela Kreyenfeld, Margarita Leon, Rob Mare, Charles Ragin, and Chiara Saraceno. Thanks also to Jennifer Hook for running overviews of multinational time use data for Spain and Germany, and Liana Sayer for doing so for Australia, the United Kingdom and the United States. Adam Burgess, Ruben Flores, and Sarah Moore made useful suggestions on earlier versions of some chapters. The then-blind reviewers of the project provided very constructive comments on both content and style; I'd like to now thank:

- Leslie McCall of Northwestern University
- Elif Andac of Kansas University
- Tom Janoski of University of Kentucky
- Paula England of Stanford University
- Janet Holland of London South Bank University
- Susan Mannon at Utah State University.

I trust Steve Rutter, the Routledge Sociology editor, has survived the process with his reliably good humor intact.

Luxembourg's La Fond supported the earliest of stages of this research as it blossomed from my 2004 doctoral thesis. The British

Academy funded part of the cost of presenting the initial ideas at the 2007 American Sociological Association annual meeting in New York City. The UK's Economic and Social Research Council provided essential financial support of the employment analyses summarized in Chapter 6, which funded the able research assistance of Pierre Walthery and Katie Hoffman.

Equally important has been my steadfast cheering squad during the moments of existential angst that occur for all writers. My bevy of beauties included Belinda Hewitt, Edie Lewis, John Goldthorpe, Olli Kangas, and John Western, all of whom offered food, wine, and/or intellectual solace as necessary.

In the end, however, writing a book is a solitary process. So there is no one else to blame but me for any remaining errors, omissions, or misrepresentations of the complex social worlds in which we live and labor.

Lynn Prince Cooke
July 2010

1

GENDER-CLASS EQUALITY OVER TIME

Introduction

Equality in industrial economies remains elusive. Gender, class, and ethnic gaps in education, employment, and domestic tasks all persist in the twenty-first century, despite the equal opportunity, affirmative action, and gender mainstreaming policies enacted during the twentieth century. Today, women often complete more years of education than men, but afterwards gender inequalities in paid and unpaid work widen across adulthood. More men than women are employed continuously and work full- rather than part-time. Men also enjoy greater average wages. Women, in turn, spend more time than men in unpaid house-work and child care whether or not they are employed. So where did we stall on the road to gender equality in paid and unpaid work?

This book answers this question by tracing how state policies structured relative gender and class equality in Australia, East and West Germany, Spain, the United Kingdom, and the United States. The state was a new entity that evolved with industrialization (Anderson 1974; Weber 1968). Yet classical liberal tenets held that any state interference in the market would undermine economic efficiency and growth (Freeden 1978). The "invisible hand" of self-interest (Smith 1970 [1776]: 184) ensured market efficiency as individuals negotiated work hours and wages directly with employers. The resulting income inequality created the necessary individual incentive for further economic growth (Kuznets 1963). States were therefore reluctant to implement any regulations or policies that affected the employee-employer relationship.

States had their own interests, however, and were not simply hand-maidens to the market. Concern over economic and military competitiveness and political stability encouraged governments to diverge from liberal tenets and introduce the first policies affecting individuals and the labor market (Freeden 1978; Glass 1967). Class-related policies regulated the training, work hours, relative wages, and benefits of those in employment. For example, England's 1833 Factory Act restricted children's employment hours and required employers to educate them (David 1980). Compulsory schooling expanded in all of the countries during this period, most rapidly in the United States. Germany introduced industrial accident insurance in 1871 and pensions in 1889 (Pierson 1998: Table 4.1). Australian men were guaranteed "family wages" with the 1907 Harvester Judgement.

The paid work of industrial production systems represented just half of modern life. Supporting it were the reproduction system and unpaid work associated with family. There are many forms of family, but state policies generally legitimated heterosexual families and different activities for the men and women within them (Collins 2000; Fink 2001; Walby 2009). Men were assumed to be the independent workers, although states frequently imposed further restrictions on immigrant men. Women were assumed to be responsible for the unpaid work that sustained families and communities (Pateman 1988). Women's responsibility for society's unpaid work limited their ability to be men's economic equal in the market, and men's responsibility for paid work limited their ability to provide equal unpaid support to families and communities.

All states therefore inserted gender, class, and other group differences in the work associated with the market and family. Yet states were not independent institutions. As detailed in this book, the specific policies implemented and the resultant group differences reflected other institutions. For example, the institutions of "family" and "market" differed across countries. In Spain and West Germany, Roman Catholic precepts strongly influenced family policy. The church was also an important provider of education and charity in Australia and England. Ethnic divides differed as well. Densely populated European countries sent migrants; the Americas and Australia received them.

The state was therefore a single institutional pole in what I call an *institutional equality frame* that structured relative gender, class, and other group equality in paid and unpaid work. The frame was not a simple border around the market and family, but an institutional cage that constrained group choices among the components of paid and unpaid work. Components of paid work included employment hours, occupations, wages, autonomy, supervision, and the like. Unpaid work components included child and elder care, cooking, shopping, house-work, running errands, and community volunteer work. These components of work complemented each other within the institutional frame, but not all work components were equally valued. As noted by Heidi Hartmann (1981: 18): "Capitalist development creates places for a hier-archy of workers, but . . . [g]ender and racial hierarchies determine who fills the empty places."

The institutional equality frame reinforced these hierarchies as state policies allocated the work of the new industrial order among social groups. Population policies affected who had children and who was responsible for their care, which reaffirmed the state's desired class and ethnic mix as well as gender differences in unpaid work. Public schooling provided the bedrock of education and skills later rewarded in the labor market (Mincer 1974), but the schooling systems systematically privileged some groups over others. The regulation of work hours, wages, and enti-tlements to sickness, unemployment, and parental benefits reflected soci-etal expectations of adults' time allocations among employment, family, and leisure activities. These time allocations, in turn, created group differ-ences in the accumulated work experience and on-the-job training that determined wages. Accumulated lifetime earnings determined individual financial circumstances in later years. State policies therefore affected relative group advantage and disadvantage from birth through old age.

Not all groups were subject to the same policies, but the group policies needed to complement one another just as the different components of "work" complemented one another (Verloo 2006). For example, policies that encouraged women to leave employment when they married created labor shortages. These shortages could be balanced by more open immigration policies. Immigration policies frequently controlled the numbers of ethnically diverse migrants, barred immigrants from bringing other family members, or restricted immigrants' access to state provisions such as education and unemployment benefits (Sainsbury 2006). Our relative advantage or disadvantage within the institutional frame therefore cannot be determined by single characteristic such as gender or class or ethnicity, but by the accumulated policy effects at what Crenshaw (1989) termed the "intersection" of our group memberships (see also Hancock 2007; McCall 2001; Verloo 2006).

Each country's frame therefore supported a given socio-economic equilibrium among the work components and social groups, but not equality for all groups. Any changes in the market, population, or policy in turn necessitated a reshuffling within the institutional equality frame to reach a new equilibrium. For example, class victories in early welfare state provisions advanced economic equality among more men, but often by limiting the employment opportunities for women, ethnic minorities, and immigrants (Freeman and Birrell 2001; Mink 1986; O'Connor 1993). Equal opportunity and affirmative action legislation implemented after World War II enabled some women and ethnic minorities to complete higher levels of education and pursue better jobs, but widened class differences within these groups (McLanahan 2004; Sobotka 2008). Growth in female employment increased class differences in unpaid work. Less-educated women and immigrant workers performed the domestic work of affluent households but could not afford to purchase such services for themselves (Anderson 2000; Gupta 2007).

In short, I argue the march toward greater equality stalled because its pursuit is a zero-sum exchange: advances for one group are invariably offset by losses for other groups or elsewhere within the frame. This offset could occur in a multitude of places. As will be shown here, policy support for greater class equality could lead to women's exclusion from the labor market, women's over-representation in part-time employ-ment, and/or more unpaid work in the home. Policy support for gender employment equality crowded out time for unpaid work, which remained gendered. As a result, those who enjoyed the greatest degree of equality in paid or unpaid work sacrificed time and/or money. In other words, there is no policy or market "silver bullet" that eradicates gender-class inequality.

The State and Institutional Equality Frames

The zero-sum nature of gender-class equality over time has eluded us to date because it is not revealed in research focused on policy effects at specific historical periods,[1] or that compared current gender equality in just one or two components of paid and unpaid work.[2] In this book I combine comparative-historical and individual-level analyses to develop a more comprehensive picture of gender-class equality in national context and over time. The emphasis throughout the book will be the policy and market effects on relative equality in paid and unpaid work at the intersection of class and gender—hence "gender-class." The comparative method is used to explore the comprehensive structures and large-scale processes that patterned social life (Tilly 1984). The outcome of interest is why gender-class inequalities in paid and unpaid work persisted across industrialized societies despite some impressive policy triumphs over the past half century.

Answering this question entails comparing how states institutional-ized a group hierarchy through initial policies, regulations, and provi-sions, and the impact of subsequent policy innovations on gender-class equality. Institutions represent strategic contexts and shared cultural understandings (Grief 1994). These understandings affect the way economic, social, or political challenges are perceived and the range of possible solutions considered acceptable (Thelen 1999: 371). Most importantly, institutions reveal and reproduce power relations within a society (Stinchcombe 1997).

This book examines these processes by revealing (1) the different insti-tutional arrangements that emerged in countries facing similar external pressures, (2) the role of institutions as coordinating mechanisms that sustained a country's socio-economic equilibrium, and (3) what happened in the aftermath of significant social or policy change—i.e. what were the new gender-class equilibria (Levi 1997; North 1990; Pierson 2000; Thelen 1999).

To accomplish this, I trace the evolution of state provisions in Australia, Germany, Spain, the United Kingdom, and the United States from the early nineteenth through the twentieth centuries. States all faced similar challenges in the process of industrialization: the best way to deal with worker mobilization (class), the new global flows of immigrants (ethnicity), and the sharp decline in fertility that accompanied industrialization (gender). As detailed here, countries differed in the level of concern generated by these changes. In the end, however, all states moved away from liberal tenets and instead took a more active role in ensuring individuals' well-being or "welfare."

States differed, however, in the nature of the new regulations and welfare provisions (Titmuss 1958). The historical comparisons reveal the diversity in policies and the institutions they complemented or created in each of the countries. The institutional equality frames also differed because of practical considerations. For example, Orloff and Skocpol (1984) argued that in the nineteenth century, the United States lacked the established civil bureaucracy of England that supported the latter's early expansion of state welfare programs. Part of the difference stemmed from the US westward expansion during this period. Yet this same local expansion that thwarted development of national welfare programs fueled development of the locally based US public schooling system far ahead of Europe (Goldin and Katz 2008). In Australia and Spain, the state met the challenge of providing education to rural communities by supporting existing religious schooling. In Australia, this resulted in a class-stratified secondary educational system that contrasted with the labor market policies that ensured greater class equality. Geographic variation in state services formed another policy dimension that affected group differences within a country.

The resulting institutional equality frames legitimated specific discursive and material relations among social groups vis-à-vis "family" and the "market" in each country (Collins 2000; Walby 2009). A detailed discussion of the political debates from which the national policies emerged is beyond the scope of this book. Instead I focus on how the specific policy choices structured each country's unique institutional frame of relative gender, class, and at times ethnic equality in paid work hours, wages, and unpaid work.

The Country Cases: Policy Effects on Class v. Gender Equality

The countries selected for comparison represent two sets of broadly similar countries in some aspects of policy, but they diverge in other policies that affect the gender-class intersections. Australia, the United Kingdom, and the United States share a British political heritage, and the first state provisions generally adhered more closely to liberal tenets (O'Connor et al. 1999). In such "liberal welfare regimes" (Esping-Andersen 1990), individuals were expected to ensure their well-being via employment. England, for example, had a long legacy of differentiating between the deserving and undeserving poor (Orloff 1993a). The United States adhered to liberal tenets in the development of corporate rather than state welfare (Kalleberg et al. 2000; Skocpol 1992). Most people in the United States were made to rely on employer-provided sickness, disability, health insurance, and other benefits, whereas the Australian and British states offered more state protections. Australia differed further from the other two English-speaking countries because of its shortage of free (as opposed to prison) labor during the nineteenth century. This restricted labor supply enhanced working-class mobilization efforts, leading to the 1907 passage of the Harvester Judgement that guaranteed Australian men a family wage sufficient for supporting a wife and three dependent children (F. Castles 1985).

With less state interference in market mechanisms, liberal markets fostered greater income inequality (Kenworthy 2008). The Gini coefficient is a commonly used measure of income inequality. It ranges from zero to one, with larger numbers indicating greater inequality. As noted in Figure 1.1, the average Gini coefficient for OECD countries in 2000 was 0.31.[3] The Gini coefficient for Australia, the United Kingdom, and the United States exceeded that, indicating greater than average income inequality in these countries. At the same time, the degree of

Source: The employment gap for 2000 is from the OECD *Employment Outlook 2002*, table 2.2 for men and women between the ages of 25 and 54. The Gini coefficient at the origin is also from OECD data, whereas the country Gini coefficients are from the Luxembourg Income Study Key Figures, www.lisproject.org/php/kf/kf.php, accessed February 25, 2010.

Figure 1.1 Relative gender-class equality in Australia, East and West Germany, Spain, the United Kingdom, and the United States

inequality across these three liberal regimes differed. As would be expected with their respective policy legacies, Australia's income inequality was closer to the average, whereas the US market imposed the greatest inequality.

Countries on the European continent implemented policies that sustained more social hierarchies than the liberal regimes. Corporatist elements required greater coordination among institutions such as employers, labor organizations, and the state (Esping-Andersen 1990; Hall and Soskice 2001). More of the population enjoyed some state welfare benefits as compared with the liberal regimes, but certain groups such as the elderly, civil servants, and skilled workers enjoyed superior benefits (Esping-Andersen 1990; Ferrera 1996).

The greater market coordination yielded greater income equality than in the liberal markets (Kenworthy 2008). This is most evident in the East and West German Gini coefficients displayed in Figure 1.1. Spain modernized much later than Germany and emerged from fascism during a period of intense global market competition (Noguera et al. 2005; Royo 2007). As a result, income inequality in Spain in 2000 was more similar to that of the United Kingdom than Germany.

The degree of class equality has been central to many mainstream welfare state theories (F. Castles 1985; Esping-Andersen 1990; Korpi 1983; Stephens 1979).[4] Feminists, however, were quick to point out that class victories were rarely socially costless (Orloff 1993b). Under the laws of supply and demand that undergird free markets, improving the working conditions or wages of some workers required limiting the employment of others. Many class victories therefore created outsider groups, usually women, ethnic minorities, and/or immigrants. The greater the early class victories, the more likely women and immigrants encountered barriers to employment (Bertola et al. 2007).

Regardless of class equality provisions, all industrialized countries imposed labor restrictions on children's and women's employment before doing so for men (Wikander et al. 1995). These policies strengthened men's position in paid work at the expense of women's. Other policies relegated women to the private sphere to maintain families and communities (Gilligan 1996; Pateman 1988; Tronto 1993). Emphasizing women's domestic duties addressed states' concerns over declining fertility and coincided with the introduction of abortion and contraception regulation (Glass 1967). Many White middle-class women's groups claimed all of society's unpaid care work as a female prerogative (Bock and Thane 1991). Women's care responsibilities also became embedded in new welfare institutions such as educational systems and health services. States supported these trends because women's unpaid or low-paid care work reduced the public cost of providing welfare (Koven and Michel 1990).

One reason state policies reinforced a gendered division of paid and unpaid work was that industrialization widened the divide between production and reproduction as work shifted from field to factory

(Reskin and Padavic 1994). The divide was more than a physical distance between employment and home (Beck 1992). The market prospered from individual action, Adam Smith's (1970 [1776]: 184) "invisible hand" of self interest. Family and the social world prospered with cooperative action, the invisible social bonds created by "reciprocity and redistribution" (Polanyi 1944: 47). State policies addressed these inherent tensions between the two by gendering paid and unpaid work.

The country cases therefore differed in relative gender employment equality, displayed as the difference between men's and women's employment rates in Figure 1.1. A larger number indicates a greater proportion of adult men than women were in employed in 2000. The average gender employment gap across OECD countries that year was 19 percentage points (OECD 2002: table 2.2).

In the less regulated UK and US labor markets, the gender employment gaps were similar and smaller than the OECD average. The gender gap in Australia, however, was larger than the other English-speaking countries and larger than average. This reflects one intersection of class policy effects on gender: policies that promoted greater class equality frequently limited the employment participation of women (Bertola et al. 2007; Pettit and Hook 2009). The Harvester Judgement dampened married Australian women's financial incentive to remain in employment as compared with similar UK and US women. The incentive was further diminished in 1919 when subsequent policies set Australian women's wages to about half the male rate (Ryan and Conlon 1989).

The continental European countries also differed in their gender employment gaps. After World War II, the two German regions were non-democratically separated. East Germany was forced to adopt a Stalinist constitution that demanded the employment of all adults, supported by a broad range of policies enabling women to combine motherhood with paid work (Cooke 2007b). In contrast, West German policies supported a male breadwinner model and made women legally responsible for the private sphere (Ostner 1992, 1993). To balance the resultant labor shortage, the West German state signed bilateral treaties for immigrant guest workers from Italy, Spain, and later Turkey

(Trappe 2000). The two German regions reunified in 1990, but markedly different gender employment gaps were still evident a decade later (Figure 1.1). The 2000 gender employment gap in Spain was the largest of the countries here, which reflected its later modernization and the conservative Roman Catholic elements embedded in policy until Franco's death in 1975 (Nash 1991).

Thus as evident in Figure 1.1, the selected country cases represent different combinations of aggregate gender-class equality.[5] The historical comparisons will reveal, however, that the structure of group differences is more complex than can be depicted in a 2×2 figure. The institutional frames yielded gender-class differences not only in employment rates, but hours of paid and unpaid work as well as relative wages of employed individuals. When looking across *all* components of paid and unpaid work, the countries represent six unique cases of relative gender-class equality.

The Resilience of Inequality Within Its Institutional Frame

Why does the institutional equality frame built in some cases more than 200 years ago still predict relative gender-class equality across these six regions? One possible argument is that today's relative equality reflects the "path dependence" of subsequent policies on the initial policy choices (Levi 1997).[6] The new state institutions faced start-up costs, learning effects, and coordination challenges (North 1990). As a result, reliance among institutions increased over time, which encouraged subsequent policies to coordinate with rather than change the existing institutional arrangements (Pierson 2000). A path dependence argument predicts that the initial institutional frame would be replicated in subsequent policy choices, as would the relative gender-class equality intersections within it. As Levi noted:

> Path dependence has to mean . . . that once a country or region has started down a track, the costs of reversal are very high. There will be other choice points, but the entrenchments of certain institutional arrangements obstruct an easy reversal of the initial choice. Perhaps the better metaphor is a tree. . . . From the same trunk, there are many different branches and

small branches. Although it is possible to turn around or to clamber from one to the other—and essential if the chosen branch dies—the branch on which a climber begins is the one she tends to follow.

(1997: 28)

The initial frame, however, resulted from a given constellation of economic, political, and social processes, all of which continued to change (Peters et al. 2005; Thelen 1999; Yuval-Davis 2006). For example, the invisible hand of self-interest tugs at everyone. Policies that privileged men in employment could not keep women or other social groups from it, either out of economic necessity or simply to enjoy the fruits of its rewards. Married middle-class women in the nineteenth century promoted their unpaid work, but after World War II this same group of women entered employment to finance luxury items such as washing machines and vacuums (Frevert 1989; Vanek 1974). The market thrives on such spirals of consumption and production. As we accumulate more, we want more, so we produce more. In a well-functioning market, catching up with the Joneses is impossible.

The political discourse and material relations also encountered "critical junctures" (Collier and Collier 1991). The atrocities of World War II resulted in a shift in political discourse to one supporting greater human rights (Hobson 1993). The change in discourse was accompanied by the introduction of equal opportunity and affirmative action policies. The 1957 Treaty of Rome that established the European Union required equal pay provisions in any member state, representing the first European move away from policy built around men's relationship to the labor market (Lewis 2006). Title VII of the US Civil Rights Act of 1964 made discrimination in education, training, and employment on the basis of race or biological sex illegal. The following year President Johnson signed Executive Order 11246, which enforced affirmative action among government contractors. The Australian trade union movement that had successfully privileged men's wages over women earlier in the century became the champion of comparable worth policies during the late 1960s.

As I argue, however, the impact of these policy innovations was constrained by the institutional equality frame and each group gain was offset by some loss. Gender differences in paid and unpaid work narrowed but did not disappear, and these gains varied along class lines. Educated women have gained the most, but at a cost of greater class and ethnic gaps among women in paid as well as unpaid work. Relative gender equality gains among less-educated women frequently occurred because of the deteriorating economic position of less-educated men. In other words, policy innovation resulted in a new gender-class equilibrium within each institutional frame, but gender-class inequality persisted.

The post-war policy "innovations" were instead compromises that improved life chances for some individuals within disadvantaged groups, but without eroding absolute advantage held by the most privileged groups (White middle-class men). Yes, more women entered employment, but primarily in part-time or public sector positions that did not threaten men's lucrative private sector careers (Mandel and Semyonov 2005, 2006; Pettit and Hook 2009). Women still dominated in care work, whether low paid (Budig and Misra, 2010; Charles and Grusky 2004) or unpaid (Bianchi et al. 2006; Gauthier et al. 2004). Equality policies themselves remain under attack. In Europe, the European Court of Justice initially ruled that affirmative action violates men's constitutional right to equality (Behning and Pascual 2001; McGlynn 2001). Similarly, a growing number of US states have reversed or proposed reversing their affirmative action laws.[7] So members of privileged social groups tolerate policies that ease some relative disadvantage within the institutional equality frame, until such a time as they perceive the changes threaten their privileged positions. These are the dynamics of social action that sustain relative group inequalities.

Book Overview

The structuring of gender-class differences in paid and unpaid work begins well before any individual sets out to get a first job. It begins before birth, extends through schooling, and continues beyond that first job as individuals form and maintain families. In the second chapter I outline the individual- and couple-level frameworks used to predict these choices. The existing frameworks depict the choices as rational decisions that are the same for all individuals in every industrialized country. The review of current evidence, however, reveals that the rational choice models explain very little of the observed gender differences in paid and unpaid work. In addition, these observed differences vary across countries. To date, cross-national analyses have generally focused on a limited number of policies that affect the gendered division of paid and unpaid work, such as the percentage of women employed, the length of parental leave, the number of public child care slots, or women's share of parliamentary seats (Fuwa 2004; Hook 2006; Pettit and Hook 2009; Stier and Lewin-Epstein 2007). These measures do not capture the full array of policies that structure gender-class inequality in paid and unpaid work. The array includes education policies, labor regulations, social insurance programs, public and private transfers, and tax and family law. This policy framework creates an interlocking system of gender-class inequality in paid and unpaid work that blocks the ability to achieve equality in either domain (Ferree 1990: 874).

The divisions of paid and unpaid work among adults therefore reflect gender-class difference in human capital that have accumulated across the life course. Policy effects across the life course are the topics of Chapters 3, 4 and 5, which examine population, education, and employment policies, respectively. I begin each chapter by comparing the issues and country policy responses during the nineteenth century that set the institutional frame of relative gender, class, and at times ethnic equality. I then trace the post-war policy innovations spurred by the civil rights and feminist movements and their aggregate effects on group inequalities. Each chapter concludes with a discussion of policy adjustments that have occurred alongside more recent demographic and globalization trends (Guillén 2001; Taylor-Gooby 2004; van de Kaa 1987; but see Wallerstein 1976).

Chapter 3 details how essentialist gender and ethnic divisions of paid and unpaid work became structured in population policies introduced during the nineteenth century. State concern over declining fertility and poor health led to early state intervention in the most private of private spheres: women's bodies. All of the countries introduced contraception or abortion restrictions during this period, with poor women more likely to be prosecuted and punished for violations (Francome 1984). The growing legion of educated but unemployed middle-class wives became the champions of women's care work in the home. Middle-class women also ran and volunteered in charitable organizations with the goal of improving the parenting skills of working-class and immigrant women (Bock and Thane 1991; Koven and Michel 1990).

Married women's exit from the labor market, however, reduced the reserve labor force available during periods of economic growth. Consequently, immigration policies provided alternative supplies of workers. These, too, contained gendered and racialized restrictions depending on the perceived ethnic similarity. After World War II, as more middle-class women remained in the labor force, population policies began to regulate the provision of low-paid immigrant domestic work that substituted for affluent women's former unpaid tasks (Bettio et al. 2006; Kofman et al. 2000; Misra et al. 2006).

Education policies also supported gender, class, and other group differences in paid and unpaid work through the structure and content of public schooling, which is the topic of Chapter 4. The expansion of compulsory schooling during the nineteenth century did not erode the elite's historical educational advantage (Wilensky 1975). As will be shown, the challenge of providing public schooling in countries with large land masses such as Australia, Spain, and the United States exacerbated class differences. In Australia and the United States, regional differences sustained racial educational disparities as well. Early compulsory schooling systems also created a care void for the years between birth and the start of public schooling, as well as in the scheduling of the school day, week, and year (David 1980; Gornick and Meyers 2003). Women were tacitly or explicitly expected to fill this care void (David 1980). Finally, the gendered assumptions about women's care work influenced girls' access to schooling, as well as the curriculum offered to them.

After World War II, countries implemented equality opportunity provisions to enhance group access to schooling. As a result, women today often complete more years of schooling than men (Shavit et al. 2007). Yet persistent gender differences in skills and subjects translate into later gender career differences. Gender educational differences start small in primary school and widen appreciably during adolescence, suggesting they are in part socially constructed. At the same time, the expansion of early education provision to fill the care void before the start of compulsory schooling has lagged behind the expansion of post-secondary education. Yet public provision of quality early child-hood education not only reduces gender differences in employment, but also reduces class differences in later educational achievement (Esping-Andersen 2004; Heckman and Masterov 2007). In contrast, post-secondary expansion generally extends the group differences embedded in earlier schooling inequalities. Thus the nature of educational expansion sustained gender-class differences.

The labor market regulations that directly shaped gender-class equality in paid work are the topic of Chapter 5. The growing working-class movement of the nineteenth century put pressure on the state to regulate employment. The success of worker mobilization varied across countries, but the earliest labor regulations restricted children's and women's access to employment (Wikander et al. 1995). The justifications ranged from moral—keeping unsuspecting women away from the sexual dangers of the workplace—to strategic, in that protective legislation could open the door to general improvements in working conditions for all workers (cf. Lewis and Rose 1995; Skocpol 1992). Protective labor market regulations, however, widened the industrial gulf between family and employment, adding the expectation that mothers must now care for rather than work alongside their children (Hartmann 1979).

After World War II, many capitalist economies witnessed a brief period when male breadwinner couples appeared to be the norm (Oppenheimer 1997). In contrast, socialist states implemented training, labor, and related policies that supported the employment of women, and mothers in particular.[8] Throughout industrialized countries, however, the call for equality grew louder and was answered in part by the implementation of equal opportunity employment policies. The resultant increase in female labor force participation, however, did not actually yield substantial gains in gender employment *equality*. Most employment growth in the post-war period was in part-time jobs, which were overwhelmingly held by women. By 2000, women comprised 80 percent of part-time workers in the OECD countries (Bardasi and Gornick 2008). Since the 1960s, the gender wage gap narrowed among full-time workers, but it did not disappear and remained wider when comparing all workers (Blau et al. 2002). In some countries, greater gender wage equality at the bottom of the earnings distribution resulted from the erosion in low-skilled men's wages and/or because the least skilled women left the labor market (cf. Rosenfeld et al. 2004). The gender wage gap has not narrowed further since the 1990s, and there is new evidence that wage differences between groups of women have widened (Pettit and Ewert 2009; Western et al. 2008). During this same period, class inequality has also generally increased (Kenworthy 2008; McCall and Percheski, 2010). These trends highlight how the post-war policy innovations did not eliminate group inequalities, but merely reshuffled them.

In Chapters 6 and 7, I explore these country effects on current gender-class equality in paid and unpaid work at the individual level. I compare women with men,[9] and assess class differences for each based on whether an individual has a university degree as compared with individuals who have secondary education or less. This definition of class ignores other factors hypothesized to differentiate social classes (see Erikson and Goldthorpe 1992; or Wright 2005). Because of occupational segregation, however, occupation-based schemas for understanding class differences (Erikson and Goldthorpe 1992) are problematic in that they conflate gender and class (Crompton 1993). Other class measures, such as cultural or social capital (Bourdieu 1977; Coleman 1988), are not available in the datasets.

In Chapter 6, data from wave 5.2 of the Luxembourg Income Study are used to assess gender, class and at times ethnic differences in employment hours and wages as of around 2000. The marginal effects of individual human capital and family characteristics on the likelihood of employment for women and men are compared across the countries.

Group differences in weekly work hours are predicted using pooled regression models and variables that capture how individual effects of education, partnership, and having children differ in their national context. The same data and two-stage regression models are used to predict women's and men's relative wages across the earnings distribution in each country. Results from these models reveal distinct class patterns in the gender wage gap across the countries. Together the employment analyses illustrate how the "individual" human capital model is not universal, but contextual.

In Chapter 7, data from the 2002 International Social Survey Program are used to compare gender differences in housework hours across social classes. I use a pooled interaction model similar to that used to predict employment hours. These analyses find a persistent gendered division of housework regardless of women's employment as reported in much recent cross-national research (see Cooke and Baxter 2010 for a review). Yet the analyses further reveal how this is uniquely structured in each country. The policy context varies the impact of individual characteristics on both paid and unpaid work hours, particularly among couples.

Chapter 8 offers a summary of the findings and their policy implications. In general, educated households enjoy greater equality in paid and unpaid work, but educated women still perform the majority of unpaid work. The greater gender equality among the highly educated is achieved by shifting unpaid tasks from the home to the low-wage service sector. Thus, equality gains for educated women are not costless in that they result in greater time poverty among dual-earner couples (Jacobs and Gerson 2004). They also hinge on low wages for service workers. As a result, countries with greater income equality have a greater burden of unpaid tasks for which there are fewer affordable market substitutes. Dual-earner households are therefore particularly time-poor in countries with greater income equality. Even East Germany's public provision of child care did not eliminate the household time burden, or women's responsibility for the remaining unpaid work hours.

The institutional and individual-level evidence suggest that policy approaches adopted in the nineteenth century, even with the post-war policy amendments, cannot further enhance aggregate equality in market economies. Modest group differences earlier in the life course widen to great disadvantage in adulthood. The accumulated disadvantage has also been increasing across generations (see Cooke and Baxter 2010 for a review). Children's life chances, for example, are diverging more and more based on their mother's education (McLanahan 2004; Sobotka 2008; Western et al. 2008).

The patterns indicated the need for a different policy approach in post-industrial economies (Esping-Andersen et al. 2002). In response, policies during the 1990s began to focus on narrowing group inequalities at critical junctures along the life course under a social "investment" strategy (Jenson 2009; Jenson and Saint-Martin 2006). For example, a critical juncture occurs during the first five years of a child's life. During this time, poverty carries the greatest negative impact on children's future outcomes (Duncan and Brooks-Gunn 1997; Gornick and Jäntti 2009). The early home environment also determines a child's cognitive ability and later educational attainment (Cunha and Heckman 2010; Esping-Andersen 2004, 2009; Heckman and Masterov 2007). Policy support for maternal employment greatly reduces the likelihood of child poverty (Kamerman et al. 2003), whereas high-quality early childhood education facilitates mothers' employment as well as children's cognitive development (Esping-Andersen 2009).

Esping-Andersen (2009) has argued that policy support for women's employment under such social investment strategies will eventually result in equality in paid and unpaid work within the home. A social investment strategy, however, does not directly narrow gender inequalities but focuses instead on improving child outcomes (Jenson 2009). For example, the evidence in Chapter 5 highlights how in many ways the recent labor activation and work-family reconciliation policies widened rather than narrowed gender employment inequalities (McGlynn 2006). The evidence from Chapters 6 and 7 also does not support that women's greater employment equality invariably begets greater gender equality in unpaid work—there are both class and gender trade-offs. Instead, a fundamental problem is that the market crowds out women's as well as men's unpaid time necessary to nurture families and communities.

Policies that support market mechanisms only serve to perpetuate the growing tension between economic and social life. So in addition to investing in individual human capital formation, the state must also find ways to reinforce the value of unpaid time along the life course for both women and men. Only by doing so can the activities currently deemed gendered no longer form the foundation of gender inequality in market economies. And only by doing so can the social investment strategies that rely on community and family action succeed.

2

Paid and Unpaid Work in Context

Introduction

Individuals make choices between paid or unpaid work across their lives, but these choices do not occur in isolation. Social influences on future work decisions begin early in life, such as when parents and the state dictate children's educational options. The influences continue as individuals select post-secondary education, training, and jobs. As adults, these decisions are usually balanced with family demands. So social circumstances strongly influence lifetime decisions relating to paid and unpaid work.

The classic "human capital" model (Mincer 1974) used to predict individual education and work decisions, however, ignores the importance of the social context at each step of the individual decision process. In this chapter I outline the basic models of labor supply and demand and what they predict for individual education and work decisions. I then provide cross-national evidence of the ways in which the basic model fails to account for gender differences in both labor supply and demand. Families are at the heart of these gender differences. Families come in a variety of forms, but I focus on dynamics between heterosexual adult couples. Sexual orientation has an important impact on individual and family decisions (McCall 2005), but this is beyond the theoretical scope of this book.

Families also differ across socioeconomic contexts. Culture shapes and reinforces a national family ideal, as well as the expected behaviors of individuals within families (Pfau-Effinger 1998, 2010). A broad range of policies reflect and reinforce the cultural family ideal (Fink 2001). The labor market, culture, and policies all therefore contribute to the institutional frame that determines not only total household hours in paid and unpaid labor, but also gender and class differences in these.

Gender Differences in Labor Supply and Demand

In the classic labor market model, the demands of production determine the labor skills required (Mincer 1974). Each industry requires certain occupations, skill levels, and hours of work. The occupational structure can differ across countries (Erikson and Goldthorpe 1992; Featherman et al. 1975), as well as across labor markets within countries (McCall 2001). Labor demand also changes over time, which in turn alters the required skills and work hours. One significant change after World War II was the shift from manufacturing to more service sector employment (Taylor-Gooby 2004). The service sector growth increased the demand for part-time work that included evenings and weekends. Another important post-war trend was the rapid growth in technology (Guillén 2001). Technology has replaced people in some jobs and has also increased the demand for educated workers who can use it to improve their productivity (Aghion et al. 1999; Autor et al. 2008). Thus, labor demand and the skills required vary across regions and over time.

People supply the labor and develop their skills through education, on-the-job training, and accumulated work experience. Together these comprise individual "human capital" (Becker 1993; Mincer 1974). Most people complete formal education early in their lives and then accrue work experience. When employed, they can enhance their skills and productivity with on-the-job training. People with greater human capital or with skills in short supply normally command higher wages (Blau et al. 2002).

The supply and demand factors theoretically work the same for members of all social groups. An employer with a "taste" for discrimination (Becker 1971), for example, would be driven out of business by employers hiring the excluded workers at lower wages. On the supply side, every person is free to pursue whatever education, training, or jobs suit his or her abilities and interests. In fact, liberal theorists beginning with Adam Smith (1970 [1776]) predicted these processes of industrialization would lead to greater equality as education became more important than family of birth in determining future prospects (Dumont 1977). Over time, class inequalities were expected to narrow as children from more disadvantaged backgrounds could, through education, attain better jobs than those held by their parents. And as technology replaced brute strength in production, more women were expected to enter employment.

Optimism in the power of education to eliminate group inequalities has waned somewhat over time. Evidence indicates, for example, that education does not necessarily enhance intergenerational class mobility (Breen and Jonsson 2005; Erikson and Goldthorpe 1992). Indeed, income inequality has continued to increase across most affluent economies (Brandolini and Smeeding 2009; Kenworthy 2008). Women in many countries now complete more years of schooling than men (Shavit et al. 2007), but distinct gender differences in employment, occupation, and earnings persist. Education could still in theory enhance group equality, but the reality is that class and gender predict systematic educational differences, either in the years of education or in the subjects studied. Societal expectations around the family also result in gender differences in accumulated work experience and on-the-job training.

These gender differences in education and work experience contribute to gender differences in wages. From an early age, girls outperform boys in reading and languages, whereas boys perform better in math and somewhat better in science.[1] The gender subject proficiency gaps widen as children continue through secondary school. In many countries, more women now attain higher levels of education than men (Shavit et al. 2007). The subject differences, however, extend into post-secondary schooling. Over two-thirds of humanities, arts, education, and social work college degrees are awarded to women, whereas men obtain over three-quarters of engineering, manufacturing, and construction degrees (OECD 2007). These gendered educational patterns are evident in all industrialized societies, although the degree of disparity differs (OECD 2008b).

Gender educational differences throughout youth translate into gender differences in occupation, work hours, and wages in adulthood. Men and women are frequently employed in different occupations (horizontal occupational segregation) and hold different levels of authority within organizations (vertical segregation). In terms of horizontal segregation, women tend to be over-represented in care-related occupations such as nursing or primary school teaching, whereas men dominate the "building" occupations such as construction, engineering, and manufacturing (Charles and Grusky 2004). The degree of horizontal segregation varies across countries, as does which gender dominates which occupation (Anker 1998). In terms of vertical segregation, men are more likely than women to be in managerial and other senior positions regardless of occupation (Blau et al. 2002; Charles and Grusky 2004).

Women and men also differ in average employment trajectories. In the first half of the twentieth century, women in industrial societies worked when single but left employment upon marrying. Immediately after World War II, women married at younger ages, creating a labor shortage that drove up female wage rates and encouraged older married women to re-enter employment (Butz and Ward 1979; Goldin 1990). These dynamics resulted in an M-shape female employment pattern: employed when single, out of the labor force during early child-bearing years, and returning to the workforce when children were older. In contrast, once men entered employment, they generally remained employed full-time until retirement.

More women entered the labor force in the latter half of the twentieth century, such that today about two-thirds of adult women across industrialized societies are employed.[2] Most of the growth in employment, however, has been in part-time jobs. In addition to providing fewer employment hours, part-time work offers fewer benefits and opportunities for advancement (Bardasi and Gornick 2008; Connolly and Gregory 2008; McGinnity and McManus 2007). Women comprise 80 percent of part-time workers, although national rates vary considerably (Bardasi and Gornick 2008). Part-time work comprises less than 5 percent of female employment in many former socialist countries. In Australia, Germany, and the United Kingdom, part-time work comprises more than one-third (Jaumotte 2003).

Because women enter and exit the labor market and are more likely to work part-time, women on average accrue less work experience than men. As predicted by the human capital model, the gender differences in education and work experience contribute to a gender wage gap. The 2006 gender wage gap for OECD countries was 18 percent, but it ranged substantially across countries (OECD 2008c: table H). The gender wage gap is smallest at the beginning of young adults' careers and largest when comparing mothers with fathers (Blau and Kahn 1992; Harkness and Waldfogel 1999; Sigle-Rushton and Waldfogel 2007). Thus, gender economic differences emerge early in the life course and increase as individuals make decisions about employment and family (Pettit and Hook 2009).

If individuals were equally likely to choose education, occupations, and employment, then these gendered human capital patterns could reflect essential differences between women and men. Gender essentialism reduces observed differences throughout life to those physically evident at birth. In their work on "occupational ghettos," Charles and Grusky (2004) argued that horizontal segregation reflects an essentialist view that women are more competent in service, nurturing, and social interaction. In contrast, men are perceived to excel in interactions with things and tasks requiring physical strength. From this perspective, vertical segregation persists under cultural perceptions of male primacy; men are considered more status worthy and appropriate for positions of authority. Essentialism would lead us to conclude gender equality cannot be achieved because a lifetime of difference is a biological *fait accompli* at birth.

From the moment of birth, however, individuals are members of social groups that interact with others over a lifetime. Simone de Beauvoir claimed that "[o]ne is not born, but rather becomes, a woman"

(1973: 301). In contrast to simply being a male, manhood in many ways is also an achieved status (Herdt 1982; Kimmel and Messner 2004). Our gender is announced at birth and then we are subjected to these cultural expectations of behavior, opportunities, and the power attributed to that gender category (Goffman 1977; West and Zimmerman 1987). Our gender identity and power relations therefore evolve from thousands of interactions across our lives, shaped by the social structure in which we live.

Gender reflects power because what is considered feminine tends to be valued less in industrialized societies than what is considered masculine (Kilbourne et al. 1994). For example, only a portion of the gender wage gap can be explained by observable differences in educational major, average work hours, accrued work experience, occupation, industry, or job characteristics (Altonji and Blank 1999; Johansson et al. 2005; McCall 2001; Rosholm and Smith 1996). Using matching to compare the small number of US women and men with nearly identical characteristics, Black and his colleagues (2008) still could not explain about 10 percent of Black and White women's wage gap (2008: 651). In addition, wages are higher when men dominate an occupation (Blau et al. 2002). For example, clerical wages were higher when US men dominated this work prior to World War II, as compared with the lower wages that characterize the occupation now that women dominate it (Goldin 1990). Jobs requiring skills considered feminine pay less than jobs demanding more masculine attributes (Budig and England 2001; Levanon et al. 2009). The social context and our gender category therefore contribute to gender differences in labor supply.

Gender differences in labor supply get reinforced by gender differentials in labor demand. Kenneth Arrow (1976) suggested that gender wage differentials result from statistical discrimination. An employer discriminates statistically when individual hiring decisions are based on aggregate information about a group. If, on average, women leave employment when they marry or have children, employers might make hiring decisions in anticipation of such an exit even if any given female applicant had no intention of doing so. Similarly, on-the-job training is not a rational business investment in employees who are expected to leave for family reasons (Barron et al. 1993; Evertsson 2004; Green 1991).

In the nineteenth and early twentieth centuries, many employers *imposed* marriage and pregnancy restrictions on women (Goldin 1990; Pedersen 1993). Women were excluded from the "queues" to the best jobs (Reskin and Roos 1990). Women were frequently required to work fewer hours than men or banned from night work (Wikander et al. 1995). If women as a group anticipated having their possibilities limited by such employment practices, their incentive to invest in their education would be reduced. The dynamics highlight the feedback effects between labor demand and labor supply (Arrow 1976). State labor market policies can amplify these feedback effects.

The State and the Labor Market

Early in industrialization, states limited their policy interventions because of widespread belief in the efficiency of markets. As noted by O'Connor and her colleagues (1999: 44): "Liberalism posits individuals as having natural rights to freedom and property, and assigns to the state the role of elaborating and enforcing those rules necessary to reconcile conflicts among the rights of individuals." Therefore, the primary role of the emerging state in liberal industrial economies was to implement and uphold property laws to facilitate economic exchange (Marshall 1950). It was not to intervene in the individual labor-supply exchange.

Yet states have their own interests in expanding, which included but were not limited to the market (Evans et al. 1985; Skocpol 1979). Economic and imperial expansion, for example, were threatened by the declining fertility rates associated with industrialization and the poor physical and mental health of the population laboring under industrial conditions (Freeden 1978; Glass 1967). Shifting people's livelihoods from the land to the factory had made human labor a commodity to be sold, much like a dozen eggs. Unlike other commodities, however, humans faced starvation and homelessness if they were unsuccessful in selling their labor.[3] Polanyi (1944) argued that selling human labor for wages also broke the "bonds of reciprocity" between peasants and feudal lords that created the obligation to help in times of need.[4] The ill-effects associated with industrial markets encouraged states to take a more active role in individual lives than liberal tenets would indicate.

Industrialization was also accompanied by new political risks as it brought large numbers of workers together in urban centers. Well-organized workers undermined the power of capitalists to unilaterally set the terms and conditions of employment, threatening the power of the ruling elite (Freeden 1978). Democratization entailed granting voting rights first to working-class men, which could strengthen class mobilization efforts (Korpi 1983; Stephens 1979). Women's groups exercised informal political power before their members could actually vote, such as by lobbying for maternity or other state payments to mothers (Koven and Michel 1993). Women's groups also frequently worked with labor organizations to improve working conditions for women and men (Pedersen 1993; Skocpol 1992).

In response to these social and political changes that accompanied industrialization, states introduced new policies to enhance people's well-being, or "welfare" (Cutright 1965; Wilensky 1975).[5] For example, many states introduced limited pensions and industrial accident insurance during the late nineteenth century (Orloff 1993a; Pierson 1998). States also expanded compulsory schooling across the nineteenth century to improve the skills of the next generation of workers. Wilensky (1975) argued education should not be considered a welfare program because higher education magnifies rather than reduces class inequalities. Yet education has the *potential* to reduce rather than replicate group employment differences, and so is included here (Bergh 2005; Leseman 2009; OECD 2010).

Thus democratic states increased welfare-related expenditures as industrialization progressed, but states varied in the nature and extent of these expenditures (Titmuss 1958). The more liberal states such as the United States justified the high class inequalities of unregulated labor markets because they theoretically provided the necessary work incentives for economic growth (Kuznets 1963). At the other extreme were socialist or communist states, which imposed total state control over production to eliminate the power of capitalists and ensure greater equality among workers (Marx 1967 [1848]). States therefore differed in the degree of welfare investment and how far policy shaped class relations among workers (Esping-Andersen 1990).

More liberal approaches resulted in more residual welfare states (Titmuss 1958). In England and the United States, for example, the aim was for policies to reinforce the work ethic and discourage individuals' dependency on the state for financial support (Orloff 1993a). State benefits were means-tested, with cash transfers dominating over state provision of services (Esping-Andersen 1990). A liberal ideology was evident as well in the class inequalities institutionalized in the Australian, English, and US public schooling systems that expanded during the nineteenth and twentieth centuries.

Liberal markets then and now require that firms respond quickly to market changes, such as terminating employees when there is a dip in demand (Hall and Soskice 2001). Workers, in turn, sell their labor to the highest corporate bidder. These dynamics create more job mobility and greater wage inequality. Greater job mobility makes firm investment in individual worker skills risky. Instead, liberal market economies reward individuals who have invested in portable general education (Estevez-Abe et al. 2001). These dynamics lead to the greater inequality associated with higher education noted by Wilensky (1975).

The degree of class inequality, however, varies across otherwise more liberal economies. For example, Esping-Andersen (1990) categorized Australia as a liberal welfare "regime" along with the United Kingdom and the United States. "Regimes" reflect a society's institutional arrangements for balancing work and welfare, with the relative reliance on the market versus the state comprising one dimension of difference (Esping-Andersen 1987, 1990). Also important are whether institutional arrangements enhanced class solidarity (through "de-commodification").[6] Early Australian legislation, the 1907 Harvester Judgement, ensured greater class equality because it required that employers pay all men wages sufficient for supporting a family, regardless of whether the employer could afford to do so (F. Castles 1985). This reflected the greater coordination among Australian labor unions and the state reminiscent of regimes found on the European continent more so than in North America or England.

Market economies in northern Europe developed around long-standing institutional relationships that resulted in more coordinated employer-employee strategies (Estevez-Abe et al. 2001). Coordinated wage negotiations, for example, reduced employers' risk of losing skilled workers to another employer paying higher wages. In this context, firms could afford to invest in developing employee skills through apprenticeships and other firm-based vocational training. The greater skills training coupled with coordinated wage agreements reduced wage inequality among workers. This meant that workers with fewer years of general education were not penalized to the same extent as in liberal markets (Blau and Kahn 2003). Workers in these economies also frequently enjoyed more favorable working conditions, such as shorter weekly work hours and longer vacations (Kangas and Palme 2005).

Mainstream theorists lauded class victories in welfare state development (F. Castles 1985; Esping-Andersen 1990; Korpi 1983; Stephens 1979). The coordination necessary for achieving greater class equality, however, created insider-outsider fissures among groups of workers. The high firm investment in employees' skills demanded a long-term commitment on both sides of the employment relationship. Consequently, firms in more coordinated market economies employed a smaller core of workers—the "insiders"—who could be relied upon to remain employed continuously (Bertola et al. 2007; Soskice 2005). The core group was chosen early in life through vocational educational systems that tracked them into the training for the best jobs (OECD 2010). Employment "outsiders" did not have access to the best training or jobs, and instead became a reserve workforce to be pulled into employment only when labor demand was especially high.

The insider-outsider distinctions were reinforced by other state policies. Many welfare regimes on the European continent offered more benefits to all citizens than the liberal regimes, but certain groups such as skilled workers, the elderly or civil servants received superior benefits (Esping-Andersen 1990). Conservative elements reflected the influence of other institutional actors, such as the Catholic political parties in West Germany (Wilensky 1981) and the Roman Catholic Church in Franco's Spain (Nash 1991). Conservative elements were reflected in policies that excluded women from employment by reinforcing their domestic obligations (Esping-Andersen 1990).

Institutional arrangements affecting relative class equality therefore cannot be disentangled from those affecting relative gender equality. The mainstream theories of the political economy remained blind to these group differences because they assumed a citizen with "masculine capacities" for paid work, self-governance, and the ability to bear arms (Pateman 1988: 185). Analyses of the impact of state provisions on workers ignored women's unpaid work in the private sphere (Dalla Costa 1972), as well as women's unpaid work in public spheres such as through volunteering (Lewis 1992a). Mapping the gender-class intersections therefore requires consideration of both paid and unpaid labor, particularly as labor is allocated between women and men within the institution of "family" (Collins 2000; Walby 2009).

The State and a Gendered Division of Household Labor

Families produce and reproduce in all societies, but industrialization increased the physical distance between where the family resides and the place of "work." At first, some families could continue to earn a living together in guilds (Hartmann 1979). Over time, the essential family tasks became more gendered and differentiated by whether they were paid or unpaid. Women became responsible for the unpaid tasks associated with the home, family, and community, which allowed men to concentrate on paid work (Dalla Costa 1972). Becker (1981) concluded that the gendered division of labor was the optimal household work allocation in industrial societies. Each partner specialized in either paid or unpaid work based on their comparative advantage, and then shared the fruits of this labor with the other. The efficiency was predicted to increase fertility and reduce the risk of family dissolution (Becker 1985; Parsons 1942).

Paid tasks by definition are valued in market economies, such that the gendered division of labor institutionalized women's lesser economic power (Blau 1960; Blood and Wolfe 1960). Gender power differences increased across the life course. Women who exited employment upon marriage became economically dependent on their husbands, a dependency gap that widened as their husbands continued to accumulate work experience and its rewards. The more extreme the gendered division of labor, the more important maintaining the marriage was for women than for men. As Hobson (1990: 238) phrased it, "the fewer the exit possibilities, the weaker the voice." Consequently, a gendered division of labor enhanced men's relative power in the family and across the life course.

A gendered division of labor, however, was not an inevitable outgrowth of industrialization. It reflected instead one solution to the competing demands of work and family in industrial societies. To enhance the bargaining power of working-class men, many labor groups first lobbied for legal restrictions on children's and women's employment (Wikander et al. 1995). As these laws spread across countries during the nineteenth century, the female labor force participation rate declined. The state also made women legally and politically dependent on men. Women were denied the right to vote in most countries for longer than most men,[7] and their legal identity was frequently subsumed within their husbands' under the common law principle of *femme couverte* (Sapiro 1990).

The state therefore helped to structure a gender hierarchy by excluding women from public spheres and defining them as dependent. At the same time, the state relied on women's unpaid work in the private sphere. The state required women's bodies to reproduce future generations of workers and warriors, and so regulated women's sexuality and contraception while almost never regulating men's.[8] New state institutions for schooling, health, and social care developed around an assumption of women's unpaid care work (Bock and Thane 1991; Koven and Michel 1993; Lewis 1992a). State policies privileging men's access to paid work and relying on women's unpaid care work comprised what Lewis (1992a) termed a "male breadwinner model."

Privileging men's access to economic resources entailed more than providing men preferential training or access to the best jobs. Related policies included tax credits for dependent spouses and family allowances that discouraged married women's employment (Cooke 2010). High marginal tax rates on a household's second earner also discouraged married women's labor force participation (Jaumotte 2003). Some states linked an employed married woman's work-related benefits to her husband's, which she would lose in the event of a divorce. In some countries, the household was made the unit of entitlement. Household-based entitlements frequently resulted in an employed married woman being unable to collect state benefits because her partner's earnings kept the household income above the minimum.

Other policies reinforced women's responsibility for and men's exclusion from unpaid work. Maternity rather than parental leave reinforced women's responsibility for unpaid child care and limited the time a man could spend with his newborn child. Extended maternity leave also reduced women's accrued work experience, reinforcing women's interrupted career trajectories and lower lifetime earnings (Aisenbrey et al. 2009; Sigle-Rushton and Waldfogel 2007). Compulsory schooling created a care void between childbirth and the time children started schooling (David 1980; Gornick and Meyers 2003). Needing to pay for private child care imposed an additional "tax" on women's wages (Michalopoulos et al. 1992). An assumption of women's unpaid care work was evident as well in public schooling schedules that were shorter than the standard work day, included extended vacation periods, or required that children return home for lunch (Buchmann and Charles 1995; Gornick and Meyers 2003).

These sorts of policies resulted in the more separate, gendered spheres of household labor depicted in the first panel of Figure 2.1. Men performed the vast majority of paid work whereas women performed the vast majority of the unpaid work, with the hours in each roughly commensurate. Because of the range of possible policies that reinforced these divisions, however, country male breadwinner models differed. West Germany implemented the most comprehensive male breadwinner model by combining class policies that ensured more men could support a dependent family with gender policies that reinforced women's responsibility for the home (Ostner 1992, 1993). Australia also implemented policies that provided men with family wages, but fewer policies directly reinforced women's domestic responsibilities. British and Spanish policies emphasized women's responsibility for unpaid care work, but no policies ensured men could earn family wages. This policy framework increased the likelihood that families would require a second income to make ends meet. The employment available to women, however, was often marginalized part-time work in the United Kingdom (Dex and Shaw 1986) and black-market employment in Spain (Barbera and Vettor 2001; Ferrera 2005).

In contrast to the above cases, East German and US policies did not actively promote a male breadwinner model. The US adherence to liberal tenets meant very few policies explicitly privileged men's employment at the exclusion of women's. In fact, the United States was the last of the liberal regimes to allow protective legislation restricting women's employment.[9] East Germany was the only country to promote the dual-earner model depicted in the second panel of Figure 2.1. Women were encouraged to continue in education and could take most of the same vocational training programs as men. Maternal employment was supported by various provisions such as public child care, which reduced the unpaid care burden on women.

Policy differences resulted in unique country configurations of gender-class equality in paid and unpaid work. West German policies

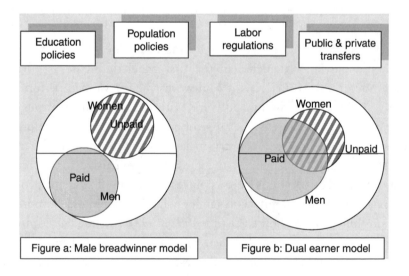

Figure 2.1 Policy effects on household production

sustained gender differences in both types of work, but minimized class differences across households. Australian policies similarly supported greater class equality while reinforcing gender differences in paid work, but policies did not necessarily reinforce gender differences in unpaid work. British and Spanish policies created greater class and gender inequalities in both types of work, but differed from each other in terms of the kind of employment available to women. In the United States, any gender and class differences in paid and unpaid work reflected the workings of the unregulated market. The East German socialist policies minimized some gender and class employment inequalities, but never fully addressed remaining gender inequalities associated with women's responsibility for unpaid work not covered by public child care (Ferree 1992).

So What Happened to the Gender Revolution?

Even strong male breadwinner policies could not keep women from employment. Women's employment helped to keep families out of poverty or buy luxury items, and also provided women with some economic independence (Blau et al. 2002; Oppenheimer 1997; Sorensen and McLanahan 1987). Household bargaining models predicted this revolution in partnered women's employment should have inspired a complementary revolution among men in that they would increase their housework and child care time (Simpson and England 1981). But by 1989, Hochschild had proclaimed the anticipated domestic revolution "stalled." Ever optimistic, Gershuny (2000) suggested the gender revolution had not stalled, but that adaptation was lagged. He argued women immediately adjusted their domestic hours as their relative time in employment increased, whereas men's domestic hours have been changing more slowly.

Between the 1960s and the mid-1990s, men across affluent economies had increased their reported time in housework and child care (Hook 2006). Yet women continued to perform the majority of housework and an even larger share of child care regardless of their employment participation (Cooke and Baxter 2010). These differences increased along the life course. Research using national longitudinal data revealed that gender differences in unpaid work were least among singles, increased when women and men formed a couple, and increased further after the birth of the first child (Baxter et al. 2008; Cooke 2007b; Evertsson and Nermo 2007; Gershuny et al. 2005; Gupta 1999).

If there has been only a modest increase in men's unpaid domestic work, what happened to the unpaid work no longer performed by women? The market forces drawing more women into employment did so in part by commodifying domestic production. As suggested in the second panel of Figure 2.1, much of women's formerly unpaid work became the paid work of other women. Unpaid child or elder care became either well-paid public sector positions dominated by women (Gornick and Jacobs 1998), or low-paid work dominated by less-skilled women and legal and illegal immigrants (Anderson 2000; Lyon and Glucksmann 2008; Misra et al. 2006; Williams 2004).

We therefore are not in the middle of a lagged adaptation toward greater gender equality, much less a revolution. Instead, group inequalities are alive and well; some have just shifted to new places. Countries continue to differ, however, in how much unpaid work shifted to the public sphere and the new gender, class, and other group intersections of work created in the process. These work reallocations occurred in the transition from industrial to post-industrial economies.

Gender-Class Equality in Post-Industrial Economies

A male breadwinner model is an artifact of an earlier industrial order, popularized by the new middle classes of the nineteenth century (Goldin 1990; Lewis 1992a; Pedersen 1993). It briefly re-emerged immediately after World War II when couples married at younger ages and went on to have more children than families had during the interwar period (Glass 1967; Oppenheimer 1997). This brief re-emergence was possible because manufacturing and trade unionism were approaching their peak in many countries (Ebbinghaus and Visser 1999), which enabled families to prosper on a single income.

Yet the civil rights and feminist movements also gained momentum in the aftermath of World War II, demanding greater group equality. Women in particular seized upon the new equal opportunity policies in education, remaining longer in secondary and then post-secondary schooling (DiPrete and Buchmann 2006; Shavit and Blossfeld 1993). Second-wave feminism reached a crescendo during the 1960s and 1970s, with more women declaring their intention of combining a fulfilling career with family. Married women's labor force participation rates continued to increase through the 1980s, most notably in the market-driven United States as well as the socialist and social-democratic countries that provided public child care and other policy supports (Blau et al. 2002; Einhorn 1993; Lewis and Astrom 1992; Szelewa and Polakowski 2008).

The shift from manufacturing to the service sector employment of post-industrial economies facilitated the increase in female labor force participation. Service sector employment required less brute strength and more people skills. The service sector also provided part-time jobs that offered flexibility for balancing paid work with family demands (Fagan and Walthery 2007; Plantenga and Remery 2005). As the welfare state also expanded in the post-war period, women's community volunteer work evolved into social work jobs dominated by women (Gornick and Jacobs 1998; Koven 1993). The increase in female employment in turn fueled growth in jobs that substituted market services and technology for unpaid domestic work. These substitutions included child care provision, as well as labor-saving household appliances, easy-care clothing, cleaning services, and restaurant and pre-packaged meals (de Ruijter et al. 2005; Vanek 1974).

As a result, the increase in female employment did not fundamentally threaten men's privileged access to employment or women's responsibility for domestic tasks. Men still dominated high-wage, full-time jobs in the private sector, whereas many women found low-wage, part-time jobs in the private sector or moderately waged jobs in the public sector (Bardasi and Gornick 2008; Budig and Misra, 2010; Mandel and Semyonov 2006). Some women managed class-based gains, but only by shifting unpaid work to less advantaged social groups. For example, a growing number of migrant women performed the domestic work of more affluent economies, with some leaving their children behind in their home country (Parreñas 2005; Zimmerman et al. 2006). Women in affluent economies also continued to shoulder the greater burden of any remaining unpaid household labor.

Within these trends, national institutional equality frames structure the total household time in paid and unpaid work, and how this differs by gender and class. In general, liberal markets encouraged labor force participation and provided greater returns to general education, which increased the total household hours in paid work. Pure market dynamics magnified any inequalities in education and work experience, however, so gender gaps in wages persisted despite high rates of female employment. Liberal markets offer the greatest reward to the highly educated, so women with more education do well in liberal markets (Estevez-Abe et al. 2001; Mandel and Semyonov 2005). At the same time, the earnings differences between women based on education are far greater than in more regulated markets (Soskice 2005).

As a result, the greater wage inequality of liberal markets leads to greater class differences in the gendered division of unpaid work, even though more women are likely to be employed in such markets. High wage inequality in liberal markets fosters the development of the low-wage service sector that can provide market substitutes for domestic tasks. Less-educated women fill these jobs, but at low wages that limit their ability to purchase domestic substitutes for themselves. In particular, purchasing private child care imposed a proportionally larger tax on these women's low earnings (Immervoll and Barber 2005). Without public provision of child care or subsidies that cover the cost of private care, low-income households in liberal market economies are more likely to rely on informal care arrangements or leave children to fend for themselves.[10] Consequently, liberal markets put less-educated women in the unenviable position of needing to engage in paid work, but at a wage penalty increased further by their remaining unpaid work responsibilities.

The lack of quality child care perpetuates the educational inequalities across generations (Esping-Andersen 2004; Heckman and Masterov 2007; Leseman 2009). Not surprisingly, Sarah McLanahan (2004) argued children's destinies diverge today more than in the past depending on their mothers' educational attainment. Part of the divergence in child outcomes stems from the greater options enjoyed by highly educated women in liberal market economies. Because people tend to marry those with similar education (Blossfeld and Timm 2003; Mare 1991), highly educated women in liberal markets can specialize in unpaid work and live well on their educated partners' high wages. Yet educated women's greater returns in liberal markets generally encourage them to work for pay. Educated women's high wages also allow them to purchase more substitutes for domestic tasks (Gupta 2007; Gupta et al. 2010), and invest in high-quality formal child care. Because educated women have the financial resources to "buy" their way out of domestic work, their educated husbands never have to increase their unpaid work hours. Thus highly educated women in liberal markets can enjoy greater equality within households because they shift the unpaid work burden to the market, where it becomes the low-wage work of women, ethnic minorities, and immigrants (Williams 2004).

Who does what in post-industrial economies is therefore determined by combinations of class and gender inequalities. The gender-class dynamics outlined above reflect those of unregulated markets, such as the United States. Policies in the other two English-speaking countries add further disparities to the pure market forces. The post-war British welfare state limited married women's employment-related benefits, whereas other regulations encouraged the proliferation of low-wage part-time work dominated by married women (Dex and Shaw 1986). The cash from family allowances and tax credits further reduced British women's employment incentive, particularly among less-educated women. These male breadwinner policies defied the reality of the British economy. During the 1970s, for example, three times as many British two-parent families would have been poor if they had relied solely on the father's employment income (Land 1976). Today, Britain and the United States have nearly identical female employment rates, but more than 40 percent of employed British women work part-time, as compared with one-quarter of US women.[11] As a result, there is greater gender paid hours inequality among less-educated UK women than in the United States. Other class and gender differences in paid and unpaid work, however, should be similar.

During the late 1960s, the powerful Australian trade unions that had earlier won family wages for men won comparable worth policies for women. The comparable worth policies required that women were to be paid the same as men for work of equal value, which increased the incentive for Australian women to remain in paid work. Their higher wages also enhanced Australian women's bargaining power when negotiating the division of unpaid work with their partners. But the policies that provided men and women with good wages also blocked the development of market substitutes for domestic work because they stymied the growth of a low-wage service sector (Scharpf and Schmidt 2000). Wage equality policies also capped the relative affluence of university-educated workers, thereby reducing the household income available for purchasing market substitutes for domestic work. Consequently, the wage equality policies that enhanced gender employment equality also increased the total hours of unpaid work. But the relative absence of post-war policies reinforcing women's responsibility for unpaid work coupled with Australian women's enhanced earnings should yield a more egalitarian division of this unpaid work than in the United Kingdom or United States.

In East Germany, socialist policies supported women's employment and mandated greater wage equality between women and men. In addition, the unpaid care work became good-wage public sector employment. Less-educated women benefited from these policies, as they were ensured relatively decent pay, whereas public provision of child care eliminated its private cost. Yet these "family-friendly" policies reflected a renegotiation of the private sphere between women and the state, not between women and men (Hernes 1987). Consequently, the East German public child care reduced some unpaid care work but did not reduce gender inequality in the remaining unpaid work of the private sphere (Ferree 1992). The under-developed service sector in socialist economies also provided very few market substitutes and the state-dictated wages offered little disposable income to "buy" out of domestic work. As a result, East German women attained greater gender equality in paid work hours, but with persistent responsibility for a rather large amount of unpaid work. In other words, East German women's greater equality in paid work came at a cost of greater time poverty as women spent more total hours in paid and unpaid work than men.

As in Australia, West German class equality policies ensured greater wage equality across men and inhibited the development of a low-wage service sector that provides market substitutes for domestic work. Conservative policy elements reinforced West German women's responsibility for this more time-intensive unpaid work (Ostner 1992, 1993). West German married women's exit from employment, however, created shortages in certain occupations such as teaching and nursing (von Oertzen 1999). This led to a series of policies that improved women's part-time civil service employment opportunities (Töns and Young 2001). A similar percentage of employed West German women now work part-time as in the United Kingdom, but these part-time workers are frequently highly educated West German women. Even employed West German women, however, retain responsibility for the greater unpaid work hours. This time burden has caused Germans to look across national borders for low-wage domestic workers. Recent legislation allows households to employ temporary Polish domestic workers provided they do not encroach on the high-wage care work of West Germans (Misra et al. 2006).

Spain industrialized rapidly after 1945, but Fascism created deeper insider-outsider cleavages than in northern Europe (Ferrera 1996). Rigid labor market rules sustained a privileged position for the small proportion of workers employed in the civil service and large industrial enterprises. Many others were self-employed or found work in the black market estimated to produce between 15 and 30 percent of Spain's gross domestic product (Ferrera 2005). A range of policies discouraged female employment, yielding one of the largest gender employment gaps of affluent economies (OECD 2002).

Today, educated Spanish women who are employed tend to work full-time in the protected sectors (Franco and Winqvist 2002). Less-educated women are more likely to find jobs in the black market (Barbera and Vettor 2001). Class differences among Spanish women are therefore greater than among Spanish men. Less-educated women also spend far more hours doing unpaid work. Educated Spanish women, particularly in urban centers, enjoy greater equality in paid and unpaid work because the latter burden is eased by immigrant domestic workers (Kofman et al. 2000; Tobio 2001). Once again, women coping under a male bread-winner model can achieve somewhat greater equality by shifting unpaid work to an even more disadvantaged group.

Summary: Policy Paths and Gender-Class Equality

Modernization theory held that the increasing importance of education would eventually yield greater group equality in industrial economies. Yet the market has in fact magnified group differences in education and subsequent human capital accumulation. Consequently, gender and class inequality persist in the most liberal markets. Highly educated women enjoy greater equality in paid and unpaid work, but by shifting domestic tasks down class and ethnic hierarchies. In addition, highly educated men in liberal markets reap greater market returns than similarly educated women because women still retain responsibility for the remaining unpaid work. Markets alone cannot eradicate inequality because they efficiently reward or penalize even minuscule group differences in education, work experience, and effort.

Class-equality policies have gendered effects on both paid and unpaid work. Greater class equality was frequently made possible by restricting the labor supply of women and other minority groups (Bertola et al. 2007). Those few women who are employed in these markets, however, generally benefit from the wage policies that benefit all working men (Pettit and Hook 2009). Cases where the state assumes some responsibility for unpaid care work lead to greater female participation rates, but via greater occupational segregation of women into public sector positions (Mandel and Semyonov 2006; Lewis and Astrom 1992). Recent evidence has shown that family-friendly policies improve the wages of less-skilled women, but in part by limiting the private sector employment of highly educated women (Mandel and Semyonov 2006).

Wage equality also inhibits the development of a low-wage service sector that offers market substitutes for unpaid domestic tasks. Consequently, class equality gains in paid work correlate with greater unpaid work hours that remain women's responsibility. State care provision reduces some of these unpaid hours, but by making them women's public sector wage work. In addition, women employed full-time retain responsibility for the remaining unpaid work, the hours of which are greater than in liberal markets. In short, employed women in more class-equal economies have a greater total burden of paid and unpaid work than men. Their burden is also greater than similar women in the class-unequal liberal markets. Without the ability to shift the unpaid work burden down the class hierarchy, women in class-equal economies increasingly use legal and illegal immigrants (Anderson 2000; Misra et al. 2006).

Thus, focusing on just class or just gender policies is insufficient for capturing the complex structure of group inequalities in paid and unpaid work. As detailed in the next three chapters, the institutional equality frame in each country was built from a range of policies affecting individuals across the life course. As industrialization gave way to post-industrialization and social hierarchies responded to social movements, relative group advantages shuffled around within the frame but without altering the frame itself.

3

POPULATION POLICIES AND GROUP DIVIDES

Introduction

Women's biological capacity for childbearing has become conflated with a gendered and lifelong responsibility for care work. Indeed, historically the two were tightly linked. In 1800, women spent much of their short lives giving birth to six or seven children, frequently dying in the endeavor. Fertility rates have steadily declined in industrialized societies since that time, whereas life expectancy increased. By 2000, people in affluent economies lived well into their seventies, with women on average bearing fewer than two children (Riley 2001). Across affluent industrial societies, one in five women foregoes childbearing all together.[1] Once born, a child can be reared by either parent, by other adults in the home, or spend part of each day in care outside of the home. As children grow older, they spend substantial time under the "care" of others within compulsory schooling systems. The capacity for childbearing, however, still dictates women's lifetime responsibility for care work.

Humans, however, share a capacity for caring. Tronto (1993: 127) differentiates among caring *about*, care *receiving, responsibility* for care, and care-*giving*. She argued that in industrial market economies, the physical labor of care-giving gets relegated to the least powerful.[2]

Accordingly, the assignment of care work to women reflects gender social hierarchies more than biological predispositions. The social hierarchy of care is evident as well in that the less-educated, ethnic minorities or immigrants are paid to perform the care work of affluent women. This enables wealthier women to enjoy the same luxury enjoyed by most men, of "care as emotion freed from labour" (Anderson 2000: 87).

These hierarchies are reinforced by a variety of social forces, including state policies. In this chapter I detail how state population policies institutionalized care hierarchies, which in turn created gender differences in access to paid work. As outlined in the first section, the declining fertility rates of the nineteenth century caused state concern over future economic and imperial growth. As a result, state policies ventured into the most intimate of private spheres: women's bodies. States mandated that the fetus was a citizen and entitled to state protection of its rights. This created a new sociopolitical issue as to whose citizenship rights should prevail: the civil rights of the fetus when protecting it, or women's right to privacy from state intervention. Also at issue were women's social rights in terms of equal access to contraception and/or abortion, as well as men's property rights over their offspring (O'Connor et al. 1999).

Policy resolution of these incendiary debates sketched out women's place within the state's reproduction hierarchy. Prioritizing fetal rights made women subservient to the reproductive capacity of their bodies, although there were class differences in these effects. For example, under the first English abortion regulations, single and poor women were most frequently apprehended for illegal abortion. In contrast, wealthy women could avoid prosecution by traveling to Paris to obtain abortions (Francome 1984). Policies requiring fathers' consent to contraception or pregnancy termination prioritized men's property rights over women. Under fascism, fetal and fathers' rights took precedence over women's, but all were in service to the state.

Policies reinforcing women's reproductive capacity dovetailed with those restricting women's employment, which reduced the reserve workforce necessary for industrial expansion. Consequently, the labor market effects of policies reinforcing women's responsibility for unpaid care work could be offset with immigration policies. During the nineteenth century, most migrant flows were young single men going from Europe to the Americas or Australia (Castles and Miller 2003). Employers generally supported immigration, as an increase in the number of workers reduced wages (Freeman and Birrell 2001). For the same reasons, organized labor resisted immigration. The political debates were frequently racialized, based on migrants' perceived religious and ethnic differences (Tataki 1990; Zinn 2005). In these ways, population policies institutionalized gender and ethnic hierarchies in early industrial societies.

The Nazis' "final solution" precipitated a change in the political discourse and post-war policy approach, as discussed in the second section of this chapter. Restrictive reproduction policies disintegrated under pressure from feminist and human rights groups, to be replaced with more state financial support for families. For a brief period in history, couples married at younger ages and fertility rates increased, resulting in the post-war Baby Boom (Glass 1967). Post-war economic growth again required young male migrant workers, but immigration flows shifted as more men from the global South migrated north. The ethnic divides of these new migrant flows sparked new political debates, particularly as immigrants from former colonies arrived in northern Europe. Thus, policies continued to restrict immigrant numbers, ethnic mixes, claims to citizenship rights, and the right to family settlement.

The evolution from industrial to post-industrial economies coincided with a "second demographic transition" (van de Kaa 1987) that presented new population policy challenges. As discussed in the final section of the chapter, introduction of the birth control pill in the 1960s and reduced abortion restrictions through the 1970s allowed women to control their fertility and enter the labor market in growing numbers. Fertility declined most sharply in the Mediterranean and former socialist countries (Kohler et al. 2002). Marriage rates also declined, whereas cohabitation and divorce rates increased (Becker 1985). Life course patterns switched sequence, with more women having children before or otherwise outside of legal marriage (Heuveline et al. 2003). The number of single-parent families grew rapidly, and these families were far more likely to be poor and require some state financial assistance than two-parent families (Daly and Rake 2003; Rainwater and

Smeeding 2004). People were also living longer after retirement, which put greater strain on public health and pension systems (Myles 2002).[3]

The rising cost of welfare provision was making the gendered division of paid and unpaid labor economically unviable (Esping-Andersen 2009; McDonald 2000). Instead, labor activation and work-family reconciliation policies began to dominate (Plantenga and Remery 2005; Taylor-Gooby 2004). "Active" labor market policies support the transition of unemployed persons into the labor force with counseling, job-seeking assistance, or additional training (Kenworthy 2008; Taylor-Gooby 2004). Active labor market policies also target groups, such as single mothers, who are more likely to be out of the labor market for extended periods of time. Work-family reconciliation policies support individuals in combining professional and family life. Such policies include child care services, parental leave provisions, flexible working arrangements, and family financial assistance (Plantenga and Remery 2005). In short, more policies now encouraged women, particularly mothers, to remain employed.

The increase in maternal employment created a new demand for care workers. Some policy rhetoric and small amendments in parental leave policies encouraged men's greater participation in child care (Gauthier 2005; Hobson 2002). Most of the unpaid domestic work, however, became the paid work of less-educated indigenous women or immigrant women from transitional and developing economies. Many immigrant women left their own children in the care of relatives in the home country, creating what Ehrenreich and Hochschild (2003) called "global care chains." Policies supported these shifts in the care hierarchy by offering families more cash transfers or tax credits with which they might pay for private care (Misra et al. 2006). The Mediterranean countries began offering periodic regularization programs for illegal migrants who were performing care work (Bettio et al. 2006; Lyon and Glucksmann 2008). Thus a social hierarchy of care work persisted in each country, with the institutional equality frame dictating its precise gender-class-ethnic configurations.

Nineteenth-Century Expansion and Women's Bodies

Industrialization, in addition to adding distance between homes and factories, spurred urbanization and the spread of infectious diseases.[4]

Most people born during this time died in infancy, not old age, with the risk of death highest among the working poor. Malthus[5] published his famous essay on population in which he argued that the epidemics, famines, and plagues offered proof of a population over-stretching its earthly bounds. Over time, public health measures improved urban living and mortality rates declined. Women also began to take more active control over their fertility, "doing by other methods what squalor and disease had done for generations" (Borrie et al. 1946: 5). Fertility rates started to decline during the eighteenth century, first in Sweden, then in France, and in other industrialized countries the following century.[6] This posed a problem for the state, which required population growth for economic and imperialist expansion. Many states therefore began to regulate the biological sources of future workers and soldiers. The state introduced new policies regulating women's attempts at contraception, as well as pregnancy termination.

Public debates over contraception and women's sexuality frequently intertwined with emerging concepts of motherhood promoted by the White and unemployed wives of the new and growing middle class. These "maternalists" valorized women's unpaid care work and claimed responsibility for the moral development of not only their own children, but also the broader community.[7] Maternalists frequently lobbied for maternity and health benefits for women, ran day nurseries and provided in-home assistance—welcomed or not—to working-class or single mothers.[8]

In contrast to liberal feminist demands for women's equal access to education and employment, maternalists promoted a "woman's morality" distinct from men's and claimed women's responsibility for care work and relationships (Beck 1992; Gilligan 1996; Tronto 1993).[9] To achieve this, the public image of woman as a sensual creature needed to be replaced with one of a demure wife offering her body to her husband only when offspring were desired. For the maternalists, sex with active birth control rendered wives no better than prostitutes. Malthus also opposed birth control, fearing it would lead to greater promiscuity. The political debate about birth control therefore frequently contained moral arguments to support the pro-natalist intentions (Besemeres 1980).

Initial state policies regulating contraception or abortion were harsh. For example, abortion in Britain was made illegal in 1803, with the penalty varying by when termination occurred. Prior to quickening,[10] the woman was subject to a maximum of 14 years transportation to one of the colonies. After quickening, abortion was punishable by death. The law was subsequently subsumed within the 1861 Offenses Against the Persons Act, which was the first law to differentiate between lawful and unlawful abortion. This allowed abortion under certain circumstances. As a British colony, Australia complied with the 1861 British Act in regulating abortion, although individual states differed in what comprised a lawful procedure. British contraception law in the first half of the nineteenth century also made it illegal to publicize birth control information. Restrictions on information eased following the Bradlaugh-Besant trial of 1876 (Francome 1984),[11] and in 1921, Marie Stopes opened the first birth control clinic in London. The Catholic Church rallied some opposition to the growing accessibility of contraception during the 1920s, but the effort faltered in the 1930s when the Church supported the Nazi population policies. Contraception debates were also muted in Australia, as the country sustained strong population growth throughout the nineteenth and early twentieth centuries (Borrie 1948).

As in Australia, US states' reproduction policies differed. In 1821, Connecticut became the first to make abortion after quickening illegal. The American Medical Association instigated an anti-abortion campaign during the nineteenth century because of worry over the fecundity of Catholic immigrants as compared with native Protestants (Beisel and Kay 2004).[12] By the end of the century, most US states had some restrictions on abortion, although only six banned it entirely.[13] In contrast, regulation of contraception information became a matter for federal law with the passage of the 1873 Comstock Law making it illegal to send information on abortion, contraception, or pornography through the mail (Francome 1984).

In Germany and Spain, Catholicism and later right-wing governments shaped the reproductive discourse. Spain's 1822 state penal code made performing abortions illegal, a position strongly supported by the Roman Catholic Church (Valiente 2001). After the Spanish Civil War of 1936, a victorious Franco promoted *grandeza*, the greatness of Spain, based on the integration of the different regions, imperial expansion, and population increase. Central to this was the notion of an *angel del hogar* (angel of the home) whose biological and social destiny was motherhood (Nash 1991). Franco's rhetoric, also endorsed by the Roman Catholic Church, denounced Second Republic gains in female suffrage and easing of divorce law. In 1941, abortion became a crime against the state.

Germany became the last of the countries here to prohibit abortion with the 1871 German Prussian Penal Code (Glass 1967). In 1897, it became the first country with an abortion reform movement. The German Social Democratic party, particularly women among rank-and-file workers, staunchly supported and practiced contraception. Yet the Catholic Church remained powerful despite Bismarck's *Kulturkampf* laws between 1871 and 1887 to reduce its influence. The 1919 Weimar Republic encapsulated this polarity. The constitution granted the socialists' demands for women's public equality, whereas the German Civil Code (*Bürgerliches Gesetzbuch*) included the Catholic Zentrum party's demands for *pater familias*: husbands' extensive and explicit patriarchal rights over their wives.[14] Socialists lobbied to amend the civil code until 1938, when Hitler declared that marriage was "no end in itself; rather it must serve a greater goal, that of expanding and sustaining the nation" (Moeller 1993: 50). In pursuit of population "quality" and "racial uplift" (*Aufartung*), the National Socialists mandated mass sterilization for 10 to 30 percent of the population in 1933, imposed non-voluntary abortion for some in 1935, and in the following year banned elective abortions among those they considered desirable—Aryans as opposed to Semites (Bock 1991; Glass 1967).

All state reproductive policies of the nineteenth and early twentieth centuries therefore restricted a woman's ability to control her fertility before and after conception.[15] These debates intermingled with a discourse promoting a White, middle-class, pious, and fertile feminine ideal. Subsequent policies reinforced women's responsibility for the

Table 3.1 Crude birth rates 1870, 1900, 1935–39

	BIRTHS/1000 POPULATION		
	1870	1900	1935–39
Australia	40	28	17
Germany	39	36	19
Great Britain	35	29	15
Spain	39	36	22
United States	37	29	17

Sources: Data for 1870 and 1990 for Australia from Spencer (1971: 249); Spain from Bacci (1968a: 227); Germany, Great Britain and the United States from Nugent (1992: 20). 1935–39 statistics from the *UN 1969 Demographic Yearbook*, Table 12.

unpaid work of private spheres, whether in the home or community. Yet fertility itself continued to decline in all of the countries, as shown in Table 3.1. Fertility declined most sharply and to a similar level in the three English-speaking countries. Declines in Germany and Spain were slightly blunted by their more aggressive pro-natalist policies. Far more crucial to population growth in all of the countries were advances in health and mortality, along with the global surge in migration.

Nineteenth-Century Immigration Policies

During the nineteenth century, the population of Britain more than tripled in size, whereas the populations of Germany and Spain doubled. Even so, these were primarily sending countries, with millions of British, German, and Spanish migrants leaving Europe for the Americas and Australia.[16] Following passage of the 1790 Naturalization Act, the US population increased from 5 to 85 million by 1900.[17] The Act established uniform rules for the naturalization of "free White persons" of "good moral character" after just two years of residence. The 1790 Act made the United States the most open receiving country, reflected in the inscription on the Statue of Liberty:

> Give me your tired, your poor,
> Your huddled masses yearning to breathe free,
> The wretched refuse of your teeming shore.
> Send these, the homeless, tempest-tossed to me.
> I lift my lamp beside the golden door.

Despite the rhetoric of open US immigration, racial divides were embedded in subsequent policies. In 1808, the US banned the importation of slaves, although an illegal trade continued in the South. Irish crop failures resulted in almost 2 million new Catholic immigrants arriving during the 1840s. At this time, the Irish were also considered one of the "dark" races and were therefore forbidden to marry "White" Americans (Beisel and Kay 2004; Zinn 2005). The disparity in family sizes between Catholics and Protestants is what spurred the American Medical Association to lobby against abortion. The medical doctors were not seeking to limit Catholic family sizes; instead they wanted Protestants to increase theirs to ensure continuation of a White Anglo-Saxon Protestant nation (Beisel and Kay 2004).

In 1849, the California gold rush attracted migrants from China. The influx of low-wage, hard-working Chinese became a threat to the fledgling US trade unions.[18] Unions lobbied for passage of the 1862 "Anti-Coolie" Act that imposed special taxes on employers who hired indentured Chinese workers.[19] Asians remained excluded from citizenship in the 1870 Naturalization Act, which expanded citizenship to Whites and African-Americans. Asians were also excluded from the Fifteenth Amendment that granted all (male) citizens voting rights. Following anti-Chinese riots in several western cities, Congress passed the 1882 Chinese Exclusion Act restricting all Chinese immigration to the United States for 10 years. Congress renewed the exclusion for another 10 years in 1892, and renewed it indefinitely in 1902.[20]

In 1917, the US Congress over-rode President Wilson's veto to pass an immigrant literacy test. That same year, Congress banned all migration from Asia. In the aftermath of World War I, Congress enacted the Quota Law of 1921, which set temporary limits on total immigration and further limited the number of migrants from any given country. Quotas were based on the number of past migrants from each country, which favored immigrants from the Northern and Western Hemispheres over those from Eastern Europe or Asia. Quotas became permanent in 1924. By 1930, the US "golden door" for immigrants was essentially closed (Timmer and Williamson 1998).

Australia was also a major receiving country during this period, and its immigration policies similarly favored Western Europeans and restricted Asians. In 1788, the first 1,000 British immigrants, including 700 convicts, landed at Botany Bay.[21] To ease the shortage of free labor and women, the 1823 Constitution Act legalized indentured labor, which provided transportation for young free British in exchange for seven years' servitude. This financial assistance continued until 1870 and was almost exclusively targeted at British nationals. British women from workhouses and charitable homes were also brought over, although "of a quality sufficient to cause the Sydney *Herald* to remark that they added pollution to a society of convicts" (Borrie 1948: 34).

As in the United States, the 1850 Australian gold discovery attracted Chinese immigrants, leading to worker violence in Victoria and New South Wales. In response, the colonial governments restricted Chinese immigration as had the US government. In 1901, the new Australian Commonwealth (federal) government passed the Immigration Restriction Act, which came to be known as the White Australia policy (Borrie et al. 1946). It prohibited employment of Pacific Islanders and required immigrants to write out a dictated passage "fifty words in length in an European language directed by the officer" (Section 3a).[22] The Australian government argued Asia was a military as well as low-wage labor threat (Borrie 1948), with the White Australia policy essential to national security.

Thus, by the eve of the Second World War, states had codified ethnic divisions within their populations through immigration policies, although racial divides shifted with each new migrant wave. With respect to gender, fetal rights dominated women's rights in all of the countries, reinforcing women's responsibility for reproduction and unpaid care work. Immigration policies eased the labor shortages caused by women remaining in the home, but favored those migrants considered more alike in terms of skin color and religion. All of this changed with World War II. The war and its atomic resolution signaled a change in modern economic and military strategy from one of population numbers (brawn) to one of technology (brains). The demand for greater human rights and the need to harness technology demanded a different approach to population policy.

Post-War Family Policies

After the war, Europe required rebuilding and governments sought to avoid the economic depression of the inter-war period. In 1944, representatives of the Allied nations met in Bretton Woods, New Hampshire, to develop a system of global financial management. The International Monetary Fund was established to bridge any temporary imbalance of payments. These agreements allowed governments to take a more interventionist approach to national markets and citizen welfare, based on Keynesian rather than liberal *laissez-faire* economic policies. John Maynard Keynes (1936) argued economic depressions could be avoided when governments invested in the public infrastructure and guaranteed full employment. Under Keynesian principles, national welfare programs expanded rapidly, making the post-war decades the "golden age" of welfare (Esping-Andersen 1996).

One of Keynes' recommendations was that governments should directly ease the cost associated with children rather than increase wages.[23] The main family policies in this regard included paid maternity leave, dependent child and spousal tax credits, and family allowances. The financial incentives in these policies reinforced varying degrees of a male breadwinner model for couple households. For example, lump-sum tax credits or family allowances offered less-skilled mothers an alternative to poor-quality employment. Rather than work for low wages, these mothers could stay at home but still bring in some money associated with their otherwise unpaid care work. Tax credits and allowances paid through wages tended to reinforce men's control of economic resources, since they were more likely to be employed than their wives. In contrast, family or carer benefits paid directly to mothers increased these women's economic resources. Such benefits could therefore narrow the gender economic gap associated with women's responsibility for unpaid care work.

As evident in Table 3.2, the United States never introduced a general family allowance,[24] although the federal tax system offered modest dependent tax deductions.[25] Employed mothers were entitled to maternity leave if they had corporate sickness benefits, but 12 weeks of unpaid family leave did not become a right for all parents until 1993. As a

Table 3.2 Summary of initial post-war family allowances

	YEAR	TYPE
Australia	1941	flat-rate universal for children above first payable to carer
United Kingdom	1945	flat-rate universal for children above first payable to carer
Spain	1945	large family bonuses payable to male breadwinner
East Germany	1950	supports for maternal employment; after 1965, childbirth subsidies
West Germany	1954	payable to wage earners with 3 or more children
United States	None	(1935 Social Security Act provided matching grants to states for means-tested benefits)

result, US post-war policy remained the least family-supportive (Gornick and Meyers 2003; Kamerman and Kahn 1997). At the same time, the lack of family financial support rendered US policy more gender-neutral in terms of reinforcing women's responsibility for unpaid work.

In 1941, Australia became the first of the countries here to introduce a universal child allowance. This allowance covered all children after the first and was payable directly to the caring parent, usually the mother. The child allowance discouraged mothers' employment, but offered some direct compensation for their unpaid care work. Britain introduced a similar flat-rate allowance in 1945 after much political wrangling before designating the mother to be the recipient.[26]

In contrast to Australia, the new British welfare state was, in fact, premised on William Beveridge's assumption that: "the great majority of married women must be regarded as occupied on work which is vital though unpaid, without which their husbands could not do their paid work and without which the nation could not continue" (1942: 50). Beveridge proposed maternity benefits 50 percent higher than single women's or married men's unemployment benefit. Yet no policies ensured British men might earn family wages as in Australia.

In Spain, the government introduced maternity insurance in 1942 and large family bonuses in 1945, both considered wage supplements and payable directly to the male breadwinner. Large Spanish families also benefited from school grants, tax exemptions, credit facilities, access to housing, sanitary assistance, and other preferential provisions

(Nash 1991). Women's dependence on a male breadwinner was also reinforced in the 1945 *Fuero de los Espanoles* that claimed the indissolubility of marriage and confirmed male authority in the family (Nash 1991). Spanish policies therefore reinforced women's responsibility for unpaid care work and her subservience to a male breadwinner.

Post-war policies of the East and West regions of Germany had very different gender effects. The western German *Länder* (states) that formed the new Federal Republic of Germany under British, French, and US occupation needed a new constitution that contained no traces of either the Third Reich or socialism. The Allies identified the Catholic Church as an institution that had not succumbed to the Nazi dictatorship (Moeller 1993, 1997). From this position, conservative West German politicians successfully argued for *pater familias* under Article 6 of the 1949 West German Basic Law (*Grundgesetz*), simultaneous with granting women public equality under Article 3 much as had been done in the Weimar Republic. During the 1950s and 1960s, other policies that reinforced the patriarchal family included a universal maternity allowance,[27] child tax rebates, and child allowances (*Kindergeld*) payable to wage earners with three or more children.[28] Technically, the sizeable post-war population of single mothers was also eligible for allowances, but only 13 percent had the requisite number of children (Moeller 1997).[29] West German married women's responsibility for the domestic sphere remained a legal duty until 1977 (Ostner 1992), similar to Spanish women's.

In contrast to West Germany, the five *Länder*[30] forming the German Democratic Republic in eastern Germany were forced to adopt a Stalinist constitution in 1949 that guaranteed women full equality with men. The 1950 Mother and Child Care and Women's Rights Acts included plans for public child care centers, kindergartens, free school meals, maternity leave at full pay, and days off to tend sick children. The infrastructure was slow to develop, however, and fertility declined in the 1950s and 1960s. More aggressive policies followed with the passage of the 1965 Family Law Code (*Familiengesetzbuch*). Between 1966 and 1972, childbirth subsidies and paid maternity leave increased, and mothers were granted pension credits and preferential access to housing.[31] These policies recognized East German women's caring responsibility and provided state support for some of it, but did not address the persistent gender differences in unpaid work within the home.

The post-war family policies therefore reinforced different gendered divisions of care work in each country, and its implications for women's economic equality. Australia's family wages reinforced the gendered division of paid work, but the care allowances payable to mothers narrowed gender economic differences. British family policy directly reinforced women's responsibility for unpaid care work, with the flat-rate family allowance similarly easing financial inequalities between women and men. The lack of US family policy or allowances allowed the gendered division of unpaid work be determined by market forces. Spanish and West German policies aggressively reinforced women's care responsibility and economic dependence on a male breadwinner, with policies in both countries infused with the *pater familias* of Roman Catholicism. East German policies took some responsibility for care work and supported women in their performance of it, but did not go so far as to encourage care work among men.

But neither male breadwinner policies nor socialist pro-natalist policies boosted fertility rates.[32] As evident in Table 3.3, the crude birth rate was lowest in post-war England and just modestly higher in the two German regions. Birth rates were higher in Australia, and highest in the United States despite its lack of policy support for families. So once again, migration was more important to population growth than fertility. As each country's welfare state expanded, however, immigrant access to the new social rights, in addition to civil and political rights, varied (Sainsbury 2006).

Table 3.3 Post-war crude birth rates 1950–54, 1960–64

	BIRTHS/1000 POPULATION		
	1935–39	1950–54	1960–64
Australia	17.2	23.0	21.9
England/Wales	14.9	15.5	17.9
East Germany	19.4	17.0	17.4
West Germany	19.4	16.1	18.3
Spain	22.0	20.3	21.6
United States	17.2	24.5	22.4

Source: *UN Demographic Yearbook 1969:* Table 12.

Immigration Policies in the Post-War Economic Recovery

New constellations of sending and receiving countries emerged after the war, although Spain would remain a sending country until Franco's death in 1975 (Freeman 1995). Reflecting the post-war democratic discourse around human rights, Australia and the United States broadened their sources of new migrants. The United States repealed the Chinese Exclusion Act in 1943, and granted Filipinos and persons from India entry in 1946. The comprehensive 1952 Immigration and Nationality Act retained something of the pre-war quota system, but race could no longer bar naturalization and immigration (Freeman and Birrell 2001). Migrants from Japan, Korea, and Indonesia finally gained entry. Amendments to the National Act in 1965 incorporated stronger anti-discrimination language, eliminated the quota system, and gave preference to re-uniting family members (Freeman and Birrell 2001). These provisions encouraged large-scale immigration from Asia and Latin America, as well as family settlement. Employed legal immigrants paid into the federal social security system through payroll taxes, and in turn were eligible to receive unemployment, disability, or pension benefits as would any employed American.

Australia dropped its White Australia policy in the 1960s (North 1984). In 1975, the government introduced a family reunion program for sponsoring immigrants' brothers, sisters, and parents. Immigrants were immediately granted access to most of Australia's welfare programs on arrival, including universal public health care and education (Freeman and Birrell 2001).

Great Britain and Germany transitioned to receiving countries with less grace (Fassmann and Münz 1992). To ease labor shortages, Britain's 1945 Atlee government recruited Polish soldiers and other refugees. The 1948 British Nationality Act allowed all citizens within the British Commonwealth to live and work in Britain, although the Irish gained special privileges. The Irish could enter and depart without restriction, and obtained the right to vote, stand for Parliament, and work. By 1961, the Irish population residing in England had increased by three-quarters of a million people (Messina 2001).

The Nationality Act also led to an influx of workers from India, Pakistan, and the West Indies. By 1961, the total population of these new migrants would be just 10 percent of the Irish population, but created more political unease (Messina 2001).[33] The 1962 Commonwealth Immigrants Act instituted a labor-voucher system to reduce colonial immigration despite continuing labor shortages. In 1968, a new Commonwealth Immigrants Act denied entry to British Asians expelled from newly independent Kenya (Joppke 1996). A subsequent 1971 Act required any new immigrants from Commonwealth nations to have at least one British grandparent, a policy that effectively excluded many ethnic migrants from the former colonies.

West Germany was required to accept more than 8 million displaced ethnic Germans from Czechoslovakia, Poland, and Hungary under Article XII of the 1945 Potsdam Agreement. These displaced persons and refugees benefited from integration measures, including housing allowances, vocational training, German language courses, and rights to public pensions (Bade and Weiner 1997). After 1953, ethnic Germans (*Aussiedler*) were differentiated from other foreigners (*Ausländer*) in the Basic Law, and automatically granted German citizenship on the presumption they were persecuted because of their German ethnicity.[34] During the decade, an estimated 4 million East Germans also fled to West Germany (Münz and Ulrich 1995; Trappe 2000). The socialists erected the Berlin Wall in 1961 to staunch the emigration.

As the flow of *Aussiedler* slowed, West Germany signed a series of bilateral agreements for guest workers, beginning with the Mediterranean countries (Italy in 1955, Spain and Greece in 1960). After the Berlin Wall went up, West Germany recruited from farther afield: Turkey (1961 and 1964), Morocco, Tunisia, and Yugoslavia (1963, 1965, and 1968). In contrast to the *Aussiedler,* these *Ausländer* could not bring dependents and frequently resided in modest employer-built accommodations (S. Castles 1985). They also were prohibited from "freedom of assembly, freedom of association, freedom of movement and free choice of occupation, place of work and place of education" (1965 *Ausländergesetzes*, paragraph 6). Despite these limitations, the number of guest workers rose from 95,000 in 1956 to 2.6 million in 1973. That same year, Germany, along with many other countries, enacted a ban on certain groups of temporary migrant workers (Fassmann and Münz 1992). The reason was not political, however, but economic. The 1973–74 oil shocks marked the end of the golden age of post-war economic and welfare state growth. In its place came a new era of "globalization" and associated economic, political, and demographic changes that reshuffled the groups within the institutional equality frame.[35]

Reproduction in the "New" Global Economy

Wallerstein (1976) argued that we have been living in a global economy for several centuries. Global economic and demographic changes since the 1970s, however, strained the institutional framework of many welfare states (Brady et al. 2005; Esping-Andersen et al. 2002). The Bretton Woods Accord faltered in 1971 as fixed exchange rates collapsed, making it difficult for countries to ensure full employment. The Accord's organizational offspring, the International Monetary Fund and World Bank, continued to flourish and encouraged expansion of neoliberal aid packages to developing countries.[36] Technological capacity in communications and transportation exploded, moving information and people more quickly across borders. Banks established international consortia, increasing global capital mobility. Full-time manufacturing jobs in affluent economies moved offshore, to countries with non-unionized and lower-waged workers. These changes put pressure on the wages of affluent economies, leading to deregulation of many labor markets. Part-time and fixed-term employment expanded (Standing 1999).

As these economic changes unfurled, a growing number of partnered women entered employment. This coincided with a "second wave" of feminism during the 1960s and 1970s (Nicholson 1997). Liberal feminists argued that to compete effectively in the public sphere, women needed to regain control of the reproductive activities that tied them to the private sphere. Under pressure from feminist activists, state restrictions on abortion began to fall away, although the nature of the amended state rights varied across countries.[37] For example, Britain and Australia modified women's civil right to abortion and also supported it as a social right through their public health systems (O'Connor et al. 1999). Britain's 1967 Abortion Act permitted legal termination of pregnancies up to 28 weeks (Lewis 1992b). Two doctors were required to certify that bringing the pregnancy to term would cause the women physical or mental harm. By 1974, all British women could access abortion and contraception for free through the National Health Service (Zweiniger-Bargielowska 2001). The 1990 Human Fertilisation and Embryology Act lowered the time limit from 28 to 24 weeks, and there have been subsequent legislative attempts to lower it further.[38]

Australia followed the United Kingdom on a state-by-state basis. The 1969 *Menhennitt* ruling in Victoria and the 1971 *Levine* ruling in New South Wales broadened the acceptable legal conditions for abortions (Coleman 1988).[39] No Australian state today requires consent of the woman's partner or an enforced waiting period, although Western Australia requires a minor to notify their parents. The Australian national health insurance system reimburses some of the cost at a fixed rate across the country. Technically, however, abortion remains illegal except in the Australian Capital Territory, which removed abortion from the criminal statutes in 2002.

In the United States, abortion became a civil, but not a social right. In 1967, California liberalized abortion when it expanded the range of circumstances under which it was deemed therapeutic.[40] By 1970, Alaska, Hawaii, New York, and Washington offered abortion on demand. The 1973 Supreme Court ruling in *Roe v. Wade* granted all US women the right to abortion within the first three months of pregnancy.[41] The initial ruling also limited states' ability to add further caveats, thus ensuring US women's constitutional right to abortion regardless of where she might live. These rights, however, remain susceptible to subsequent contestation (O'Connor et al. 1999). The 1976 Hyde Amendment upheld by the Supreme Court limited the expenditure of federal funds on abortion.[42] So in contrast to Australia and the United Kingdom, US women's civil right to abortion retained a class bias, mediated by a woman's financial ability to pay for the procedure.[43] The Supreme Court also upheld the "gag rule" in 1991, which prohibited personnel in federally funded family planning clinics from providing information on or counseling for abortion.[44] Other subsequent Court rulings allowed states to regulate abortions during the first trimester or ban elective abortions beyond the first trimester.[45] As of 2000, the majority of states required some type of waiting period and counseling, and 34 required parental consent or notification for minors (McBride 2007: 197–98).

Abortion never became a civil right in Spain or Germany. After Franco's death, the new Spanish constitution explicitly granted gender equality, yet the question of abortion divided left and right political factions (Valiente 2001).[46] To achieve consensus, abortion was removed from the constitutional discussion. Instead, the penal code was reformed to decriminalize abortions under a limited range of circumstances (Glendon 1987). Similarly, the 1974 attempt to decriminalize first trimester abortion in West Germany was overturned by the Federal Constitutional Court. The Court ruled that the new law violated the fetus's right to life and the state's responsibility to protect that right as it had not done during the Third Reich (Glendon 1987: 30). In the subsequent 1976 law, abortion remained a crime, but terminations up to 12 weeks for medical necessity or serious emotional or mental distress could be approved by two doctors. The law further required a three-day waiting period and counseling that encouraged a woman to keep the fetus (Glendon 1987).

In contrast to other socialist countries,[47] East German policies also restricted women's rights to abortion. Article 11 of the 1950 Mother and Child Care and Women's Rights Act restricted abortions to pregnancies that severely threatened the life or health of the pregnant woman, or if a parent suffered from a grave inherited condition. The number of legal abortions approved annually dropped to just 1,000 by 1956, whereas the annual number of illegal ones soared to 100,000 (Harsch 1997). During the 1960s, the Politburo amended abortion restrictions as women's paid labor became more critical for production. On December 22, 1971, with little public fanfare, the Politburo announced a resolution in favor of legalizing abortion in the first trimester of pregnancy. The resolution took effect in 1972, following the only non-unanimous vote in the Volkskammer as of that date (Harsch 1997).[48]

Reunification of the two German regions stalled as the German Democratic Republic representatives refused to accept the more limited

West German abortion law (Banaszak 1998). Following reunification, a new 1992 law allowed abortion on demand in the first 12 weeks, subject to the counseling and waiting period. Again conservatives legally challenged the law. The following year, the Federal Court again ruled that it must protect the rights of the fetus, but Parliament was free to pass a law eliminating punishment of women who aborted in the first trimester. Parliament did so in 1995. So as in Spain, abortion remains illegal in reunified Germany, but a woman's punishment is waived if she receives counseling (Rahman et al. 1998).

The varying levels of policy restriction were evident in the abortion rates listed in Table 3.4. Spain and Germany had the fewest abortions per 1,000 women of childbearing age, and East German rates fell dramatically after reunification. The incidence in Australia and the United Kingdom edged up the latter part of the twentieth century. The United States retained the highest incidence rate among advanced industrial economies. Yet when comparing the information in Table 3.4 with the fertility rates in Table 3.3, there is little direct relationship between abortion and fertility rates, which are also highest in the United States.

Women's greater control over their fertility in the post-war period was one hallmark of the "second demographic transition" of industrial societies (van de Kaa 1987). Fertility control enabled women to participate more in the labor market, enhancing women's direct access to economic resources. Related to these trends were other demographic

Table 3.4 Abortions/1000 women age 15–44 in 1986, 1996, 2003

	1986	1996	2003
Australia	15	22	20
England and Wales	13	16	17
United States	27	23	21
East Germany	27	18e	11e
Germany (West)	7	8	8
Spain	*	6	8

Source: Rates for 1986 from Henshaw (1986: Table 1); 1996 from Henshaw *et al.* (1999: Table 2) except East Germany; rates for 2003 from Sedgh *et al.* (2007: Tables 1 and 2) except East Germany. The 1996 and 2003 estimates for East Germany derived from average relative ratio of abortions/1000 births across the *Länder* based on data from *Statistisches Bundesamt Deutschland* (Federal Statistics Office Germany).

changes that have proven particularly challenging to the male bread-winner model (Esping-Andersen et al. 2002; Taylor-Gooby 2004). Marriage rates declined by one-third or more across the countries between 1970 and 2007, as indicated in Figure 3.1. The proportion of cohabiting couples increased. As of 2000, two-thirds of all East German couples aged 25–34 were cohabiting (Kiernan 2004b: 38). About half of Australian, British, West German, and US couples, and 40 percent of Spanish couples in this age group were cohabiting rather than married.[49] Many cohabitants, particularly those who have children, eventually marry, although this transition is less likely in the United States (Heuveline and Timberlake 2004). All co-residential relationships have become more unstable, with cohabitation less stable than legal marriage (Andersson 2003; Liefbroer and Dourleijn 2006).

Associated with the increase in cohabitation is the sharp increase in nonmarital births since 1970 as displayed in Figure 3.2. Almost one-sixth of German and US births are to single mothers without a co-residential partner (Heuveline et al. 2003: 56). The aggregate figures

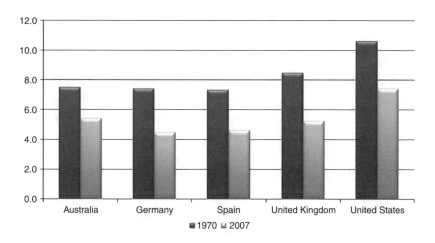

Source: From OECD Family Database, www.oecd.org/els/social/family/database. Retrieved June 25, 2009; 1970 data for Germany for West only.

Figure 3.1 Number of marriages/1,000 population, 1970 v. 2007

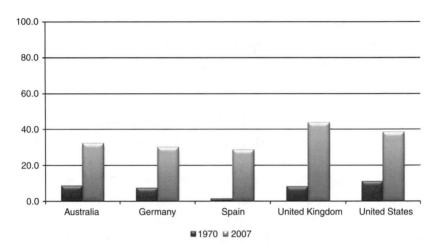

Source: From OECD Family Database, www.oecd.org/els/social/family/database. Retrieved June 25, 2009; 1970 data for Germany for West only. At the time of reunification, over one-third of all babies born in the East, and over half of all first-births, were to unwed mothers (Einhorn 1993; Rueschemeyer 1989).

Figure 3.2 Nonmarital births as percent all births, 1970 v. 2007

hide group differences within countries. Across countries, less-educated women have become more likely to have a nonmarital birth whereas educated women tend to bear children in marriage (McLanahan 2004; Sobotka 2008). In the United States, Blacks and Hispanics are also more likely to have a nonmarital birth than Caucasians or Asians (Millar and Rowlingson 2001). As a result of these trends, a growing proportion of children are now likely to reside with a single mother at some point in their lives (Heuveline and Timberlake 2004). This represents an increased financial exposure for the welfare state, particularly those that historically reinforced men's privileged access to employment. Single female-headed households are more likely to live in poverty and require state financial assistance than two-parent households (Daly and Rake 2003; Rainwater and Smeeding 2004). Poverty now, as in the past, bodes poorly for children's future life chances (Kamerman et al. 2003).

These new risks have resulted in states implementing labor activation policies for all groups at risk of unemployment or reliance on state transfers (Kenworthy 2008; Taylor-Gooby 2004). Mothers' employment in particular reduces the risk of child poverty (Kamerman et al. 2003). Many states have therefore introduced a range of work-family balance policies to support maternal employment. These policies, however, rarely challenged a male breadwinner model. European states enhanced paid parental leave provisions and Australia and the United States introduced unpaid family leaves, but men in all countries take a small proportion of leave as compared with women (Cooke and Baxter 2010; Hobson 2002). The women who entered the labor force were more likely to take up the part-time or fixed-term jobs (Bardasi and Gornick 2008; Plantenga and Remery 2005). As women in affluent economies entered employment, more of the formerly unpaid domestic tasks were commodified to the market. The remaining domestic work in the home increasingly became the work of less-educated women or one of the growing legion of female migrants (Williams 2004). The growth in immigrant domestic workers reflected just one of several changes in migration over more recent decades.

Immigration in the "New" Global Economy

In the 1970s, family reunification policies replaced the migrant worker policies of the 1960s (Castles and Miller 2003; Kofman et al. 2000). As a result, ethnic communities from former guest worker pools swelled in all of the countries: Mexicans in the United States, Turks in Germany, Asians in Australia, and Asian colonials in the United Kingdom. The Berlin Wall came down in November 1989, with East and West Germany reunified after 28 years. With the 1993 Maastricht Treaty, a single European market was established, ensuring "four freedoms" of movement: goods, services, people, and money. The disintegration of socialism in the Soviet bloc resulted in a further influx of migrants into the European Union. Immigration from outside of the expanded European economic area became increasingly limited to refugees and asylum seekers, leading to allegations of "Fortress Europe" (Geddes 2008).

Similarly, the US 1990 Immigration Act limited legal entry to the highly skilled, asylum seekers, and family members. Despite these restrictions, 9 million new immigrants arrived during the 1990s, primarily from

Asia and Latin America (Bade and Weiner 1997; Castles and Miller 2003). During that same decade, Australia imposed new quotas, skill requirements, and re-introduced language tests, whereas asylum seekers were subject to mandatory detention (Freeman and Birrell 2001). In both countries, substantial funds went into border control in an attempt to limit the number of illegal migrants coming in (Castles and Miller 2003; Freeman and Birrell 2001).

Table 3.5 displays the percentage of the total 2005 population in each country that was born in other countries. Almost one-quarter of Australia's population was foreign-born that year, with most coming from Asia. Over the twentieth century, Germany became one of the most popular destination countries, such that its percentage of foreign-born residents now equals that of the United States. The largest proportion of the German foreign-born population hails from the former socialist countries. More of today's migrants are transnational, with cultural, familial, and physical connections to more than one country (Bryceson and Vuorela 2002). This leads to greater diversity in families within a country, but not necessarily any change in the national family ideal (Fink 2001).

More women now migrate than ever before, migrating as workers as well as wives (OECD 2008a). A growing number of migrant women (and men) migrate as legal or illegal care and domestic workers (Parreñas 2005; Zimmerman et al. 2006). Policies directly or indirectly encourage this, often without extending citizenship rights to these care workers. For example, a series of UK immigration policies in the 1960s recruited

Table 3.5 Foreign-born population 2005

	% TOTAL	PRIMARY POPULATION SOURCE
Australia	23	Asia
Germany	12	EUA10
United Kingdom	8	Asia
Spain	5	EU15
United States	12	Latin America

Source: OECD 2008a: Table 0.1. The EU15 includes Austria, Belgium, Denmark, Finland, France, Germany, Greece, Ireland, Italy, Luxembourg, Netherlands, Portugal, Spain, Sweden, and the United Kingdom. The EUA10 includes Czech Republic, Estonia, Hungary, Latvia, Lithuania, Poland, Slovakia, Slovenia, Cyprus, and Malta.

Filipino women to ease a nursing shortage. In the late 1970s, however, quotas were imposed that restricted their entry, followed by some deportations in the early 1980s (Anderson 2000). More recently, neoliberal restructuring in Poland resulted in high unemployment levels, encouraging more migration to Germany for work (Misra et al. 2006). Germany extended some work permits for Polish elder care workers, provided they did not compete directly with German-trained homecare employees. Permits were not given for other domestic workers, who were more likely to enter and work illegally on tourist visas (Anderson 2000; Kofman 2003). Similarly, families in Mediterranean countries increasingly employ illegal migrants from Central Europe and Africa to provide elder care, paid for by state care transfers (Lyon and Glucksmann 2008). The practice is so common that since the 1990s, the Spanish government has offered "regularization" programs to allow such workers to become legally recognized by the state (Bettio et al. 2006).

New World, Old Social Order

In the latter half of the twentieth century, there was a reconfiguration within households around the world. Fertility rates had declined as countries industrialized (Mason 2001). Unpaid time in the private sphere declined in most affluent economies, with women as well as men spending more time in paid work (Gershuny 2000; Jacobs and Gerson 2004; Medalia and Jacobs, 2008). The type and duration of family forms continued to evolve (Heuveline et al. 2003; Sobotka 2008). More people migrated across national borders, with women now comprising a large proportion of temporary and permanent immigrants (Castles and Miller 2003). Populations were on the move, from the home to the workplace and across national borders.

Yet the spokes of the institutional equality frame set by nineteenth century population policies remained in evidence. Initial policies codified women's responsibility for reproduction and unpaid care work. Other policies mapped which migrant groups had equal access to work in immigrant-receiving countries, and whether they might settle as families. As more married women in affluent economies remained in or entered employment, the gendered domestic work became the paid work of the less-educated or immigrants. Despite these changes, the male breadwinner model privileging White native-born men's access to the best jobs remained unchallenged. Whatever unpaid work had not been commodified was almost as gendered as it was 50 years prior (Cooke and Baxter 2010). Consequently, as the spheres of paid work expanded, the social hierarchy reflected in initial population policies still determined who performed more or less valued work.

Population policies alone, however, did not construct the institutional equality frame. The social hierarchies and inequalities were also reinforced by a range of policies affecting individuals across their life courses. As discussed in the next two chapters, education and employment policies were key to sustaining gender, class and ethnic differences in the paid and unpaid work of industrialized economies.

4

EDUCATIONAL FOUNDATIONS
OF EQUALITY[1]

Education and the Institutional Equality Frame

Industrialization increased the importance of education over birthright in determining life chances. As a result, the modernization process was predicted to bring about a more meritocratic opportunity structure (Erikson and Goldthorpe 1992).[2] Class inequalities were expected to decrease as children from any background could obtain the education necessary to enter the most desirable occupations. Liberal feminists applied a similar logic to women's position in industrial society, arguing equal access to education and subsequent employment opportunities would provide the pathway to gender equality (Williams 1989).

Education offers the potential to enhance individual opportunity, but as discussed in the first part of this chapter, the educational systems that developed during the eighteenth and nineteenth centuries institutionalized rather than ameliorated group differences in industrialized societies. In 1763, Frederick II of Prussia implemented free compulsory schooling for all children between the ages of 5 and 13. *Volksschule* (people's schools) provided the basics of reading, writing, and arithmetic considered essential in the evolving industrial society. Yet Frederick also noted, "We do not confer upon the individual or upon society any benefit when we educate him beyond the bounds of his social class and vocation" (Reisner 1922, in Ramirez and Boli 1987: 5).[3] Access to education therefore bestowed individuals with skills essential to future success, but educational institutions frequently reinforced group differences in possible future employment.

The new public educational systems also reinforced women's responsibility for an enlarging sphere of unpaid care work. Compulsory schooling requirements complemented the early labor laws that restricted children's employment (Lewis and Rose 1995; Thompson 1991).[4] As younger children could no longer spend the days in the workplace alongside their parents, compulsory education created a new societal need for child care (David 1980). Compulsory primary schooling filled some of this need, but most national schooling systems did not provide preschool. In addition, compulsory schooling schedules did not span the work day and frequently offered a disjointed annual calendar that conflicted with full-time employment (Gornick et al. 1997). Heretofore, I refer to this as the "care void" created by educational systems.

Women became responsible for filling the care void, within and outside of formal schooling systems. Young single women comprised a growing percentage of primary school teachers. If they married or became pregnant, female teachers were forced to leave employment. Mothers, in turn, were assumed to care for children in the years prior to compulsory schooling and outside of school hours once children were enrolled. These assumptions were reflected not only in the paucity of public preschool, but also in gendered curricula and women's limited access to higher education. In these ways, public schooling systems institutionalized the gendered division of unpaid labor across the life course.

This newly created care void also replicated class inequalities in that the early home environment was critical to later academic achievement (Bradley et al. 1988; Leseman 2009). Educated households offered more resources such as books that supported children's educational success (Lareau 2000). Working-class women still had to work, and so their children were frequently left to fend for themselves. Even today, parents with more education often spend more time with their children, regardless of their employment (Bianchi et al. 2006; Sayer et al. 2004).

As a result, the new schooling systems for enhancing economic competitiveness often replicated class educational inequalities even before the start of formal schooling.

The exact mix of gender and class schooling differences varied across the countries, and reflected their unique administrative challenges. The challenges persisted during the educational expansion that followed World War II. As discussed in the second part of the chapter, countries modestly expanded educational options before the start of compulsory schooling. Secondary and post-secondary opportunities, in contrast, expanded rapidly. Countries introduced programs or amended structures to reduce some group inequalities. These initiatives resulted in greater educational attainment across countries and for social groups within them (Breen et al. 2010). Women in particular made great strides in educational attainment (Shavit and Blossfeld 1993; Shavit et al. 2007). As revealed in the comparisons of current group performance and achievement, however, it is clear that educational expansion has not eliminated inequalities.

Group Differences in Educational Foundations

Frederick's vision of preparing people for their place in society evolved into Germany's highly stratified secondary educational system administered by the individual *Länder*. By the early twentieth century, the German system contained four distinct secondary tracks, including a separate track for girls. Students were assigned to their tracks by the age of 10 with no possibility of switching between tracks later in schooling. The lower secondary tracks fed into the renowned German vocational training and apprenticeship system (Cooke 2003). A small minority completed the upper secondary track (*Gymnasium*) and passed the *Abitur* credentialing exam that allowed students to attend university. As in most of Europe, the German university remained an elite male pursuit until well after World War II.[5] In 1930, less than 3 percent of the relevant German age group was enrolled in higher education (Guruz 2008), with women a minority of this group.[6] Despite the overall elitism of the German educational system, the vocational training ensured that a large proportion of male school leavers had sufficient technical skills to subsequently earn a decent living. The vocational training system simultaneously barred women's access to the training for the best jobs (Geschka 1991). None of the other countries implemented a public schooling system that so tightly slotted class and gender educational opportunities.

At the other extreme was the US public schooling system, which evolved from local initiatives. General rather than vocational education dominated US mass schooling, reflecting Horace Mann's vision of schooling for the "democratic uplift" of an educated citizenry (Brint 2006). Mann argued education should embrace all children, be free of religious influence, provided by well-trained professional teachers, and paid for, controlled, and sustained by an interested public (Mann 1850). The constitutional separation of church and state effectively precluded US public funds being used to support private religious schooling.[7] By 1918, all US states provided free public education and required that children attend at least elementary school. Each US state developed a department of education and regulated the financing, personnel hiring procedures, and curriculum. Most financing, however, derived from local property taxes within 130,000 independent school districts.[8] Funding levels and quality of public schools therefore varied within as well as across US states.

The decentralization of the US public schooling system had both positive and negative effects on group inequality. On the negative side, poorer districts could not offer the same educational services as wealthier ones, such that the US public schooling system geographically repli-cated existing class hierarchies. Decentralization also embedded racial hierarchies (Woodward and McFeely 2001). In 1896, the US Supreme Court ruled that "separate but equal" facilities for Blacks did not violate the Constitution.[9] School reliance on local financing and more limited training options for teachers of color meant educational facilities for Blacks were markedly inferior to those available to most White students (Card and Krueger 1992b). In 1928, high school graduation rates were appreciably lower in southern US states with a large Black population (along with New Mexico and its high proportion of Native Americans) than in northern states (Goldin 2001).

On the positive side, local control of US schooling allowed it to expand rapidly as US settlement expanded westward. This included post-primary educational expansion. In the first decades of the twentieth century, the US high school movement resulted in impressive educational attainment among the youth population. By 1940, 50 percent of 18-year-old children had their upper secondary high school diploma (Goldin and Katz 2008). The widespread availability of upper secondary schools also facilitated further educational expansion via locally based junior and community colleges. By 1930, 15 percent of the relevant US age group was enrolled in university, a percentage indicative of mass higher education several decades ahead of Australia and Europe (Guruz 2008).

US women benefited from this educational expansion. The country's development into its western territories created a demand for new teachers for new local school districts that drew more women into advanced education. As early as 1880, one out of every three undergraduates in US universities and colleges was female (Sklar 1993). Yet US women's post-secondary enrollment clustered within the community colleges offering teaching certificates. In addition, the elite universities such as Harvard segregated women, or allowed them to study while refusing to grant them degrees, as was the case at Columbia University (Solomon 1986).

Class hierarchies were also replicated in the Australian and English educational systems, but by creating public-private schooling divides. Australian educational initiatives began early in colonization, in part to address concerns over the large proportion of convicts that comprised Australia's population (Bassett 1970). In 1821, Commissioner Bigge argued for greater expansion of public education in New South Wales and Tasmania, "so that as little control as possible shall be left to the parents over the time, habits, and the disposition of their children."[10] As in the United States, individual Australian states passed public school acts in the late nineteenth century that ensured free, compulsory, and secular education to all residents and abolished public financing of religious schools. When the Commonwealth formed in 1901, the new constitution mandated separation of church and state. But in contrast to

the United States, Australia's large landmass and harsh interior conditions inhibited rather than fostered the expansion of public schooling.
Instead, church organizations frequently offered basic schooling for
free settlers away from the coast (Austin 1961). As a result, religious
schools continued to receive state subsidies into the twentieth century
(Boyd 1987).

Many rural schools in Australia employed one teacher for all grade
levels.[11] If a child had to walk more than three miles to reach a school,
the attendance requirement was waived. Rural educational attainment
therefore continued to lag behind that in urban areas. In addition, the
Aboriginals that populated the interior often remained outside of the
public education system or left schooling earlier than settlers. Where
schools drew mainly from the Aboriginal population, the curriculum
emphasized "handicrafts."[12] So as in the United States, racial educational
differences were pronounced.

Class and gender differences also became embedded in the public-
private mix of Australian secondary schooling provision that differentiated between the upper quartile and remaining secondary students.
The upper quartile of Australian students was served almost entirely by
private schools, segregating the best students (Boyd 1987). Many
Australian schools were also sex-segregated and offered a gendered
curriculum. In the nineteenth century, Australian girls in secondary
school were significantly more likely than boys to take painting and
music, in addition to instruction in domestic arts (Jones 1985).

England also supported private educational provision, and was in fact
the last affluent market economy to offer publicly financed compulsory
schooling (Glennerster 1995). The 1833 Factory Act that limited children's working hours required factories to educate children, but few
actually did. That same year, the British government began to provide
grants to religious voluntary societies that delivered elementary instruction (David 1980). Local school boards were established in areas not
served by the religious organizations, creating a dual system of religious
and public education, both at least partly funded by the government.
During the 1880s, schooling for children aged 5–10 became compulsory, but remained fee-based until the 1890s (Glennerster 1995). Girls'

elementary curriculum included reading, writing and arithmetic, along with domestic training (David 1980). A 1904 report following Britain's near-defeat in the Boer War (1899–1901) suggested the need for still greater emphasis on developing girls' domestic skills to enhance the quality of future British soldiers (Tinkler 2001).

Secondary education for a select minority in England predated elementary, with some schools established under Alfred the Great in the ninth century. These schools prepared pupils for the universities and the learned professions, becoming known as grammar schools as they taught Latin grammar. The 1662 Act of Uniformity placed these schools under the purview of the Church of England. Some attracted students from well beyond their local area and became known as "public" schools, although they were in fact private. The most elite boarding schools were for wealthy boys through the age of 18 or 19 and provided the path to university. In the first half of the twentieth century, less than 2 percent of English birth cohorts went to university (Glennerster 1995). Day schools with a leaving age of 16 existed for the sons of merchants, businessmen, and other petty bourgeoisie. A third type of day school served the sons of small tradesman, artisans, and tenant farmers, with a leaving age of 14. The Education Act of 1902 allowed the state to support both private and public secondary schools. Some secondary schools for middle-class girls existed, but they were not state-endowed and had a very short school day (David 1980). As in the United States, English women had limited access to university education. Not until 1914 could women study in all English universities, although some departments retained restrictions even after that time (David 1980). Oxford began granting women degrees in 1920. Cambridge refrained from doing so until 1948, almost 100 years after first allowing women to attend classes and take examinations (Zweiniger-Bargielowska 2001).

The 1944 National Education Act finally implemented publicly funded compulsory schooling for English and Welsh children aged 5–15.[13] The Act established a centralized Ministry of Education, although programs were administered by local elected authorities. The Act instituted a tripartite system based on an "eleven-plus" exam at age 10,[14] the same age at which German students were sorted into the different secondary tracks. British students scoring in the top 10–25 percent could continue to public or private grammar school;[15] those scoring below this continued to public "secondary modern" schools. The proposed third track of secondary technical schools never garnered more than 2 or 3 percent of enrollment (Timmins 1995). As in Germany, Britain put in place a stratified secondary schooling system. But in Britain, the different tracks did not necessarily impart useful skills. In the words of Oscar Wilde's Lady Bracknell, "The whole theory of modern education is radically unsound. Fortunately in England, at any rate, education produces no effect whatsoever. If it did, it would prove a serious danger to the upper classes" (1950: 359).

Spain's expansion of public education preceded its modernization by two centuries,[16] but shared some of the challenges faced by Australia. Spanish progressives in the eighteenth century promoted public education as a means of minimizing the influence of the Roman Catholic Church. In Madrid, elementary education was placed under official control in 1740. King Charles III (1759–1788) expanded public elementary schools with a gendered curriculum: "Boys should not read novels, poetry or stories which do not impart useful knowledge; girls should be kept clean and quiet and learn handiwork."[17]

The 1812 Constitution accorded the state responsibility for education, but a public system was not introduced until the 1857 Moyano Law (Boyd 1997). The law, following the French model, stipulated public provision of primary, secondary, and university education. The minister of development was responsible for all personnel, curricula, textbooks, and secondary and university examinations and degrees. The state financially maintained the 10 universities.[18] Spanish municipal and regional *comunidades autonoma* authorities funded and administered primary and secondary schools. Children in towns with more than 500 residents were entitled to sex-segregated primary education. As in Australia, rural areas proved more challenging to serve. Many Spanish public primary schools in rural areas were age-integrated, with 70 or 80 students aged 6–13 being taught by one poorly trained and badly paid male teacher (Boyd 1997).

In deference to conservative interests, the Moyano Law mandated religious instruction for all primary and secondary students, with the Catholic Church retaining the right to review the moral and doctrinal content (Castilliejo 1937). The law also permitted private schools that were subject to state regulation, leading to the proliferation of religious schools in the latter half of the nineteenth century. As in Australia, this proved a practical compromise given the limited financial resources of local governments, with 20 percent of primary students enrolled in religious schools (Boyd 1997).

As in most countries, Spanish secondary schooling targeted the middle and upper classes. Fifty-eight *institutos* located in provincial capitals delivered almost all public secondary schooling. These offered one track leading to a *bachillerato* degree. Public *institutos* did not provide boarding facilities and students were only required to pass annual subject exams, not attend lectures. Religious *colegios* strove to outperform their public counterparts and more frequently offered boarding facilities. Yet educational expansion continued to lag behind that of the other countries. By the end of the nineteenth century, just 2 percent of Spanish boys aged 10–14 were studying for the secondary *bachillerato* in either public or private schools. Girls could not officially enroll until the early 1900s, and as of 1910, only 353 girls nationwide were studying for a secondary degree (Boyd 1997: 14).

Spain teetered between church and state control of schooling during subsequent political upheavals. In the aftermath of the uprising of General Primo de Rivera in 1923, church control of education was reinstated (Castilliejo 1937). Control again reverted to the state under the socialist influence that dominated the Second Republic (1931–36). Article 26 of the new Spanish constitution prohibited religious orders from teaching, yet the new government had no money to fund public places for the 350,000 students who would have been affected. Thus religious provision continued,[19] accompanied by intensified animosity between reformers and the church (Boyd 1997). After seizing power in 1936, Franco reversed the Second Republic educational reforms and reasserted the cultural hegemony of Catholic schooling. This educational policy persisted until 1953 (OECD 1965).

The educational foundations in all of the countries therefore embedded combinations of group inequalities. Class-tiered schooling structures dominated all national educational systems except the United States, where *de facto* tiers derived from the reliance on local financing. In conjunction with its tiered structure, the vocationally intensive German system ensured most young men possessed marketable skills upon completion. Class differences in the Australian and English systems were reinforced via state support for elite private secondary schools. Australia and Spain struggled to provide education to rural populations, which resulted in on-going state support for religious schools. Local provision embedded stark racial disparities in Australia and the United States. All educational systems institutionalized gender differences, with women's education assumed to benefit primarily the next generation through teaching and mothering.

Post-War Expansion of Pre-Primary Provision

After World War II, middle-class families clamored for more education for their children[20] and social activists demanded policies for minimizing educational inequalities. Enhancing educational equality had several attractive benefits for the state. A highly skilled workforce could ensure economic competitiveness within a global market place. Minimizing group educational disparities could reduce future welfare state expenditures. Consequently, as welfare states expanded, education was increasingly regarded as a state investment that garnered both public support and positive economic effects (Bergh 2005; Jenson 2004, 2009; Machin 2009).

States differed, however, in the nature, timing, and goals of educational expansion. Most states invested heavily in expanding secondary and post-secondary options. It is the latter in particular that Wilensky (1975) argued replicate class inequalities. In contrast, the core of compulsory schooling systems remained remarkably unchanged over time. Children would begin compulsory schooling at age 5 or 6 and frequently attend a half-day for the first year. Weekly schooling hours ranged from 28 in Australia to 35 in Spain,[21] and no schooling system expanded to year-round primary education.[22]

Non-compulsory private and public early childhood education programs expanded in the post-war period. The initial goal in most countries was to enhance children's educational performance, not to fill the care void between birth and the start of compulsory schooling. Only East Germany implemented a public child care system that enabled mothers to engage in the public spheres on a more equal footing with men. In Germany, half-day provision had dominated primary schooling since 1872. Both regions retained the half-day primary schooling after the war, but East Germany simultaneously expanded child care provision for the other half of the day (Hagemann 2006). The 1946 East German School Law integrated preschools into a unified state system, reflecting the commitment throughout the Eastern bloc to societal rather than individual responsibility for the education of the youngest children.[23]

Yet as in West Germany, the new East German constitution defined childrearing as a parental right, so preschool provision at first developed no more quickly than in West Germany. Soviet pressure on East Germany to expand preschool provision intensified during the second half of the 1950s. One reason for the pressure was the production system's growing reliance on female labor given the high male out-migration to West Germany (Budde 1999; Trappe 2000). By 1960, almost half of East German 3–6-year-olds were in all-day care, a proportion rising to two-thirds by 1970 (Hagemann 2006: 240). The 1965 Family Law Code (*Familiengesetzbuch*) further expanded provision for younger children. By the late 1980s, East Germany had public child care places for 80 percent of children under 3, and near universal provision for 3–6-year-olds (Einhorn 1993: 262).

In contrast, the West German minister of the family claimed that children needed their mothers at home to avoid psychic damage (Kolbe 1999).[24] Rather than expanding public preschool, West Germany first expanded maternity leave provisions. In the mid-1960s, as part of broader educational reforms, West Germany included some preschool for 3- to 6-year-old children as the first rung on the educational ladder. By 1990, less than 5 percent of West German children aged 0–3 were in either public or private care, and only one-third of children aged 3–4 were in public preschool (Zimmerman 1993). The nature of public provision in West Germany also differed from East Germany. Most West German *Länder* offered part-time preschool, whereas East German care centers were open from 6 a.m. to 6 p.m. (Ahnert and Lamb 2001).

Thus from a similar schooling base, East Germany's educational system supported maternal employment whereas West Germany's supported a male breadwinner model. Yet the renegotiation of care work between East German women and the state did not directly challenge the gender care hierarchy (Hernes 1987). The state assumed some responsibility for unpaid care work, but the assumption that this was women's work and not men's did not change. The failure of East German policy to encourage greater equality within the home led to feminists founding the *Unabhaengiger Frauenverband* in 1989. This group lobbied for policies demanding equal responsibility for child care not covered by the state (Ferree 1992).

As in West Germany, the other countries at first expanded preschool provision to enhance children's educational preparation. Reflecting their more liberal ideology, the United States and Australia offered public pre-primary education targeted for disadvantaged groups. In the United States, the 1962 Act revising Aid to Families with Dependent Children authorized child care programs for children of people receiving, or at risk of receiving, government aid. The 1964 Economic Opportunity Act[25] authorized a school-readiness program, which was launched in 1965 as an eight-week summer program that served more than a half million children.[26] "Head Start" expanded to a year-round program the following year and has sustained subsequent legislative support. The US federal government funded Head Start as a grant to individual states, which were responsible for overseeing and administering contractors. Across states, a wide range of public and private, non-profit and for-profit agencies provided the comprehensive child development services to economically disadvantaged children and their families.[27] Head Start expanded in 1995 to serve children younger than 3, but as of 2007, only 10 percent of the 1 million children served annually were in this age group.[28]

Evidence generally indicates that Head Start improved the children's outcomes along a variety of measures.[29] But the success of Head Start did not encourage universal expansion of US public preschool. A 2002 review by *Education Week* found that only Georgia offered public preschool for most 4-year-old children. Oklahoma and New York reported similar goals but less success thus far in implementation.[30] In the liberal US market, private preschool provision grew to dominate (Morgan 2005). Since the 1970s, employed parents have been eligible to claim a modest child care credit for private care costs on their federal income tax.[31] As of 2007, the percent of US 3- to 4-year-old children in preschool ranged from 25 percent in Nevada to over 60 percent in Connecticut and New Jersey.[32] Preschool as well as kindergarten hours also varied across states, from part-time to full-time (Gornick and Meyers 2003).

In Australia, parental demand in the late 1960s prompted passage of the 1972 Child Care Act that provided Commonwealth funding for more long-day child care places (Cox 1988). By 1991, 250,000 places had been created to serve the 2 million children requesting places.[33] Despite the unmet demand, subsequent Commonwealth support reverted to after-school rather than pre-primary programs.[34] Australian states administer preschool programs, which primarily serve children aged 4–5. As in the United States, Australian preschools tend to be separate from primary school and run by local councils, community groups, or private organizations.[35] Since the 2000 introduction of the sliding child care benefit, employed parents could claim some government subsidy for the cost of care. A 2002 survey found approximately 59 percent of 4-year-old children attended preschool, and an additional 25 percent attended long-day care.[36] Despite the noted benefits of pre-primary schooling for disadvantaged groups,[37] these groups have been least likely to attend Australian preschools. As of 2004, participation rates of indigenous children and children in more remote and poorer households were lower than those for other children. The rural-urban gap was 15 percentage points, the racial enrollment gap was 11 percentage points, and the income gap almost 17 percentage points.[38] So, as in the United States, participation in early childhood programs is uneven.

The UK's membership in the European Union resulted in greater early childhood education provision than found in the other two English-speaking countries. EU directives since the 1957 Treaty of Rome have required member states to implement policies that minimize group, and in particular gender differences. Conservatives under Thatcher (1979–90) resisted compliance with these directives, whereas New Labour more readily followed suit.[39] Yet it was Thatcher who, as minister of education in 1972, first promoted increasing the number of public preschool places for 3- to 4-year-old children. She emphasized the benefits of preschool in minimizing class differences in later educational attainment, but her goal was to derail the growing political pressure to close the elite grammar schools (Timmins 1995).

Budget constraints stalled the UK's public preschool expansion until the election of New Labour in 1997. New Labour's 1998 National Child Care Strategy contained a combination of public provision, government financing of local provision, and a child care tax credit[40] to ensure coverage of all children aged 0–14.[41] In 1999, the government committed to providing places for all 4-year-olds. The European Union raised these targets at the 2002 Barcelona summit. By 2010, member states were to provide places for at least 90 percent of children between the age of 3 and the start of compulsory schooling, and for at least one-third of children under 3 years of age. The United Kingdom was close to achieving the Barcelona targets by 2008, in part by funding places at voluntary and private providers. Yet the public preschool places were for just 2.5 hours per day, 33 weeks per year (León 2007).[42] Consequently, the United Kingdom adhered to the letter of the EU targets without eliminating the state's historical reliance on British women's unpaid care work.

In Spain, the 1970 General Law on Education addressed pre-primary education for 3- to 6-year-old children (*educación infantile*). Franco did not intend a seamless system to further gender equality, but to differentiate education from women's motherhood duty (Nash 1991; Valiente 2003). Public preschool expanded rapidly, with Spain achieving near universal enrollment among children aged 4–5 by the late 1980s (Ministerio de Educación y Ciencia 1990). As in West Germany, however, the male breadwinner model was evident in that only 5 percent of children younger than 4 were in either public or private care (OECD 2004). In anticipation of joining the European Union, Spain further expanded early childhood education in 1990. *Educación infantile* was divided into two cycles: the first cycle for children aged 0–3, and the second cycle for children 3–6 years of age. Educational provision for all ages of children was therefore technically included as part of the national system.[43] As with other elements of the Spanish schooling system, however, these programs were administered by the autonomous communities and regions. This decentralization perpetuated substantial variation in early childhood education provision across the country.

Each cycle of *educación infantile* was also covered under different branches of public policy within each region (León 2005, 2007). For most children aged 3–6, the government provided preschool, which has been free since 2005. The private sector provided services for the youngest children, the cost of which was subsidized by government grants. Despite this financial assistance, many low-income families could not afford formal care and instead relied on familial networks, particularly grandmothers.[44] Borra Marcos (2006) estimated that coverage for children under 3 was less than 10 percent, with wide regional variation. Coverage was higher in the cities, particularly Madrid and Barcelona, and much lower in Andalucía in the south (León 2007). As a result, early childhood education might be included in Spain's formal schooling system, but as in the past, its availability and usage differ by parental socio-economic status and region.

Each country's expansion of pre-primary schooling therefore sustained the group inequalities evident in other policies. Only East German provision filled the care void created by compulsory schooling, but without policies that directly tackled the gendered division of unpaid care. The three English-speaking countries offered targeted or part-time public preschool that reinforced gender and other group differences. The lack of public care provision encouraged the development of private care provision, made possible by the greater class income inequality (Morgan 2005). Yet greater class inequality did not result in affordable private care. The estimated cost of private care in 2001 for a

2-year-old was 18 percent of average earnings in the United States, 21 percent in Australia, and 25 percent in the United Kingdom (Immervoll and Barber 2005).[45]

As evident in Figure 4.1, the private cost of care inhibited 2004 preschool enrollment of 3- to 4-year-old children in the three English-speaking countries, with the percentage smallest in the United States. Public provision, in contrast, led to greater participation rates. Both East Germany and Spain had almost universal enrollment of children aged 3–4 in 2004, followed closely by West Germany. The cost of private care for younger Spanish and German children was more affordable than in the English-speaking countries, 6 percent and 12 percent of average earnings, respectively (Immervoll and Barber 2005). These countries' institutionalization of a male breadwinner model was also evident, however, in the very small percentage of the youngest age group

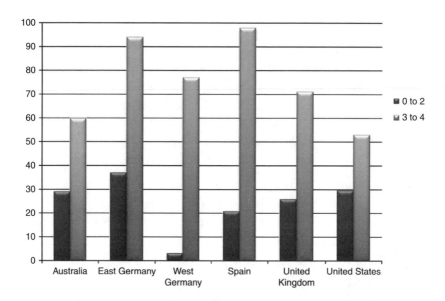

Source: East and West Germany are 2002 public places per 100 children from *Deutsches Jugendinstitut.* Spain and the United Kingdom (2005) and Australia and the United States (2005) from the OECD databases: www.oecd.org/document/4/0,3343,en_2649_34819_37836996_1_1_1_37419,00.html

Figure 4.1 Percentage of age group enrolled in public or private child care, circa 2004

(0–2) enrolled in formal care. West Germany had the smallest percentage of the youngest age group enrolled in formal care in 2004, with the percentage in Spain slightly greater. Enrollment among the three English-speaking countries was not substantially greater than in Spain, suggesting new mothers must choose between high-cost private care or unemployment in these countries. East Germany retained the highest proportion of infants and toddlers enrolled in formal care, despite the availability of the same generous maternity leave provisions as in West Germany.

Thus with the exception of East Germany, the post-war expansion of pre-primary education and care provisions sustained the national gender-class divisions of the initial compulsory schooling systems. Group inequalities in early childhood education structured subsequent educational opportunities and outcomes (Esping-Andersen 2004; Heckman and Masterov 2007; Leseman 2009). Yet as countries expanded secondary education and beyond in the post-war period, some group inequalities began to narrow.

More Secondary Education for All

Public investment in secondary schooling expanded rapidly in the years after World War II. As illustrated in Figure 4.2, the United States had the greatest proportion of young people aged 15–19 enrolled in high school in the 1950s. Part of the reason for the national enrollment disparities was that the other countries differentiated between lower and upper secondary education. Germany's vocational tracks required only 9 or 10 years of formal schooling (Cooke 2003), categorized by UNESCO as lower secondary (ISCED Level 2).[46] After the war, Australia, England, and Spain raised the leaving age for students to nine years from age of entry. The majority of students in these countries completed only lower secondary, yielding the relatively lower enrollment rates evident in Figure 4.2.

In the non-US systems, education from the age of 15 or 16 leading to specialist labor market skills or to university was categorized as upper secondary (ISCED Level 3). By 1970, Australian, German, and British total secondary enrollment would approximate that of the United

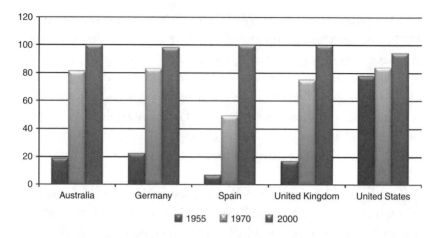

Source: Calculated as percentage of 15–19-year-olds enrolled in secondary education. Australia data from Australian Bureau of Statistics for 1958 and calculated as those age 15 and older in government and non-government secondary schools as a percentage of the 15–19-year-old population. Other country data pertain to 1955. German data apply to West Germany only, including Saar and West Berlin. The European estimates are from Dewhurst et al. (1961: table 10.2 and appendix 10.1, table A). The United States estimate is from Goldin (2001: figure 1) based on US census data. 1970 and 2000 data from the UNESCO 2008 (table 2), except 1970 Germany, which is the West German figure from Basic & Structural Data 2001–2002, German Federal Ministry of Education and Research.

Figure 4.2 Secondary education gross enrollment ratios, 1955, 1970, 2000

States. Because of the continuing challenge of serving rural areas, Spain's total secondary enrollment would not reach parity until the end of the century.[47] In contrast to the United States, most upper secondary students in the other countries were in vocational rather than general education (OECD 2007).

While the other countries expanded secondary provision, the United States grappled with its institutionalized racial differences. The landmark 1954 US Supreme Court decision in *Brown v. Board of Education of Topeka* ruled that school segregation violated the Fourteenth Amendment of the Constitution by denying Black children equal educational opportunities.[48] To overcome the differences associated with local financing, both federal and state investment in poorer districts increased. During the 1970s and 1980s, some school districts were forced to address racial disparities through mandatory student busing.[49] Yet geographic disparities continued to grow as businesses and other organizations disappeared from the most troubled US neighborhoods, enlarging the resource vacuum for the "truly disadvantaged" (Wilson 1987; see also Massey and Denton 1993). As of 2007, ethnic educational performance gaps persisted, narrower among younger children and widening by the end of compulsory schooling.[50] Also in 2007, the US Supreme Court ruled that schools could not select students solely to achieve racial integration.[51] Many school districts throughout the United States have begun to "resegregate," with the racial disparities in educational outcomes anticipated to widen further.

The other countries also implemented policies to reduce educational disparities. In the 1970s, some West German *Länder* introduced comprehensive schools, *Gesamtschulen*, to decrease the rigidity of the secondary tracking system. Similarly, the 1963 Robbins Report in the UK revealed that class differences in educational attainment had not changed much from the 1920s.[52] Most local education authorities abolished the eleven-plus exams and were directed to convert the elite grammar schools into open-access comprehensive schools.[53] University entrance, however, still required attending upper-secondary "sixth form" school and passing Advanced-Level (A-level) exams, just as university entrance in Germany still required attending upper-secondary *Gymnasium* and passing the *Abitur*.

The public-private secondary divides persisted in Australia, England, and Spain, with many private schools still sex-segregated.[54] As evident in Table 4.1, a sizeable minority of Spanish lower secondary students attended private religious schools financially supported by the government in 2004. A large percentage of Australian lower and upper secondary students attended state-supported private schools that same year.[55] Almost half of English upper-secondary students attended private schools, the majority of which received state funds.[56] In contrast, German and US private schools served less than 10 percent of all secondary students in 2004.

Despite the policies and programs for improving educational opportunity, group educational performance differences remained evident at the end of the twentieth century. Since 2000, the OECD's Program for International Student Assessment (PISA) has coordinated assessments every three years of the reading, mathematics, science, and

Table 4.1 Percentage of secondary students in private and public schools, circa 2004

	LOWER SECONDARY			UPPER SECONDARY		
	PUBLIC	PRIVATE		PUBLIC	PRIVATE	
		GOVERNMENT SUPPORTED	INDEPENDENT		GOVERNMENT SUPPORTED	INDEPENDENT
Australia	67.5 %	32.5 %	–	78.6 %	21.3 %	0.1 %
United Kingdom	93.7	0.9	5.4	52.2	41.9	5.9
United States	91.6	–	8.4	92.0	–	8.0
Germany	92.1	7.9	–	91.4	8.6	–
Spain	68.1	28.9	3.0	78.3	11.1	10.6

Source: UNESCO *Global Education Digest 2008*, Table 17.

problem-solving skills of several thousand randomly selected 15-year-old children in participating countries.[57] Students enrolled in pre-vocational or vocational secondary programs performed less well than students enrolled in general education (OECD 2007).

There was also evidence of intergenerational class effects on educational performance. As displayed in Figure 4.3, the extent of these differed across the countries. In all of the countries, students with more educated fathers performed better.[58] The difference in student performance based on fathers' educational attainment was not appreciably greater in the United States (17 percent) than in Germany (16 percent) or the United Kingdom (15 percent).[59] But the US class differentials were large because students whose fathers had completed only high school performed worse on average than similar students in the other countries. Class educational performance differences were smallest in Spain (4 percent) and moderate in Australia (10 percent). The latter two differences were more modest because of the better performance of the students with less-educated fathers, and also because Spanish students with more educated fathers did less well than similar children in the other countries.

Despite Australia and Spain's relatively good aggregate student performance, rural–urban divides persisted. Figure 4.4 contrasts urban and rural 15-year-old student performance in 2003 (upper panel) with student performance in 2006 (lower panel). The dark gray

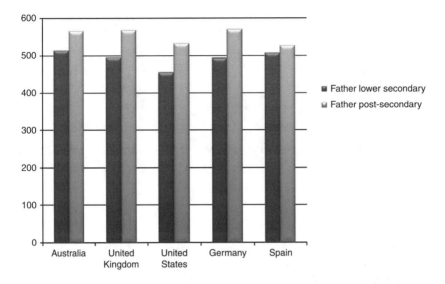

Source: Author calculations based on data from OECD, http://pisa2003.acer.edu.au/interactive.php. Displayed are average country scores for 2003 in reading, math, science, and problem-solving together. Lower secondary school equates to ISCED Level 2; Tertiary is ISCED Level 5A, which is roughly equivalent to a university degree, but might include some master programs. For specific definition of the ISCED levels, see http://stats.oecd.org/glossary/search.asp.

Figure 4.3 Average country PISA scores by father's educational attainment, 15-year-olds in 2003

bar displays the average performance of students attending schools in cities of 1 million or more people. The light gray bar displays the difference in scores for those residing in small villages. In Australia, there was almost no change in either the average urban performance or the rural gap between 2003 and 2006. In contrast, Spain's 2006 rural gap was half that of 2003, with no decline in urban students' performance. Germany's small rural gap in 2003 widened in 2006. At the same time the average German urban students' score declined slightly.

A rural–urban gap also existed in the United Kingdom and the United States, but displayed the opposite pattern of the other countries. British and US rural students performed better than students who resided in the largest cities. The urban penalty was particularly acute in the United States. This might reflect the concentration of both the poor and ethnic minorities in urban centers. Unfortunately, the US PISA data did not allow for ethnic comparisons.

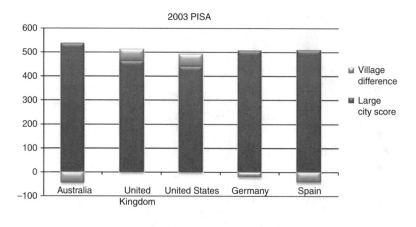

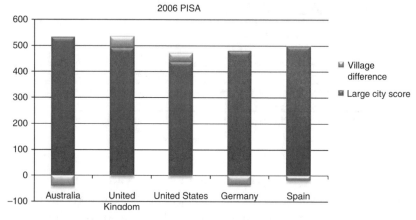

Source: Author calculations based on data from OECD, http://pisa2003.acer.edu.au/interactive.php, accessed June 30, 2009. 2003 data are the average mean scores for 15-year-olds in reading, math, science, and problem-solving for students residing in a large city, and the average difference from this for students residing in a village. 2006 data are average of reading, math and science, except in United States, which is the average of math and science only.

Figure 4.4 Rural-urban difference in average PISA scores, 15-year-olds in 2003, 2006

Immigrants often migrate first to urban centers and can face language issues that affect their children's school performance. As evident in the top panel of Figure 4.5, immigrants in all of the countries performed worse in 2003 than did non-immigrant students, particularly in reading. The immigrant student performance gap was greatest in Germany and smallest in Australia. In each country, however, the category of "immigrant" is not homogeneous. Among the top five source countries,

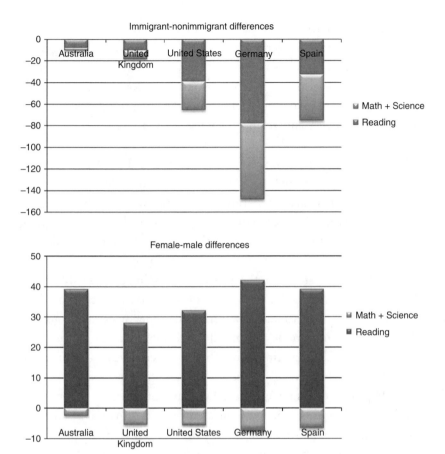

Figure 4.5 Between-group equality: Immigrant and gender differences in average PISA scores, 15-year-olds in 2003

immigrants from some countries tend to be more highly educated whereas others tend to be less educated than the native population.[60] As a result, the country immigrant educational differences evident in Figure 4.5 reflect mixes of language difference, parental education differences, and relative cultural differences. Educational integration and language proficiency policies also vary considerably within a given country's schooling system.[61]

As evident in the lower panel of Figure 4.5, girls continued to display significantly greater reading proficiency than boys. The gender reading differential was smallest in the United Kingdom and most pronounced in Germany. In contrast, boys performed only slightly better than girls in math and science. Australia had the smallest gender differential in math and science, whereas it was most pronounced in Germany.

In summary, with the exception of Australia, the 2003 disparities in secondary educational performance reflected differences institutionalized in each country's initial schooling system. The stratified German educational system still yields pronounced class, immigrant, and gender educational disparities, although they have narrowed since the 1960s. Class differences remained large in the United Kingdom and the United States, but the processes sustaining these differ. All US students performed less well than British students, regardless of their parents' educational attainment. In other words, US general education did not benefit the middle and upper classes to the same extent as in the United Kingdom. US general education also provided less benefit to children of less-educated parents. The Spanish system similarly provided less benefit to the children of educated parents, but did not penalize those of less-educated parents. Australian students performed well regardless of their parents' educational attainment. Consequently, the structure of class educational inequalities varied across countries.

Indicative of the complex structuring of group inequalities, gender and immigrant or ethnic differences did not necessarily follow the class patterns. Spain had the smallest class differences, but gender and immigrant educational disparities were almost as large as in Germany. Educational performance differences between US immigrants and native-born children remained sizeable, but the gender performance gap was among the smallest. Despite the large UK class differential, gender and immigrant performance differences were relatively small as compared with the other countries. Immigrant disparities were smallest in Australia, as was the gender gap in math and science. These differences highlight that gains (or losses) for one social group do not necessarily predict similar gains (or losses) for all groups, and the specific group differences vary in the institutional equality frame.

Expanding Educational Attainment

The expansion of secondary schooling provided the platform for post-secondary expansion. In the immediate post-war period, Australian, British, and West German governments focused on technical education and training options (tertiary type-B).[62] Vocational training programs were dominated by men and some post-war initiatives aimed to improve female enrollments. Yet gender differences persisted in both supply and demand. For example, there were 455 recognized skilled occupations in West Germany as of 1977, with the training for half of these restricted to men (Münch 1991). Among the more than 200 occupations for which West German women might train, most women selected one of ten traditionally "female" occupations such as retail sales, secretarial work, and hairdressing (Münch 1991: 43–44). The German federal government sponsored a pilot program between 1978 and 1985 to attract women into training for technological and manufacturing-based occupations, but the percentage of female trainees did not increase appreciably (Münch 1991). Similar gender differences were found in socialist East Germany. Only 30 of 225 East German training programs were closed to women, but most young women chose one of 16 vocational tracks similar to those selected by West German women (Budde 1999; Korn et al. 1984; Nickel 1992).

Overall enrollments in post-secondary vocational training in most countries, however, declined across the ensuing decades. In 2005, only 9 percent of the relevant age cohort in OECD countries graduated from a post-secondary vocational program (OECD 2007: 58). Germany's graduation rate was only slightly higher than average, and Spain's was at 15 percent following reforms that took effect in 2002/3. These reforms ensured free basic technical training and introduced new apprentice-based training (Hidalgo et al. 2002).

The greatest post-secondary expansion occurred in degree-granting colleges and universities (tertiary type-A).[63] By far the most impressive growth was in the United States. The same year that England introduced public compulsory schooling, the United States introduced the Servicemen's Readjustment Act of 1944 that granted returning veterans financial support for pursuing post-secondary education or training. By the time the first "GI Bill" ended in 1956, almost 8 million World War II veterans had participated.[64] Middle-class demand for higher education also burgeoned (Trow 1973).

Between 1950 and 1990, the number of US colleges and universities increased from 1,851 to 3,535 (Lazerson 1998: 66). This growth included a diverse assortment of public and private institutions (Douglass 2005). The locally based community and technical colleges offered a more affordable educational path.[65] The majority of these colleges received some public funding and offered short-term certificate programs or two-year associate degrees. The average annual tuition fee at US community colleges in 2009 was about $2,400.[66] The other alternative was one of the 2,400 four-year institutions, 75 percent of them private. Annual tuition fees of these institutions were appreciably higher than those of community colleges, but ranged widely.[67]

The United States is unique in the private cost of higher education. As of 2000, over 66 percent of US higher education expenditure originated from private sources, evenly split between households and private enterprise (OECD 2004). This compared with the average OECD private expenditure of just 22 percent (OECD 2004). The US federal government initially provided grants for qualified students who could not afford tuition and fees, similar to the grants provided to veterans under the GI Bill. Beginning in the 1970s, however, federal grants were replaced by federally guaranteed student loans (Douglass 2005). US university students now graduate with ever-increasing debt (Lazerson 1998).[68] Despite the financial barriers, almost two-thirds of US cohorts completing secondary education enter post-secondary education, well above the OECD average of 50 percent (OECD 2004). About 40 percent enter one of the community colleges, whereas slightly more than half enroll in one of the four-year institutions. Only half of the US students who enter university complete a degree, but this still represents a slightly higher rate than the OECD average (OECD

2004). As of 2004, the United States had the greatest percentage of the adult population with college degrees, along with Israel and Norway (OECD 2007: 38).

Tertiary type-A educational provision expanded in all of the countries. The Australian Commonwealth government established new suburban universities and Colleges of Advanced Education during the 1960s, which became degree-granting institutions in the 1970s (Mahony 1993). The United Kingdom upgraded three technical colleges and sanctioned seven new universities during the 1960s.[69] West Germany established 13 new universities and medical schools between 1957 and 1970 (Taylor Cole 1973: 46). In Spain, the number of public and private universities doubled since the 1978 Constitution enshrined regional autonomy and academic freedom (OECD 2009a).[70]

In contrast to the United States, however, university education in these countries was financed by the government.[71] As post-secondary provision expanded, this state underwriting of the privileged classes became financially and politically untenable. In 1988, Australia introduced a flat fee for all students based on the argument that university education improved graduates' future earnings. A three-tier system introduced in the late 1990s charged greater fees to students on courses for occupations with greater salaries, such as medicine and law. The government subsequently introduced a deferred repayment program.[72] In 2005, the Commonwealth deregulated fees and allowed universities to increase them by up to 25 percent.

In the United Kingdom, the 1998 Teaching and Higher Education Act introduced modest university tuition fees for all but the poorest students. Fees the first year (1998/9 academic year) were a little more than £1,000 for all UK universities and all courses of study. The following year, the government raised the number of funded student places, with Prime Minister Tony Blair pledging a target of 50 percent of UK youth going on to higher education in the next century.[73] The Higher Education Act of 2004 replaced the fixed fee with variable fees and introduced an income-linked deferred repayment system as in Australia. In the wake of the 2008 financial crisis, however, the UK government has cut the number of university places, with further cuts pending.

In Spain, autonomous communities and regions are responsible for their universities, leading to significant regional variation (OECD 2009a). Each region is free to set its student tuition fees within a nationally mandated range, which as of 2002 varied from 600 to over 700 euros per year (OECD 2009a).[74] The individual German *Länder* similarly manage their universities. In 2002, however, the federal government under Chancellor Gerhard Schröder passed a law forbidding German universities to charge fees to undergraduates. The Federal Constitutional Court overturned the law in 2005, upholding the *Länder's* administrative authority. In 2007, seven *Länder* announced the introduction of modest university fees.[75]

Financing university education, therefore, now requires more private resources in all of the countries. On the one hand, private financing of higher education reinforces class differences in access to higher education, both in terms of cost as well as perceived risk (Breen and Goldthorpe 1997; Jackson et al. 2007). On the other hand, public financing uses taxes to provide a benefit enjoyed primarily by the children of the middle and upper classes (Blanden and Machin 2004; Le Grand 1982). In either case, higher education policies institutionalize class inequalities. To exclude higher education from the discussion of the welfare state as suggested by Wilensky (1975), then, ignores the state's role in structuring the relationships among education and class equality and individual welfare.

Although class differences in education remain, gender differences have narrowed.[76] For example, as of 1965, only 3 percent of West German women of a graduating cohort went to university as compared with 7 percent of men (Geschka 1991). As of 2005, more than one-third of West German women in the age cohort entered university, the same percentage as men (OECD 2007: 294). In the other countries, women's enrollment has surpassed men's (OECD 2002, 2007; 2009a; UK Women's Equality Unit 2005). In the United States, this occurred more than 30 years ago (Lazerson 1998). In 1984, women also outnumbered men in US post-graduate programs (OECD 2004). But the greater participation of women in higher education has not coincided with a substantial reduction in gender differences in subject majors. As of 2000, Australian women dominated health, education, and creative arts majors. Australian men were more likely to major in information technology, engineering, and related technologies (Australian Bureau of Statistics 2001). Spanish women remain over-represented in health and welfare, the humanities, arts, and education, and under-represented in computer science, engineering, manufacturing, and construction (OECD 2008b). US gender subject differences were smaller than in most affluent economies, whereas British women's were slightly greater (OECD 2004). The gender differences in university subjects presage later gender occupational differences, which can reduce women's relative returns to university education as compared with men.

The distribution of educational attainment in the adult population as of 2005 provides a snapshot of the institutionalized class and gender differences across the national schooling systems (see Figure 4.6). Australia and Spain's provision challenges are evident in the large

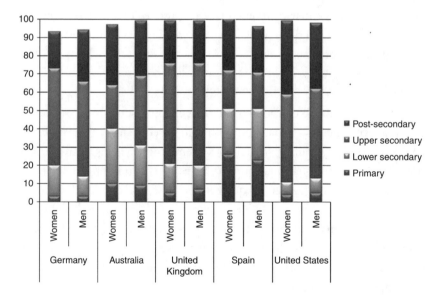

Source: Author calculations based on 2005 data from OECD's 2007 *Education at a Glance*. In the United States, lower secondary completion indicates persons who dropped out of high school at the age of 16.

Figure 4.6 Educational attainment as of 2005, 25- to 64-year-olds

percentage of persons between the ages of 25 and 64 in 2005 who had completed only primary or lower secondary education. In Spain, more than 20 percent of men and a slightly higher percentage of women had completed only primary schooling. In both countries, however, a relatively large percentage of women had completed post-secondary schooling, a larger percentage than men. The United States had the largest percentage of adults with post-secondary education as of 2005, with the percentage again greater among women. In contrast to Australia and Spain, most of the remainder of the US population had completed high school (upper secondary education).

Similarly, the vast majority of the British and German population in 2005 had completed only upper secondary. In contrast to the other countries, a smaller percentage of British and German adults had completed post-secondary education. Gender differences persisted in Germany, with the percentage of German women in 2005 with post-secondary education the smallest among the countries here. A commensurately small percentage of the British population had post-secondary degrees, but the gender difference was negligible. In short, the gender and class educational disparities persisted in all of the countries, but the exact group differences varied.

Educational Structures and Relative Group Equality

All of the countries considered in this chapter sought to meet the challenge of industrial expansion with a more educated citizenry. Each cobbled together a public schooling system from existing institutional options and specific national opportunities or constraints. The eclectic approaches institutionalized unique gender, class, and ethnic educational differences in each country. The critical gender difference was that mass schooling systems institutionalized women's responsibility for unpaid care work of infants and children outside of compulsory schooling schedules. Having children cared for in the home several years before the start of compulsory schooling also perpetuated class differences in children's educational readiness that predicted future educational success.

Early schooling systems ensured that the middle and upper classes retained their privileged access to better educational options, although the structures for doing so varied. Class differences were embedded in the highly stratified German schooling system, the public-private schooling divide in Australia and the United Kingdom, and in the local financing of US schools. Australia and Spain faced a rural-urban divide that affected regional educational access and quality. In these cases, wealthier rural families could send their children to private boarding schools, many supported by state funds, whereas less well-off families had only the age-integrated public option.

Post-war policies and reorganizations improved equality of educational access in these countries, but at best narrowed group inequalities in the educational outcomes that predict later life chances (OECD 2009a). Women attained higher levels of education, but primarily within care-related subjects such as teaching, nursing, and social services. More of the population entered secondary schooling and then post-secondary education, but the middle and upper classes retained their privileged position. In the United States, this class advantage derived from the high private cost of higher education. In the other countries, tax dollars financed the upper secondary and university education of middle- and upper-class children. So although more of the population remained in formal schooling for longer periods of time, relative group positions within the educational hierarchy endured.

The different national schooling systems resulted in different gender-class distributions of educational attainment in the adult population that predict relative advantage in the labor market. In Germany and the United Kingdom, the relatively small percentage of adults with post-secondary degrees created an educated elite. German women were least likely to attain post-secondary degrees, whereas UK gender differentials in the elite were small. This suggests subsequent labor market advantage among the elite, but minimal differences among the remainder of the population because the majority had completed upper secondary schooling in each case.

In contrast, a sizeable proportion of Australian and Spanish adults had completed lower secondary or less, at the same time that a sizeable percentage of women had completed post-secondary education. This bifurcated distribution suggests the potential for substantial class differences among women in these countries. A bifurcation was also found in the US educational system, but it derived from educational performance rather than attainment. The United States had the largest percentage of adults with post-secondary degrees, slightly greater among US women than men. Yet the educational performance of US high school students was markedly worse than similar students in the other countries. This suggests, as in Spain, an acute class disadvantage among those with less education.

A growing body of evidence suggests that a lack of educational human capital among the least advantaged groups in a society undermines economic growth (Aghion et al. 1999; Machin 2009; Voitchovsky 2009). These class inequalities stem in part from the early-years care void. A great deal of research supports that quality early childhood education narrows class differences in educational outcomes by evening out differences in parenting skills or the home environment (Scarr and Eisenberg 1993) and supporting children's early cognitive development (Cunha and Heckman 2010; Esping-Andersen 2004, 2009; Heckman and Masterov 2007). Of the countries discussed here, only East Germany offered public early childhood programs that bridged the gap between infancy and the start of compulsory schooling. Spain, West Germany, and to a lesser extent the United Kingdom, expanded public preschool for children aged 3–6, although not necessarily full-time provision. Private options dominated the care of younger children in these countries, and for all preschool-age children in Australia and the United States. Private care provision, however, perpetuates class differences in mothers' ability to afford quality child care. Thus, private care provision increases the risk of household poverty for already less-advantaged families (Gornick and Jäntti 2009). These gender-class dynamics suggest that education policy can either ameliorate *or* exacerbate group inequalities.

5

POLICY FOUNDATIONS OF GENDER-CLASS EMPLOYMENT EQUALITY

Introduction

No government of an industrial economy aims to undermine employment. Compulsory education and training systems prepare citizens for future work. Sickness or unemployment benefits offer some financial support during what are expected to be temporary interruptions in employment. Public pensions represent the reward for a lifetime of employment and taxes paid into the state. Countries differ in the degree of government intervention in market mechanisms to support citizen welfare—what Esping-Andersen (1990) referred to as the state-market nexus—but not in their fundamental expectation of employment.

The particular state-market nexus in each country institutionalized differences in group employment equality. The absence of policy intervention typical of more liberal regimes, coupled with minimal social protection, encouraged labor force participation regardless of group membership. Unregulated markets also led to greater income inequality associated with education. In these labor markets, educated members of any social group could reap greater returns associated with that education. At the same time, even small group differences in the substance or quality of education would result in group wage differentials (Card and Krueger 1992a; Hall and Farkas 2008). So, too, would group differences in accumulated work experience (Sigle-Rushton and Waldfogel 2007; Tomaskovic-Devey et al. 2005). Unregulated markets therefore encouraged employment participation, but exacerbated inequalities in the wage returns to that employment.

In contrast, policies that enhanced wage equality raised the cost of labor, which theoretically reduced labor demand and stymied employment growth. For example, Neumark and his colleagues (2004) found that increases in the US minimum wage between 1979 and 1997 were followed by higher unemployment among the least-skilled adolescents and adults. Kenworthy (2008) found a modest negative relationship between aggregate wage equality and employment growth between 1970 and 2000 across OECD countries. Within a country, policies that supported greater wage equality were usually sustained by limiting labor supply to a core group of workers (Katz and Murphy 1992; Hall and Soskice 2001). Women were often excluded from the labor market (Bertola et al. 2007; Blau and Kahn 2003) or segregated into particular occupations (Mandel and Semyonov 2006). In the first case, women remained economically dependent on a male breadwinner. In the second case, women often found jobs in the public sector, which were contingent on sustained political support for state spending.[1] Policies supporting greater class equality for some workers therefore reinforced gender differences in paid work.

In this chapter I outline how each country institutionalized particular gender-class employment inequalities through labor market regulations and related employment policies. In the second section of the chapter, I contrast Australian and US employment policy approaches during the nineteenth century. Esping-Andersen (1990) categorized both as more liberal welfare regimes and both had more open immigration policies (Freeman and Birrell 2001). In each country, the success of worker mobilization efforts varied across individual states and colonies. The two countries differed, however, in the overall strength and strategies of worker mobilization. The Australian labor movement took a more political approach to win class-equality legislation, whereas such efforts ultimately failed in the United States. The divergent mobilization strategies resulted in greater class equality in Australia but greater gender employment equality in the United States.

All states intervened more in labor markets after World War II. As discussed in the third section of the chapter, East German socialist policies supported greater class and gender equality within the state employment system, but occupational segregation and gender wage differentials persisted (Nickel 1992; Sorensen and Trappe 1995). British, Spanish, and West German policies excluded women from employment and instead assigned them responsibility for the unpaid work of the domestic sphere. The feasibility of the respective male breadwinner models varied, however with only West German policies ensuring men's family wages. The British and Spanish labor markets provided women with very different employment alternatives for augmenting household wages.

Neither the market nor gender relations were static. During the 1960s, more middle-class married women re-entered employment so families could afford the growing array of household luxuries. Family sizes continued to shrink, young women remained longer in education, and second-wave feminists demanded still greater gender economic equality. In the fourth and fifth sections, I contrast the national equality policies of this period. The historical institutional differences in Australia and the United States again resulted in quite different equality policies and processes, with the Australian union strategy in this period favoring rather than penalizing women. The expanding European Economic Community issued numerous equality directives, which Spain, West Germany and the United Kingdom adapted in ways that did not fundamentally threaten their post-war male breadwinner models.

As discussed in the sixth section of the chapter, equality directives by the end of the century became subsumed within state efforts to minimize spiraling welfare costs. Periods of high unemployment after the 1970s oil shocks drained state resources (Kenworthy 2010; Kvist 1999). Divorce and nonmarital birth rates climbed, with female-headed households more reliant on state transfers than male-headed households (Daly and Rake 2003; Heuveline and Timberlake 2004; Rainwater and Smeeding 2004). The aging population strained the public health and pension systems (Myles 2002; Taylor-Gooby 2004). The low fertility rates indicated that the financial situation would worsen in subsequent generations with their smaller pools of workers and larger pools of retirees (Esping-Andersen 1999, 2009).

Thus, labor activation and work-family balance policies that addressed these issues came to dominate during the 1990s and into the twenty-first century (Kenworthy 2008, 2010; Plantenga and Remery 2005). Within these policies, greater gender equality became a political means to an end rather than an end itself (Jenson 2009; McGlynn 2006). As summarized in the final section, these policy initiatives have narrowed but not eliminated gender inequalities in paid work.

Australian Versus US Nineteenth-Century Worker Mobilization

Worker mobilization occurred in all industrializing economies during the nineteenth century, but varied in strength and tactics even across more liberal states. One common tactic of organized labor was to seek protective legislation that limited the employment of children and women (Wikander et al. 1995). Protective legislation passed as part of trade union efforts to reduce British men's working hours (Lewis and Rose 1995), enhance Australian men's wages (Howe 1995), and gain greater occupational protections for US workers (Sklar 1993; Skocpol 1992). Australian and British trade unions in the garment industry also won minimum wage legislation that forced piecework done by women in the home back into male-dominated factories (Pedersen 1993; Ryan and Conlon 1989).

The strength of organized labor and the relative success of such efforts differed across the three English-speaking countries. As of 1900, 106 per 1,000 Australian inhabitants were members of a trade union, as compared with 86 per 1,000 in Britain and 27 per 1,000 inhabitants in the United States (Sutcliffe 1967).[2] In Australia, protective legislation restricted the already limited supply of free (as opposed to prison) labor, further enhancing union bargaining power. For example, stonemasons in Melbourne and Sydney won an 8-hour work day during the 1850s, almost three decades before all British workers won a 10-hour day (Shannon 1992; Sutcliffe 1967).[3]

In 1907, the powerful Australian trade unions were also able to accomplish a singular legal victory. The Harvester Judgement of the

Commonwealth Conciliation and Arbitration Court ruled that Australian employers must pay men a family wage sufficient to support a man, his dependent wife, and three children (Ryan and Conlon 1989). The wage was to be paid regardless of an employer's ability to do so, and regardless of a man's family status (F. Castles 1985; Lake 1993). A 1912 ruling legally differentiated between women's and men's jobs, with women's jobs not covered by the 1907 wage ruling (Baldock 1988). In 1919, the Court formally ruled that women's wages would be approximately half the basic male wage and that men would receive greater pay premiums for the same skills (Baldock 1988). Were a man to take a "woman's" job, he was to be paid the male wage given his assumed family responsibilities. A woman in a man's job was paid the higher wage only if paying the female rate threatened the male wage scale (Ryan and Conlon 1989). In short, the stellar working-class victory represented by the Harvester Judgement codified Australian women's occupational segregation and inferior wages.

As in Australia, US workers' organizations were somewhat successful in introducing legislation in individual states. Local trade unions frequently lobbied with women's organizations and used gender to further class strategies (Sklar 1993). For example, these local coalitions lobbied for minimum wages, 8-hour work days, and other protective legislation for women in hopes of eventually obtaining similar legislation for all employees (Sapiro 1990; Skocpol 1992). In contrast to Australia, however, the separation of powers among the executive, legislative, and judicial branches of US government provided employers with a litigious avenue of resistance (Skocpol 1992). Many legislative gains won at the local and federal levels were legally challenged by employers and subsequently overturned by the courts. For example, through the 1905 *Lochner v. New York* decision,[4] the US Supreme Court repeatedly overturned state attempts to pass protective legislation, holding instead that women under the Fourteenth Amendment had the same right as men to enter into employment contracts. This interpretation of the Constitution changed in 1908 when the Court upheld an Oregon law limiting women's working hours. In *Muller v. Oregon*,[5] Justice Brewer ruled that "in the struggle for subsistence she is not an equal competitor with her brother. . . . she is properly placed in a class by herself, and legislation designed for her protection may be sustained, even when like legislation is not necessary for men" (412: 423).

The influence of US courts induced the American Federation of Labor (AFL) to reject a strategy of political action in favor of industrial action (Skocpol 1992). The AFL opposed a guaranteed family wage because a high wage for all workers would reduce the benefit of using a union for wage negotiations. The AFL was also unique in that it formally supported gender employment equality during the first part of the twentieth century (Kessler-Harris 1995). At the same time, however, the AFL did nothing to stop the local unions from lobbying for protective legislation (Sklar 1993; Skocpol 1992).

The US labor movement's rejection of a political tack led to the development of corporate rather than national welfare programs. Most US states enacted workers' compensation laws between 1911 and 1920, and by 1929, 40 states had mothers' and widows' pensions (Michel 1993; Skocpol 1992). But in general, employment-related benefits were negotiated directly with the employer. Unionized industries generally offered better wages and benefits than non-unionized industries. As a result, US workers faced greater wage and benefit inequality than in Australia. Without the exclusionary class policies, however, US women faced fewer employment limitations than Australian women in the wake of the Harvester Judgement.

The Great Depression deepened the US gender divide. The 1932 Economy Act barred two spouses from being employed by the US civil service, with wives overwhelmingly the spouse asked to leave. Using the Economy Act as precedent, numerous states subsequently introduced local marriage bars that forced married women to resign from employment (Hobson 1993). The National Labor Relations Act of 1935 and the Fair Labor Standards Act of 1938 central to Roosevelt's New Deal discriminated against women in jobs and training (Sapiro 1990; Sklar 1993). When dire economic circumstances finally forced the US state's interventionist hand, it, too, implemented labor policies privileging male over female workers.

The issues leading up to the Second World War, however, heightened concerns about human rights. Hobson (1993), for example, argues that the fascist policies reinforcing women's motherhood roles made the US Congress question policy barriers to women's employment. Congress repealed the Economy Act in 1937, ending the proliferation of state marriage bars. The political call for greater employment equality grew louder in all countries after the war, but policy responses differed.

European Post-War Employment Policies

In 1946, the Soviet military administration decreed equal rights in all spheres and equal pay for equal work, policies which became applicable in the newly constituted East Germany (Budde 1999). East Germany's 1950 Mother and Child Care and Women's Rights Acts included plans for public child care and other services that supported maternal employment, which were expanded further with the 1965 Family Law Code (Einhorn 1993; Gerhard 1992; Münz and Ulrich 1995). The Code called for a new male consciousness in child care and childrearing, but policies in fact discouraged it (Budde 1999). For example, fathers had no right to claim part-time work, paternity leave, or a reduction in working hours before retirement (Ostner 1993). As a result, East German child care remained the obligation of mothers and the state (Heineman 1999).

The policies and provisions enabled East German women to work full-time across more of their adult lives (Einhorn 1993). Women's right to parental leave and other "mother-friendly" provisions, however, made them less productive in the eyes of employers (Nickel 1992). As in free market economies, East German women were denied key promotions and on-the-job training (Einhorn 1993). East German women also dominated the same occupational sectors as West German women—education, health, retail, and service sectors—and lower-level positions in all sectors (Nickel 1992). Even the government wage-setting within the socialist equal pay mandate narrowed but did not eliminate a gender wage gap (Sorensen and Trappe 1995). Consequently, gender employment inequality persisted because of the persistent gendered division of unpaid work.

In West Germany, the specter of nationalism and East German socialism gave conservative Christian politicians an advantage in fashioning policies acceptable to the Allies (Moeller 1993, 1997). Conservatives successfully argued that the new political system needed to be based on a "pre-political" patriarchal order ordained by God (Moeller 1993). Under Article 6 of the 1949 Basic Law (*Grundgesetz*), West German women were required to obtain their husband's permission before seeking employment (Ostner 1993). The 1957 Equality Act officially lifted this ban, but most policies continued to favor men's employment. For example, post-war labor agreements contained higher wage categories for men, as in Australia. The equality guaranteed under Article 3 of the Basic Law was used to legally challenge the lower female wage groups (*Frauenlohngruppen*). In 1955, the Federal Labor Court ruled that any agreement paying women less than men for the same work indeed violated the principle of equality. The Court went on to rule, however, that wage levels could be more precisely calculated based on the level of physical difficulty (Frevert 1989). *Frauenlohngruppen* were replaced by new *Leichtlohngruppen* (light wage groups) that yielded no substantive change in women's wage levels.

The coordination of the West German labor market among trade unions, employers, and the state ensured a large proportion of men earned family wages within a more equal wage structure (Cooke 2003, 2007b). Greater wage equality, however, did not fully sate families' appetite for consumption. In 1960, almost one-third of married West German women were employed (Frevert 1989). A survey carried out in the 1950s found that only 13 percent of employed married women worked out of economic necessity; half did so to finance luxury items such as televisions, washing machines, and vacuums, or otherwise raise the family's standard of living (Pfeil, as reported in Frevert 1989).

In addition, the immigrant guest worker policies introduced so that married West German women could stay at home were not a satisfactory political solution to all labor market needs. Women's exit from employment upon marriage created shortages in teaching and nursing, occupations deemed too socially important to be filled by immigrants. In 1953, the civil service, of which teachers comprised more than half, made it unlawful to force married women to quit. The Protestant Church promoted part-time work arrangements for married women to resolve a severe shortage of nurses (von Oertzen 1999). A 1969 federal civil service reform bill improved the part-time opportunities for women in the public sector. The bill was amended in 1971 so that fathers might apply for part-time civil service work, but very few did (von Oertzen 1999).

Consequently, West German women dominated part-time employment, a modified employment scenario that did not fundamentally threaten the male breadwinner model (Ostner 1993). West German part-time jobs, however, were not marginal ones (Kolinsky 1989). Most part-time workers were incorporated into the social security system and retained a statutory right to proportional pay and allowances related to working time (Drobnič et al. 1999). As a result, the pay penalty associated with part-time employment was smaller in West Germany than in the United Kingdom or United States (Bardasi and Gornick 2008; McGinnity and McManus 2007).

In Britain, the 1946 National Insurance Act gave employed married women the option of paying reduced contributions to the new social security schemes and instead rely on their husbands' entitlements were they to become unemployed or disabled. Even if a British married woman continued to pay full contributions, her benefits were not equal to men's or single women's benefits (Land 1976). Also in contrast to men, British women could only claim disability benefits if they proved they could no longer perform household duties. These policy incentives resulted in three-quarters of employed married women opting out of paying contributions into the national employment insurance system (Pascall 1997). The UK policies consequently made British women financially vulnerable to any interruptions in employment or their marriages.

The definition of British married women as dependent on a male breadwinner defied post-war economic reality. British economic growth remained sluggish relative to the rest of Europe (Maddison 2003). Alternating periods of inflation and unemployment led to the government enacting limits on wage rises (Timmins 1995). In the 1960s, three times as many two-parent families with dependent children would have been poor had they relied solely on the father's wages from full-time employment (Land 1976). The British male breadwinner model therefore reinforced women's economic dependence, but did not ensure men could earn family wages as in Australia or West Germany.

Other regulations in Britain led to the proliferation of marginal part-time jobs overwhelmingly taken up by married women. Until 1999, British employers were not required to pay social security contributions for employees whose weekly take-home pay was lower than a Lower Earnings Limit (Dex and Shaw 1986). This policy made it less expensive for employers to offer several low-wage jobs of less than 15 hours per week rather than a full-time position (McKnight et al. 1998). Even when employees worked more than 15 hours per week, part-time jobs were associated with pay penalties (Joshi et al. 1999). In 1977, the National Insurance regulations changed to require that married women pay contributions, but few women working part-time earned above the required threshold for doing so (Pascall 1997). Many married British women therefore earned little money in dead-end jobs and, if unable to work, were not entitled to state unemployment or disability benefits. In short, the modified male breadwinner model that evolved in Britain exacerbated gender employment inequalities beyond those resulting from class inequalities inherent in a liberal labor market.

Spain developed a third version of a modified male breadwinner model that resulted in greater class inequalities among women. The 1938 *Fuero del Trabajo* legal statement excluded women from employment in the formal labor market (Nash 1991). Beginning in the 1960s, Franco's government introduced protective employment policies that created a highly segmented labor market (Noguera et al. 2005). Rigid hiring and termination rules, job stability, and good wages tied to seniority characterized the core employment sector (Ferrera 1996). In contrast, flexible entry and exit rules, job instability and greater wage inequality characterized the peripheral sectors (e.g. small enterprises, building sectors, etc.). A substantial informal black market developed as well, estimated to produce between 15 and 30 percent of total gross domestic product (Ferrera 2005).

As a result of these policies, Spanish workers faced wider insider-outsider employment divides as compared with northern European countries. This market polarization also accentuated gendered divisions of paid work, between men and women and among women. Spanish women were less likely to be employed than other women in OECD countries. Many who were employed, however, were in full-time jobs and in the privileged sectors of the labor market. At the same time, Spain's gender wage gap among full-time workers was one of the largest in the OECD countries (Caprile and Escobedo 2003). Another aspect of the gendered division of labor in Spain was that less-educated married women needing paid work were more likely than men to find it in the informal or black market sectors (Barbera and Vettor 2001). Spain's employment policies thus structured not only an acute gendered division of paid work, but also larger class inequalities among women than men.

In short, the policies shaping gender and class employment equality complemented the group inequalities reinforced in the population and educational policies. East German socialist policies minimized class inequalities and supported maternal employment, but without addressing persistent gender inequalities in unpaid work. Class inequality was greatest in Spain, the United Kingdom, and United States. Spanish policies further exacerbated employment inequalities among women, whereas UK policies exacerbated employment inequalities between women and men. Australian and West German policies enhanced wage equality among working men, but by implementing policies that discouraged women's employment. In Australia this was accomplished with policies that inserted gender differences in paid work, whereas in West Germany this was accomplished with policies that reinforced the gendered division of both paid and unpaid work.

Political voices demanding greater gender employment equality strengthened in the decades after World War II. The first surge came from second-wave feminists of the 1960s and 1970s who argued for greater equality in employment opportunities as well as outcomes. Supranational organizations such as the International Labour Organization, the European Union, and eventually even the Organization for Economic

Co-operation and Development promoted the economic if not ideological benefits of greater gender employment equality. The institutional frame undergirding gender employment inequalities, however, determined the policy approach for rectifying them.

Australian Versus US Post-War Equality Initiatives

The equality policies introduced in Australia and the United States during the 1960s and 1970s differed in ways reminiscent of their past worker mobilization efforts. Of particular note is that the institutions that had undermined some group equalities early in the twentieth century—Australian trade unions and US courts—were used by later activists to enhance gender employment equality. The Australian and US cases serve to highlight that the institutions that structured the equality frame can be used to *narrow* the group distances within it, even though they sustain *relative* group positions.

Women's employment in war-time industries intensified gender pay equity issues, which persisted in the post-war era. In 1937, Australian trade activist Muriel Heagney and the Australian Labor Party set up the Council of Action for Equal Pay. During the war, the Council and Australian employers argued women should be paid men's wages when performing men's work, but the Commonwealth Women's Employment Board disagreed (Ryan and Conlon 1989). After the war, public sector trade unions were the first to win pay equity. The Teachers Federation of New South Wales agitated for a five-year phase-in to the male basic wage rate, which became effective in 1959 (Ryan and Conlon 1989). The Tasmanian public sector followed suit in 1966, as did the remaining states shortly thereafter.

In the Australian private sector, women's basic wage was raised to 75 percent of men's in 1950 (Ryan and Conlon 1989). Responding in part to employers' demands for a more streamlined wage system, the Conciliation and Arbitration Commission in 1967 granted men and women the same wage increase. Trade unions brought equal pay cases to arbitration and won a 1969 Commission decision that called for equal pay for equal work. The Commission limited the impact of the ruling by imposing equal pay only on those jobs "upon which male employees may also be employed" (129 Commonwealth Arbitration Report 1158).

Australia's occupational segregation limited the impact of subsequent decisions as well. A 1972 decision called for equal pay for work of equal value, but applying this rule affected only 18 percent of female workers (Baldock 1988). In 1973, the Commission set a single minimum wage rate, but only for female and male workers who performed the same job. The Commission also encouraged work-value comparisons between male and female classifications, but very few were ever conducted (Pocock 1995). At the same time, the Commission rulings effectively narrowed the Australian gender wage gap among full-time workers to be one of the smallest of the OECD countries (OECD 2002: 97).[6]

In the United States, pay equity arose as a civil rights rather than a trade union issue. Congress passed the Equal Pay Act in 1963 that prohibited gender wage discrimination for the same job in the same location (Costain and Costain 1987). Title VII of the Civil Rights Act in 1964 made employment discrimination on the basis of race, color, national origin, religion or sex unlawful in firms of 25 or more employees. The Act established the Equal Employment Opportunity Commission (EEOC) to enforce anti-discrimination laws. At its inception, the EEOC was a "toothless tiger" because its activities were limited to collecting statistics, conciliation, education, and technical assistance.[7] Congress strengthened Title VII in 1972 by giving the EEOC litigation enforcement authority, a move which made the US courts a battleground for group equality. With litigation authority, the EEOC filed lawsuits on behalf of individuals and also on what the Commission found as a general practice or pattern of discrimination. With this new purview, the EEOC investigated or filed suit against large employers or trade unions thought to be systematically discriminating. The EEOC brought cases against General Electric, General Motors, Ford Motor Corporation, United Airlines, the nation's nine largest steel producers, and the United Steelworkers Union. The 1974 steel industry settlement included $31 million in back-pay for 40,000 employees.[8] Steel companies and the union also agreed to affirmative action goals and timetables for hiring women and minorities in the privileged trade and craft jobs.

In 1972, the EEOC categorized pregnancy as an employment-related disability. Any employer that failed to include pregnancy as a temporary disability in its corporate benefit plan was regarded as discriminating against women. Employers contested the new regulation to the US Supreme Court, with the Court retaining its historical employer bias. For example, the Court ruled in 1976 that failing to cover pregnancy-related disabilities did not discriminate between men and women, but between pregnant and non-pregnant persons.[9] The following year, the Court ruled that sick pay could be refused to women unable to work because of pregnancy or childbirth.[10] The EEOC, however, successfully pursued legislative redress. Congress passed the Pregnancy Discrimination Act of 1978 as an amendment to Title VII. The Act prohibited discrimination against pregnancy in all aspects of employment and required those employers who had disability policies to include pregnancy. Critics disliked that pregnancy became considered a disability under this legislation, but the law granted some employed US women a paid maternity leave. Not until the 1993 Family and Medical Leave Act were all US parents eligible for up to 12 weeks unpaid parental leave, the least generous leave provisions among the OECD countries (Jaumotte 2003: 31).

US second-wave feminists therefore successfully used the courts and legislation to ensure greater gender equality in employment opportunity within the context of greater class inequality and a corporate welfare system. In this context, part-time employment remained less desirable because it was more uncertain, paid lower wages, and frequently carried no disability program, health insurance or pension (Kalleberg et al. 2000). US women's part-time employment as a share of women's employment has consequently declined since the 1960s (Drobnič et al. 1999).

No US policies addressed the persistent gender division in unpaid work that resulted in gender differences in accumulated human capital. The United States therefore had a high female employment rate, large class differences in earnings, and one of the largest gender wage gaps among OECD countries (Blau and Kahn 2003). Because US women were more likely to work full-time, even as mothers, the accumulated lifetime earnings gap between US mothers and nonmothers was not as large as in Germany or the United Kingdom (Sigle-Rushton and Waldfogel 2007: 76).

Thus the Australian and US institutions that had initially hindered group equality were central to achieving greater gender equality later in the twentieth century. These institutions narrowed but did not eliminate gender equality in either context, leaving the relative gender-class inequalities intact. Australian policies instigated by trade union efforts resulted in greater gender wage equality in the context of greater class equality, but also persistent gender occupational segregation. US policies that resulted from the nip-and-tuck of litigation supported greater gender equality in employment participation and work hours, but also persistent income inequality between women and men and among women.

Equal opportunity, equal treatment, and affirmative action policies therefore gave members of disadvantaged groups the right to act like a member of the dominant group (Rees 1998). The labor market itself, however, was considered androcentric (Smith 1987). Across industrialization, the selfish, competitive, work-obsessed traits rewarded by the market increasingly became equated with masculinity (Tronto 1993). The European Union would use its growing influence to not only further national equal opportunity legislation, but also to promote assessment of the gendered structure of employment that inhibited increasing female labor force participation in member states.

The European Union and Gender Equality

The European Economic Community was established when West Germany along with Belgium, France, Italy, Luxembourg, and the Netherlands signed the 1957 Treaty of Rome. Article 119 of the treaty was a single paragraph that required member states to ensure equal pay for equal work, a policy that was legally enforceable in the European Court of Justice (McGlynn 2001). Member states largely ignored Article 119 during the 1960s, which caused the European Community[11] to issue subsequent binding directives. Member states, or those vying for membership, were legally required to comply with directives by introducing national legislation.

The first directives were for equal pay for work of equal value (1975), equal treatment in access to employment, training, promotion and working conditions (1976), and equal treatment in social security matters (1978) (Rees 1998: 52). Non-binding recommendations and resolutions were also issued, such as the promotion of positive action programs to help women compete in the labor market (1984), the promotion of dignity at work (1992), and promotion of equal opportunities through European Structural Funds (1994) (Rees 1998: 55).

States retained latitude in how they complied with the EU directives and recommendations. As a result, neither resulted in national policies that fundamentally altered the bases of the British, Spanish or West German male breadwinner models. For example, the United Kingdom passed the Equal Pay Act of 1970 in anticipation of joining the European Community in 1973 (Glennerster 1995), but occupational segregation limited the impact of the Act (Lewis 1992b). Other UK equality policies of the period were similarly perfunctory. The Sex Discrimination Act of 1975 established an Equal Opportunities Commission to promote equality of opportunity in education, employment, housing, and the provision of goods, facilities, and services (Zweiniger-Bargielowska 2001). But the Act required no reporting or other assessment of the extent to which discrimination existed. In addition, individuals needed to bring forward complaints at personal cost, which were heard and decided by an industrial tribunal (Walby 2001). The Act allowed for positive action programs that trained women to compete more effectively with men, but not positive discrimination that required representative outcomes as with Australian and US affirmative action policies (O'Connor et al. 1999).

At the same time, British activists were able to use the European directives to force greater policy change than had been achieved through national efforts alone. For example, the Conservative government under Thatcher (1979–90) resisted most directives pertaining to equality or social well-being.[12] In the 1980s, the United Kingdom and several other member states were taken to court by the European Commission for failing to have sufficiently strong equal opportunities legislation (Gregory 1987). This resulted in the United Kingdom being forced to pass the 1984 Equal Value Amendment that extended the legal meaning of equal pay to compensate for the problems arising from occupational segregation (Walby 2001).

The European Commission needed to bring even greater legal pressure on West Germany to move it away from its policies that privileged men in the labor market. Between 1970 and 2000, one-quarter of the European Court of Justice rulings on gender policy were referred by the German courts (Liebert 2003). Despite being one of the founding members of the European Economic Community, West Germany did not introduce equal pay legislation until 1980. German legislation banned sex discrimination in hiring and promotion, but imposed such limited sanctions that the issue was referred back to the European Court of Justice. The Court subsequently ordered the German labor courts to establish damages for violations. They did so in 1989, at the lowest level advised (Töns and Young 2001).

Germany's equal opportunity efforts generally reinforced women's segregation into part-time public sector positions. The 1994 Second Act on Equality for Men and Women provided more comprehensive regulations to eliminate discrimination and advance women's careers in the public but not private sector (Töns and Young 2001). Part-time employment and family leave became a right for every government official. *Länder* affirmative action policies that guaranteed women priority over men in the labor market, however, were also challenged in the European Court of Justice (Rees 1998).

In 1995, however, the European Court of Justice ruled that any positive discrimination policies were contrary to the EU's Directive on Equal Treatment.[13] The ruling threatened similar policies enacted in other member states and was criticized for impeding EU women's employment equality (Magnusson et al. 2003). The Court subsequently ruled in *Marschall v. Land Nordrhein-Westfalen* (1997) that positive discrimination was allowed where there were fewer women than men at the level of a relevant post in the public service and when applicants were equally qualified.[14]

The two German regions continued to differ after reunification, despite the imposition of West German male-breadwinner assumptions on the East. For example, East German firms privatized by the *Treuhand* in 1991 granted only 3,400 of 20,800 vocational training places to girls (Ostner 1993). Less than one in four new jobs went to women and unemployment among women was disproportionately high (Gerhard 1992). Despite these policies, East German women exhibited a stubbornness (*Eigensinn*) in retaining "the German Democratic Republic standard biography" that included motherhood and full-time employment (Adler 2004: 1171).

Spain complied with European equality directives to remain eligible for structural adjustment funds so it might join the Community in 1986. The 1978 Constitution adopted after Franco's death had explicitly granted gender equality, including equality in employment, working conditions, and careers (Escobedo 2001). The 1980 Workers' Statute established the principle of equal pay for equal work, although the first constitutional ruling was not issued until 1991 (Caprile and Escobedo 2003). The *Instituto de la Mujer* (Institute for Women's Affairs) was created in 1983 to support gender equality at the national level. As in the United Kingdom, however, this agency had insufficient power and budget to effect much change (Escobedo 2001).

Spain's letter compliance with the equality directives did not compensate for labor market factors that widened gender divides during this period. Mediterranean countries faced particularly high structural unemployment in the aftermath of the 1970s oil shocks (Ferrera 1996). To protect men's wage levels, collective bargaining agreements through the 1990s contained male and female categories for the same work (Caprile and Escobedo 2003). Because of Spain's high unemployment in addition to its stringent labor market regulations for permanent jobs, the government introduced temporary, fixed-term contracts in 1984 (Noguera et al. 2005). These temporary contracts expanded more rapidly in Spain as compared with northern European countries (Polavieja 2006). Thus, in addition to being more likely to be unemployed, Spanish women who entered employment were more likely than men to be offered a temporary position (Escobedo 2001).

The European Union therefore promoted gender equality into the 1990s as a policy ideal, and its directives enhanced the level of gender employment equality in many member states. But as in Australia and the United States, countries' institutional equality frames maintained relative group positions. In 1996, the European Commission formally adopted "gender mainstreaming" in addition to the directives and recommendations (Rees 1998). Gender mainstreaming recommended that member states review the roots of gender inequalities in all aspects of policies, rather than just remediate the effects of gendered foundations (Behning and Pascual 2001). Gender mainstreaming sparked national reviews of different employment initiatives, but rarely extended into other policy areas (Hafner-Burton and Pollack 2009).

Employment, however, became central to the European Union's growth strategy with the 1997 Treaty of Amsterdam. The treaty revised and expanded Article 119 (renumbered 141), and proclaimed equal opportunities for women and men in all aspects of life as central objectives of the European Union. New guidelines issued that year urged member states to rectify gender employment inequalities that represented, "labour-market rigidities, which impede Europe's capacity for growth and job creation." (Commission of the European Communities 1997: 16). Member states were to prepare annual National Action Plans on employment strategies, including ones to tackle the gender wage gap, work–family balance, and women's return to employment after an extended absence (Behning and Pascual 2001). Gender equality became part of labor activation strategies and supported by work-family reconciliation policies (Fagan and Walthery 2007; Plantenga and Remery 2005).

Work-family Reconciliation Policies and Gender Equality

Post-war welfare states faced rising costs associated with inflation, high unemployment, and an aging population. As evident in Table 5.1, welfare costs remained relatively low in the more liberal regimes of Australia and the United States, where fertility rates were also higher (Sleebos 2003). Welfare costs were higher in Germany and the United Kingdom where a larger proportion of the adult population was unemployed or under-employed. German reunification had increased welfare costs, with unemployment in East Germany rising sharply as the socialist

Table 5.1 National social expenditures and percent of children under 17 living in poverty, circa 2000

	TOTAL	CASH		SERVICES		% CHILDREN < 17 IN POVERTY	
	AS % GDP	PENSIONS	INCOME SUPPORT TO ADULTS	HEALTH	ALL SOCIAL SERVICES EXCEPT HEALTH	ALL HOUSE-HOLDS	FEMALE-HEADED HOUSE-HOLDS
Denmark	29.2	6.5	8.7	7.1	5.4	2.7	6.1
Sweden	28.9	7.4	7.0	7.4	5.8	4.3	12.9
France	28.5	11.9	6.0	7.2	2.0	7.9	28.8
Germany	27.4	11.2	4.5	8.0	2.6	9.0	38.1
Switzerland	26.4	13.1	5.1	6.4	1.4	8.9	22.3
Austria	26.0	12.9	6.0	5.2	1.2	7.8	21.4
Finland	24.8	8.0	7.3	5.3	3.2	3.0	8.1
Italy	24.4	13.8	3.3	6.3	0.6	16.6	19.0
Greece	24.3	13.4	3.1	5.2	2.4	12.7	33.5
Norway	23.9	4.8	6.8	6.8	4.7	3.4	10.9
Poland	23.0	10.6	7.3	4.4	0.6	13.5	21.9
United Kingdom	21.8	8.3	5.9	6.1	1.2	19.0	44.9
Netherlands	21.8	6.4	6.9	5.7	1.2	6.3	37.9
OECD-30	**20.9**	**8.0**	**4.8**	**5.8**	**1.7**	**12.1**	
Luxembourg	20.8	8.0	6.5	4.8	1.4	9.1	29.1
Czech Republic	20.1	7.6	4.8	6.7	0.8	6.6	36.2
Hungary	20.1	7.7	5.3	5.1	1.5	8.1	13.6
Spain	19.6	8.7	4.1	5.4	0.6	16.0	32.8
Australia	18.0	4.3	5.5	6.2	1.5	14.9	35.2
Canada	17.8	5.3	2.8	6.7	2.7	15.5	42.3
United States	14.8	6.1	1.8	6.2	0.5	21.9	49.5
Mexico	11.8	7.6	0.4	2.7	1.1	26.9	24.5

Source: Social expenditure data from OECD, http://www.oecd.org/els/social/expenditure, retrieved 4 April 2009. Child poverty is the percent of children under 17 living in households with less than 50% median household income, from LIS Key Figures, wave 5, http://www.lisproject.org/php/kf/kf.php, accessed 6 May 2010.

production system struggled to compete in free markets (Sleifer 2006).[15] In addition, more of the German population was over the age of 65, resulting in higher pension (column 2) and health (column 4) costs, whereas fertility rates remained low in both regions (Kreyenfeld 2003).

The growing number of female-headed households in the latter part of the twentieth century were also more likely to be recipients of state welfare transfers than other households, with these state transfers representing a larger share of their total household income (Daly and Rake 2003). As indicated in the final two columns of Table 5.1, one-fifth of all British and US children under the age of 17 lived in poverty in 2000, whereas one-half of children residing in female-headed households lived in poverty. The poverty rate of female-headed households was one-third or more in the other case countries. Poverty has been shown to affect a child's future success in education, transition into employment, and family formation patterns (Heuveline and Weinshenker 2008; Hout and DiPrete 2006; Pong et al. 2003). Evidence has also suggested that poverty carries the greatest future penalty when experienced during the first five years of life (Duncan and Brooks-Gunn 1997; Kamerman et al. 2003). Children are most at risk of poverty during these early years where mothers face a tradeoff between care responsibilities and employment (Gornick and Jäntti 2009). As a result, cross-national comparisons revealed that policy support for maternal employment, not just generous welfare transfers, was a more effective strategy for reducing child poverty (Christopher et al. 2002; Kamerman et al. 2003).

Many OECD countries introduced or expanded "active" labor market policies in the 1990s to further lower welfare costs. Labor activation policies placed more conditions on receiving state unemployment benefits, or reduced benefit amounts and duration (Serrano Pascual 2004; Standing 1999). Labor activation policies also targeted groups more likely to receive state benefits, such as single mothers, the disabled, and the elderly (Taylor-Gooby 2004). To further encourage maternal employment and reduce welfare costs, the EU endorsed work-family reconciliation as a part of the European Employment Strategy (McGlynn 2006). The 2000 Lisbon Treaty included a goal of a 60 percent female labor force participation in all member states simultaneous with sustained fertility levels. The 2002 Barcelona child care targets were set in support of this goal, in particular to facilitate the employment of mothers with small children (McGlynn 2006).

The 1996 adoption of gender mainstreaming noted above also became part of the process to review national barriers to greater female employment participation. In the United Kingdom, the 1999 National Action Plan adopted gender mainstreaming, proposed "New Deals for Lone Parents and Partners of the Unemployed," and introduced a minimum wage as well as a working families tax credit (Walby 2001). The New Deals increased employment incentives among those who received welfare benefits, but did not address the needs of women re-entering the labor market after years spent in childrearing (Walby 2001). The minimum wage legislation benefited British women who were over-represented in low-wage occupations, but the working families tax credit discouraged rather than encouraged two-earner families (Bennett 2002). The 2003 work-family reconciliation policy encouraged UK employers to consider requests for flexible employment arrangements "seriously."[16] Flexible employment allowed parents to reduce working hours and has been taken up by more mothers than fathers.[17] The UK policies therefore continued to promote part-time female employment primarily to minimize state transfers to single mothers or households with unemployed male heads.

The German federal government adopted the gender mainstreaming principle in 1999, led by the Federal Ministry for Family, Senior Citizens, Women and Youth.[18] One initial suggestion was to extend the equal rights legislation of the public sector to the private sector. The proposal garnered little political support and met with direct opposition from the employers' federation (Töns and Young 2001). To address rising welfare costs, Germany introduced new employment incentives for single mothers (Henninger et al. 2008). During the 1990s, the German government also introduced "mini-jobs" that were not subject to social security regulations (Wanger 2006), similar to the British part-time jobs. In contrast to the British jobs, however, mini-jobs were intended for marginal male workers (Wanger 2006). German policy therefore continued to support a core group of privileged male workers, even as that core shrunk in size (Palier and Thelen 2009). The net effect would be an increase in overall income inequality, although not to the same extent as in unregulated markets.

Eastern *Länder* continued to embrace gender equality more fully. For example, the *Land* of Mecklenburg-Vorpommern passed a regulation in 2000 stipulating that all decisions and programs in all policy areas were to be subject to gender impact assessment and monitoring.[19] That same year, the Saxony-Anhalt *Land* plan included a five-step process for checking the gender equality dimensions of all policies.[20] All East German wages were lower than in the western *Länder*, but so, too, was the gender wage gap in those wages (Rosenfeld et al. 2004). Ten years of reunification had not eliminated the historical gender employment differences across East and West regions of Germany (Adler 2004).

Spain introduced the concept of gender mainstreaming in its third National Plan for Equal Opportunities (1997–2000). Within the context of high unemployment, however, women were more likely to receive career counseling rather than the more expensive training measures (Escobedo 2001). A key work-family reconciliation policy was the expansion of part-time employment, but as with temporary contracts, it was driven by employers' rather than parents' need for flexibility (Behning and Pascual 2001). Part-time work did not expand as rapidly as in Northern Europe, but Spanish women were still more likely than men to be employed part-time (Jaumotte 2003). Spanish work-family reconciliation policies therefore did not attenuate the country's deep gender-class divides.

Australia liberalized its labor market policies during this period in ways that eroded women's employment gains, and some of men's class gains. Two-tiered wage systems were introduced in 1987 that hurt the wages of workers in less powerful trade unions, usually those that represented women's occupations (Ryan and Conlon 1989). In 1991, "enterprise bargaining" between employees and employers pre-empted the family wages set by the Commission. The 1996 Workplace Relations Act increased incentives for Australian women to work part-time. Australian part-time jobs, as in Britain, offered lower pay, and two-thirds came with no benefits such as pensions, sick leave or paid holidays (Australian Bureau of Statistics 2002: table 6.45). By 2002, the rate of Australian female full-time employment had declined 10 percentage points from its high in the 1970s (Australian Bureau of Statistics 2005;

Edwards and Magarey 1995). Instead, almost half of employed Australian women worked part-time (Jaumotte 2003). Part-time jobs did not receive the full benefit of the comparable worth policies (Cass 1995; Pocock 1995; Preston and Crockett 1999). As of 2000, however, Australia's gender wage gap for all employees remained among the smallest in the OECD countries (OECD 2002: 97).

US unemployment policies were already draconian as compared with the other case countries, such that welfare reform focused on welfare-to-work. The 1996 Personal Responsibility and Work Opportunity Reconciliation Act was based on the premise that the existing welfare system created dependency and intergenerational poverty, in addition to providing incentives for nonmarital births.[21] The Act replaced "Aid to Families with Dependent Children" with "Temporary Assistance for Needy Families" (TANF). Under TANF, the federal government provided block grants to states, which were free to design their own systems provided they adhered to several requirements. These requirements included the need for recipients to begin employment after two years of benefit receipt, a lifetime limit of five years of benefits paid by federal funds, promotion of two-parent families, and enhanced child support enforcement. Goals and timetables were specific. For example, single parents were expected to be active for at least 20 hours per week the first year, increasing to at least 30 hours per week by 2000. By July 1, 1997, two-parent families were expected to have a total household employment of 35 hours per week.[22] The Act provided additional supports for employment such as child care and transportation. States could also, using non-federal funds, continue to provide benefits beyond the imposed time limits.

Early analyses indicated that the US welfare changes did make work "pay" for former welfare recipients, but the effects occurred during a time of general economic growth (Danziger et al. 2002). Rebecca Blank (2007) subsequently noted the failure of TANF to address the needs of single mothers with greater barriers to employment. The number of single mothers who were neither employed nor in receipt of welfare benefits had grown substantially since 1997, which Blank (2007: 183) estimated to be about 2.2 million US mothers responsible for 4 million children. The 2008 financial crisis and ensuing worldwide economic slump could only increase the number of vulnerable families.

The labor activation and work-family reconciliation policies in all of the case countries therefore emphasized employability without resolving women's continued responsibility for unpaid care work that blocks their ability to achieve equality in paid work. Indeed, McGlynn (2001, 2006) argued the EU work-family reconciliation policies further institutionalized women's responsibility for unpaid care work. EU directives and recommendations related to men's equal sharing of care work were weaker than those relating to women's employment. For example, the EU's 1992 Pregnancy and Maternity Leave Directive required member countries to provide 14 weeks of paid *maternity* leave. In contrast, the more gender-neutral 1996 Parental Leave Directive did not require that the leave be paid, which significantly decreased the likelihood fathers would take parental leave (McGlynn 2006). The European Court of Justice was even more conservative with rulings that overturned national policies supporting fathers' right to parental leave, or that restricted care-related rights to single fathers (McGlynn 2001, 2006). In short, the increased expectation of female employment shared by affluent economies at the dawn of the twenty-first century was not combined with policy support for greater shared responsibility for unpaid work, the same dilemma faced by East German women 20 years previously.

Gender-Class Employment Equality in the Twenty-First Century

The same institutions that exacerbate group differences at one period in time, such as trade unions or the courts, can at other times be forces for achieving greater equality. Yet relative group advantage or disadvantage within the institutional equality frame is remarkably robust across time. The coordination between trade unions and the state in Australia and West Germany resulted in greater class equality among men, won in part by excluding women from employment and reducing the wages of women who were employed. The Australian trade unions subsequently championed comparable worth policies for women employed full-time, but these were followed by other policies that began to promote women's part-time employment. Similarly, West Germany modified its strong male breadwinner policies by creating high-quality part-time public sector jobs for women. Each country's greater class equality among men, therefore, has been sustained by subsequently supporting women's part-time work. UK policies similarly encouraged women's part-time employment, but in the context of greater class inequality that undermined most men's ability to earn breadwinner wages.

In contrast, East German, US, and Spanish women who were employed were more likely to work full-time than women in the other countries, but under very different gender-class arrangements. East German policies supported women's full-time employment for more of their lives, albeit within persistent occupational segregation and a related wage gap. Being subsumed under the West German state did not dramatically alter East German women's expectations. The US corporate welfare system and liberal labor market similarly encouraged more women to work full-time, but the same factors exacerbated both class and gender wage differentials. The bifurcated Spanish labor market further exacerbated gender inequalities, and greater class inequalities among women than men.

The country differences in relative gender and class equality across several components of paid and unpaid work as of 2000 are summarized in Table 5.2. This table highlights the more complex nature of gender-class equality than depicted when using just the Gini coefficient and male-female employment gap, as was done in Figure 1.1. Table 5.2 also includes each country's gender wage gap, the percentage of employed women who worked part-time, men's share of housework, and women's total housework hours, along with the OECD average for each of these measures. An "A" indicates when the country was above-average in equality on the measure, whereas a "B" denotes below-average equality on the measure. The strong male breadwinner countries of Australia, Spain, and West Germany had more Bs than As. The United Kingdom had an equal number of each, whereas US women enjoyed greater equality in full-time employment. The greatest degree of gender-class equality was found in East Germany.

Table 5.2 Relative class and gender equality in paid and unpaid work in the case countries, circa 2000

COUNTRY	GINI COEFFICIENT[1] 2000	GENDER EMPLOYMENT GAP (MALE-FEMALE) 2000	GENDER WAGE RATIO 2000	GENDER GAP PART-TIME EMPLOYMENT (FEMALE-MALE) 2000	MEN'S SHARE HOUSE-WORK 2002	WOMEN'S AVERAGE WEEKLY HOUSE-WORK HOURS, 2002*
East Germany	A (.28)	A (6)	A (91)	A (20)	B (30)	= (12)
West Germany	A (.28)	B (30)	B (77)	B (32)	B (28)	B (15)
Australia	B (.32)	B (25)	A (90)	B (32)	A (35)	B (19)
Spain	B (.34)	B (31)	B (82)	A (13)	B (33)	B (17)
United Kingdom	B (.35)	A (16)	B (76)	B (35)	A (38)	A (8)
United States	B (.37)	A (16)	B (76)	A (12)	A (39)	A (9)
Average 17 countries	**0.29**	**17**	**83**	**21**	**34 %**	**12 hours**

Source: Gini coefficients are from Luxembourg Income Study Key Figures accessed 10 September 2009 (http://www.lisproject.org/php/kf/kf.php#kf). Australia and US employment and unadjusted median wage gaps between all employed women and men aged 25 to 64 are from OECD *Employment Outlook 2002*; these data for the other countries are from Eurostat: http://epp.eurostat. ec.europa.eu/portal/page/portal/labour_market/earnings/main_tables, accessed 15 January 2010. The wage information is for 2006 and represents the difference between women's and men's average gross hourly earnings of among all paid employees in enterprises with 10 or more employees. The East German wage gap is from Rosenfeld et al. (2004); East German part-time gender gap is from Matysiak and Steinmetz (2008: 333). Housework share and hours based on author calculations of the 2002 International Social Survey Program data. "A" indicates the country is above average in gender equality on this indicator; "B" indicates the country is below average. For the housework hours measure, greater equality means women spend fewer hours performing housework than average, whereas less equality means they spend more hours.

Also evident when comparing the As and Bs, however, is that no two countries were exactly alike. In other words, the combinations of As and Bs reflect each country's unique institutional equality frame. How policy structured these gender-class differences in paid work at the individual level is explored in the next chapter.

6

CURRENT GENDER-CLASS EMPLOYMENT EQUALITY[1]

Introduction

The historical policy trajectories outlined in earlier chapters served to support two basic points. The first point is that the "individual" human capital predicting labor supply is in fact shaped by the social context. The state and other institutions within the institutional equality frame reinforce gender, class, and other group differences in the education and work experience that affect relative wages. The second point is that subsequent equal opportunity policies enhanced relative equality for some, but were counter-balanced by losses elsewhere within the institutional equality frame. The gains and losses could be exchanged among social groups, and/or among the individual components of paid and unpaid work. For example, advances for one group (e.g. women) along one dimension (e.g. employment hours) were offset by losses in other dimensions (e.g. wages or unpaid work) or for some other group (e.g. immigrants).

In this and the next chapter, I demonstrate how the individual predictors of paid and unpaid work differ across the country cases. In this chapter, I use Luxembourg Income Study (LIS) data from around 2000[2] to show how the effects of education, partnership, and children on women's and men's predicted employment hours and wages differ within each country, as well as across the countries.[3] The next section provides a descriptive overview of adult women and men's employment participation by educational attainment. The third through fifth sections present results of statistical analyses using the LIS data. The third section reveals the country differences in how individual characteristics such as educational attainment or having a small child change the likelihood men or women are employed at all, whereas the fourth section offers a similar comparison of the effects of individual characteristics on paid work hours. The results of the relative wage analyses presented in the fifth section also reveal unique country patterns of gender-class wage inequality. The final section summarizes how gender in its social context affects employment hours and wages.

The Institutional Equality Frame and Employment Status

Population, education, and labor market policies in each country resulted in different configurations of gender-class equality in paid and unpaid work. For example, class inequalities in education were sustained through a stratified vocational tracking system in Germany, rural-urban divides in Australia and Spain, public-private schooling divisions in Australia and the United Kingdom, and local financing in the United States. Educational expansion resulted in more of the population remaining longer in formal schooling, but without appreciably narrowing other class or gender differences. Middle- and upper-class children still attended the best schools and attained higher levels of education, which improved their later employment success and exposed them to more desirable marriage partners. Gender differences in academic subjects also persisted, which in turn led to gender differences in later occupations.

Compulsory schooling systems also institutionalized a care void that widened gendered divisions of unpaid work and in turn relative equality in paid work. After the war, only the East German educational system provided comprehensive childhood care provision before and after the start of compulsory schooling. In the United States, private care filled some of the void, whereas a spotty mix of public and private care filled some of the void in Australia, Spain, West Germany, and the

United Kingdom. In all countries, women retained responsibility for any remaining unpaid care. Male breadwinner policies also encouraged partnered women's exit from employment, whether or not they had children (Ferree 1995).

Country differences in the distribution of adult women and men's employment status as of 2000 are displayed in Figure 6.1. These suggest two general employment patterns common to all of the countries. First, educational attainment mattered. For both genders, those with low education (top panel) were much more likely to be out of employment (white bar), whereas women and men with a university degree (bottom panel) were likely to be employed full-time (black bar). Second, gender differences in paid work persisted. Regardless of educational attainment, more women than men were out of employment and fewer women than men were employed full-time.

Country variations on these general themes are also apparent. In 2000, East German women's employment patterns continued to reflect the socialist legacy despite the region's high unemployment rate.[4] Among East German women with no more than lower secondary education (top panel), half were employed full-time. The full-time employment rate of university-educated East German women (lower panel) was even higher and reminiscent of pre-unification levels. The East German public child care system might be credited with the high female employment rate, particularly among less-educated women. Yet a similar percentage of less-educated women worked full-time in the United States, a country which does not have a comprehensive public child care system. Instead, the liberal US labor market and corporate welfare system, coupled with the meager social safety net, demanded that less-educated women work full-time to ensure individual and family welfare.

At the same time, only two-thirds of US women with university degrees were employed full-time, as compared with over 80 percent of similar East German women. Similar albeit smaller employment differences were apparent across university-educated men in the two countries. The country differences suggest the greater class inequality in the US labor market provides highly educated individuals with sufficiently high wages so they can reduce their paid work hours—what economists call "income effects" on labor supply (Blau et al. 2002). East German wages, in contrast, are rarely so high as to invoke income effects among men or women.

Spain's strong male breadwinner model and rigid labor market were reflected in the country's employment distributions. As evident in the top panel of Figure 6.1, less-educated Spanish women faced the greatest employment gap of the countries considered here. Almost two-thirds of Spanish women with less than lower secondary schooling were out of the labor force in 2000, compared with less than one-fifth of similar Spanish men. Fewer university-educated Spanish women were employed as compared with the other countries. Regardless of educational level, however, Spanish women who were employed generally worked full-time. Australian women were those next most likely to be out of the labor market, indicating that comparable worth policies did not trump the initial male breadwinner model. The more recent policy support for part-time work, however, was apparent. In contrast to Spain, almost one-half of less-educated Australian women who were employed worked part-time. In both countries, a similar proportion of employed university-educated women worked part-time.

West German and British policies also promoted women's part-time work under their respective modified male breadwinner models. Regardless of educational level, only a slightly smaller proportion of West German women were employed as compared with East German women. But more than half of employed West German women with lower secondary education worked part-time, as did more than one-third of employed university-educated women. Somewhat fewer British women were employed, but a similar proportion of less-educated British women were employed part-time as in West Germany. Among university-educated women, more British women worked full-time, similar to the proportion of university-educated Australian women.

Individual Characteristics and Employment in Context

How might policies and other institutions alter the effects of individual characteristics on employment? Women in all of the countries carry the

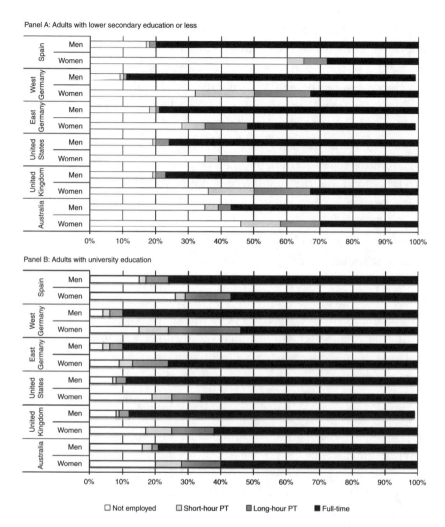

Figure 6.1 Usual weekly employment, men and women age 20–54, circa 2000

primary responsibility for unpaid care work, meaning that children should reduce women's employment. These care effects on women's employment should be more marked in strong male breadwinner states. Partnered men in male breadwinner states should be more likely to be employed, whereas partnered women should be less likely to be employed. Those women who are employed in male breadwinner states represent a select group of women who invest in education and work experience despite the policy discouragement (Pettit and Hook 2009). University-educated women in male breadwinner countries should therefore be significantly more likely to be employed than educated women in more liberal labor markets. Liberal labor markets offer greater wage rewards for education, but high rewards can result in the income effect that reduces the employment incentive. Also, people tend to marry persons with similar education (Blossfeld and Timm 2003; Mare 1991), so a highly educated partner's earnings could induce the income effect on employment among other members of the household. In economic models, these other household income effects should be gender-neutral. In other words, a wife's high earnings should be just as likely to reduce her husband's employment hours as his high earnings would be likely to reduce her employment hours. Institutional reinforcement of a male breadwinner model would lead to husbands' high earnings having a greater effect on wives' employment than vice versa.

Women and men's predicted probabilities of employment using the Luxembourg Income Study data are displayed in the first row of the two panels of Table 6.1. Women's probability of employment was always lower than men's, but the probability each gender was employed varied across the countries. Only 46 percent of Spanish women between the ages of 20 and 54 were likely to be employed, as compared with 77 percent of East German women. Australian men had the lowest probability of employment at 75 percent, whereas West German men had the highest at 92 percent.

As indicated in the remaining rows of Table 6.1, the marginal effect of each individual characteristic on the probability of employment differed across countries and usually for each gender within a country. Having a university degree had a greater effect on women than men, although the East German gender difference was just one percentage point. This finding suggests that employed women were a select group of varying size in all of the countries compared here, not just the strong

Table 6.1 Marginal effects of individual characteristics on likelihood of being employed, circa 2000

	AUSTRALIA		UNITED KINGDOM		UNITED STATES	
	MEN	WOMEN	MEN	WOMEN	MEN	WOMEN
Predicted probability of employment	75 %	64 %	86 %	71 %	88 %	74 %
University	0.15***	0.22***	0.11***	0.19***	0.09***	0.13***
Partner	0.15***	0.05**	0.15***	0.13***	0.12***	−0.01
Child<3	−0.05*	−0.33***	−0.002	−0.29***	0.00	−0.16***
Other household income (000)	−0.008***	−0.004***	−0.002***	−0.002***	−0.001***	−0.002***
Immigrant	−0.08***	−0.10***	−0.16***	−0.25***	0.003	−0.13***
US black					−0.09***	−0.04***
N	4,025	4,300	12,806	14,079	29,402	31,814

	EAST GERMANY		WEST GERMANY		SPAIN	
	MEN	WOMEN	MEN	WOMEN	MEN	WOMEN
Predicted probability of employment	86 %	77 %	92 %	73 %	83 %	46 %
University	0.14***	0.15***	0.05***	0.09***	0.07***	0.31***
Partner	0.13***	0.11***	0.07***	−0.07***	0.23***	−0.10***
Child<3	−0.02	−0.38***	0.02	−0.47***	0.07**	−0.03
Other household income (000)	−0.003***	−0.005***	−0.002***	−0.005***	−0.001	−0.004***
Immigrant	—	−0.47*	−0.12***	−0.23***	—	—
N	1,553	1,586	4,828	5,048	2,545	2,861

* $p<=0.05$; ** $p<=0.01$; *** $p<=0.001$
Source: Sample of individuals aged 20 to 54 not still in school. Controlling for age (see technical appendix).

male breadwinner ones. The largest effect of a university degree was evident among Spanish women, increasing their probability of being employed by 31 percentage points. A university degree increased Australian and British women's probability of being employed by 22 and 19 percentage points, respectively. In West Germany, however, having a university degree increased a woman's probability of being employed by just 9 percentage points, not much more than the 5 percentage point effect for West German men. The relatively small impact of university education on West German women or men's employment might reflect the West German institutional training support for individuals with less general education (Estevez-Abe et al. 2001). The university effect on Spanish men was also modest, which could reflect the very high rate of self-employment among men in Mediterranean countries (Ferrera 2005).

Other strong male breadwinner effects were more pronounced in West Germany as well as Spain. Having a partner decreased a West German woman's probability of employment by 7 percentage points, whereas partnership increased West German men's probability by a similar amount. In Spain, having a partner decreased women's probability of employment by 10 percentage points, and increased Spanish men's by 23 percentage points. Thus, having the wife out of the labor market and economically dependent on a male breadwinner still typified Spanish and West German partnership arrangements.

Having a partner also increased Australian and British men's probability by 15 percentage points and US men's by 12 percentage points. In contrast to Spanish and West German women, however, having a partner had no effect on US women's employment probability. Partnered Australian and British women in fact had a higher probability of employment as compared with single women. Having a partner increased the probability a British woman was employed by 13 percentage points, two points more than the partnership effect on East German women. Partnership in the three English-speaking countries and East Germany, therefore, did not signify women's exit from employment and total economic dependence on men as it did in Spain and West Germany.

Partnership effects have always been a class privilege in that they hinge on the household's ability to survive on a single income—the "family wage." But the "other household income" effect listed in the fifth row of Table 6.1 suggests that each $1,000 increase in household income other than the individual's own earnings decreases the likelihood of employment for both men and women. In other words, income effects work similarly on men and women. What differs across the countries is the magnitude of this household income effect for each gender. As would be expected under a male breadwinner model, the effect of other household income on employment was four times greater for Spanish women than men, and twice as great for West German women as compared with men. The household income effect was also twice as great for US women, indicating that the liberal US labor market sustained a muted male breadwinner model if the household could afford it.

The other household income effect was also larger among East German women than men. This suggests that the most wealthy East German households were also more likely to live under a male bread-winner model, despite the 50 years of socialist policies that promoted female employment. The household income effect on East German men, however, was also greater than in most other countries. This raises another possible interpretation of these effects. In the high regional unemployment as East Germany struggles to transition to a free market economy, the quality of available jobs might be sufficiently poor such that either gender exits the labor market if they can afford to do so. Unfortunately, the LIS data contained no measures of job quality with which to assess this possibility.

Australia and the United Kingdom have moved further away from the male breadwinner model than the United States. Partnered British women had a greater probability of employment than US women, and the other household income effects were identical for each gender. Beveridge's premise notwithstanding, second earners have always been an economic if not ideological necessity in most British families (Land 1976). The British male unemployment rate also generally runs higher than the female unemployment rate.[5] These trends suggest British men did not or could not fully embrace their economic responsibility for the household.

The effect of other household income on Australian adults suggests that country's male breadwinner model did not hinge on men's high earnings. Each additional $1,000 in other household income reduced Australian men's probability of being employed twice as much as it reduced women's. The low overall employment probability among Australian men and women indicated in the first row of the table suggests employment in general is less central to Australian life than in other market economies. In other words, high wages for both genders allow Australians to enjoy more time outside of paid work, an option that is desirable to both men and women.

The results noted above suggest some erosion in the economic effects associated with a male breadwinner model in some of the countries (see also Crompton 1999), but the gendered effects of care work persisted in all of them. The effect of having a child younger than three was greatest in West Germany, decreasing a woman's employment probability by 47 percentage points. In 2000, East German women shared the same generous maternity provisions as West German women, but a young child did not decrease their probability of employment quite so much (38 percentage points). Having a young child reduced the probability of employment among Australian and British women by 33 and 29 percentage points, respectively. Young children had a more modest but still significant effect on US women's employment probability, decreasing it by 16 percentage points. Only in Australia did the presence of a small child significantly reduce men's employment likelihood as well, although the gender gap in the care effect remained large at 28 percentage points. Clearly the largest, but not the only barrier to gender equality in paid work in most countries is the persistent gender inequality in unpaid care work.

In Spain, effects of women's care responsibility manifested differently than in the other countries. The direct effect of a small child on women's employment probability was insignificant, within the context of women's overall lower employment probability. The child effect on female employment reflects the rigidities in the Spanish labor market that discourage employed women from exiting work following childbirth (Ariza et al. 2003). At the same time, Spain was the only country where the presence of a small child significantly increased the probability of men's employment. The two effects together point to the perverse effects that strong male breadwinner policies have on fertility in post-industrial labor markets (Dalla Zuanna and Micheli 2004; McDonald 2000). Few post-industrial economies offer the secure, high-wage employment necessary to a male breadwinner model, but these models offer few policy supports for female employment. As a result, aggregate levels of female employment and total fertility rates are both low in strong male breadwinner countries (Brewster and Rindfuss 2000; McDonald 2000; Sleebos 2003). The female employment-fertility trade-off becomes more acute as male employment becomes more precarious, as it is in the Mediterranean countries (Ferrera 2005). Thus female employment and fertility tend to be lower in the southern versus northern European male breadwinner states (Adsera 2003; Cooke 2009).

Gender-class differences are the primary group effects of interest here, but the LIS country datasets have some measures that allow me to illustrate how all group memberships matter. Controlling for education and family characteristics, being an immigrant usually reduced the probability of employment (Table 6.1, sixth row). Immigrant women were generally less likely to be employed than either immigrant men or nonimmigrant women. The immigrant penalty in Australia was fairly small and similar for both genders, reducing the probability of employment by 8 percentage points for immigrant men and 10 percentage points for immigrant women. The immigrant penalty for both genders was greater in West Germany and the United Kingdom, and substantially greater for immigrant women than men. In contrast, immigrant men in the United States faced no significant barrier, although being an immigrant woman reduced the probability of employment by 13 percentage points. In the United States, however, ethnicity has historically been a greater social divide than immigrant status per se.[6] As displayed in the seventh row of Table 6.1, being a US Black man reduced the probability of employment by 9 percentage points, whereas the penalty for US Black women was 4 percentage points.

Thus in all of the countries, the highly educated were privileged in employment over the less-educated, as were noncarers over carers, nonimmigrants over immigrants, and in the United States, Whites over Blacks. Gender differences in education and employment have narrowed over time, but women's unpaid care responsibility continued to shape gender differences in employment participation. Each country's institutional equality frame dictated the nature and size of these group differences. Class inequality was greater among Spanish women than men, and accompanied by the largest partnership effects in the context of lower overall female employment. West Germany's class equality policies minimized educational effects, but the strong male breadwinner model was evident in sharp gender differences in partnership and parenthood effects.

In contrast, education and partnership effects were positive and similar for East German men and women, although parenthood still had gendered effects despite the availability of public child care. The significant differences in the effects of a university degree, partnership, and motherhood on women's employment across the two German regions highlight the importance of the policy context in shaping the factors that predict labor supply. The German regional differences also suggest that the effects of earlier policies promoting women's employment can persist after many of the policies themselves have changed (Adler 2004). At the same time, the gender difference in the effects of young children on employment highlights that East German policy did not shift the unpaid care burden.

Vestiges of a male breadwinner model remained in the other countries, primarily among the most affluent households as in East Germany. Australian men were least likely to be employed, particularly if other household income allowed it. Australia was also the only country where having a small child significantly reduced men's probability of employment. These effects hint that high wages for Australian men and women created more "space" for non-employment time. Whether both genders benefit equally from this additional non-employment time is explored in the next chapter.

Weekly Work Hours of Employed Individuals in Context

Relative employment participation is just one component of gender equality in paid work. Equally important are any gender differences in the work hours of those who are employed, as these contribute to the accumulated work experience that predicts wages. The evidence presented in this section illustrates that the policy context also alters the effect of individual characteristics on weekly work hours (see the technical appendix to this chapter for details of measures and the model). The country effects contrast with those in the United States. The

United States was selected as the baseline because of its minimal policy interference in the labor market and the prevalence of full-time employment among employed women and men (Drobnič et al. 1999; Kalleberg et al. 2000). The statistically significant individual and country effects on weekly work hours are displayed in the panels of Figure 6.2 (full results are in Table 6A.1).

The first panel illustrates the effects of education, partnership, and children on US men's and women's weekly work hours controlling for their age. The constant term signifies that in 2000, a single US 20-year-old employed woman with some post-secondary education but no children worked about seven more hours each week than a similar US man. Possessing just a high school degree or less did not significantly alter either gender's weekly work hours. Having a university degree increased employed US men's and women's predicted work hours by about two per week, with the university effect infinitesimally greater for US women.

Controlling for human capital, the gendered effects of family characteristics on US weekly work hours were similar to their effects on employment probability, but again very modest. Being partnered and having a young child predicted employed US women worked about two fewer weekly hours, whereas these family characteristics predicted employed US men worked one or two hours more. Although still gendered, the small magnitude of individual-level effects highlights the similarity of work hours in the United States regardless of education and for both employed men and women.

The remaining five panels of Figure 6.2 highlight how these effects differ in each of the other countries. The weekly work hours of employed Spanish men and women were the most similar to the United States. The overall country effect indicates that Spanish men worked slightly fewer hours on average than US men, whereas there was no significant difference in the weekly work hours of employed women in the two countries. Less-educated employed Spanish men actually worked almost five more hours each week than similar US men. Both less and more education predicted slightly fewer work hours among employed Spanish women as compared with US women. Thus, although Spanish

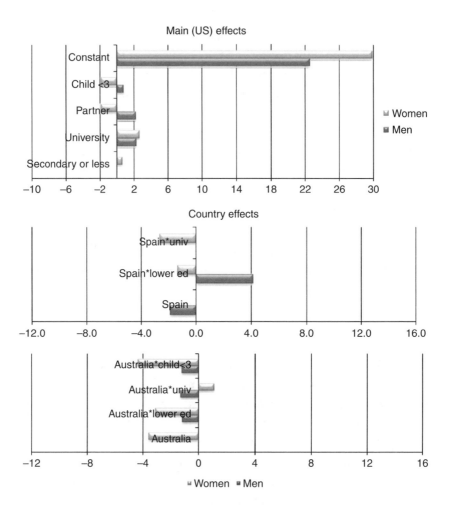

Source: Coefficients from pooled regression model predicting weekly employment hours, including country indicator variables and interaction terms, LIS wave 5.2, 20–54-year-olds not in school. See technical appendix, Table 6A.

Figure 6.2 Main and country effects of individual predictors of weekly employment hours by gender, circa 2000

women were far less likely to be employed than US women (Table 6.1), those who were employed worked similar weekly hours as employed US women.

The institutional frames in the other countries elicited larger individual and family effects on weekly work hours as compared with the

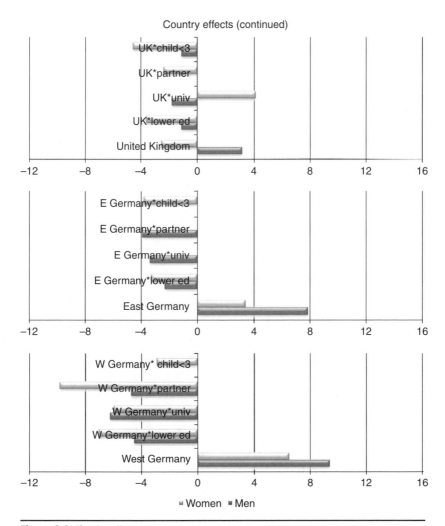

Figure 6.2 (Continued)

United States.[7] The third and fourth panels display effects for Australia and the United Kingdom, respectively. As immediately apparent when comparing these two cases with the United States, gender differences across the English-speaking countries were greater than any class differences captured by the education measures. The educational differences in weekly work hours were also greater among Australian and

British women than men, suggesting greater class differences among employed women in these countries as compared with men in either country or women in the United States.

Employed Australian women worked fewer hours than their US counterparts regardless of individual or family factors, as evidenced by the main Australia effect for women. There was no such country effect for Australian men. The work hours penalty for having less education was greater among employed Australian women than employed US women. Less-educated Australian women also worked fewer hours than less-educated Australian men. Australian women with a university degree worked about one hour more than similar US women, whereas university-educated Australian men worked about one hour less than their US counterparts.

Another gender-class pattern is evident among British men and women. The British work hours penalty for those with secondary schooling or less was greater for British women than men, with the magnitude of gender difference similar to that found in Australia. Also similar to Australia, employed British men with university degrees were predicted to work slightly fewer hours than similar US men. Yet employed university-educated British women were predicted to work almost five more hours per week than their US counterparts. Thus, the gender differences in educational effects on weekly work hours were greater between employed British men and women than they were between either Australian or US men and women. Less-educated Australian and British women worked similarly fewer hours than less-educated US women, but educated British women worked appreciably more hours than educated Australian or US women.

Partnership effects also differed across the three English-speaking countries. Employed British women with a partner were predicted to work even fewer hours than partnered US women, whereas there had been no incremental effect of partnership on employed Australian women's weekly work hours. Partnered British women were therefore more likely to be employed than partnered Australian or US women (per Table 6.1), but those in employment worked fewer hours. These effects reflect the UK's post-war policy reinforcement of married women's part-time employment under their modified male breadwinner model.

Australian and British parenthood effects also differed from US parenthood effects. Employed mothers with a young child worked about four (UK) or five (Australia) fewer hours per week than US mothers. A young child also predicted a significant but more modest reduction in Australian and British men's weekly work hours as compared with US fathers. Employed Australian and British parents therefore worked fewer hours than employed US parents. Yet only Australian mothers and fathers spent appreciably more time in primary child care as compared with US or British parents (Bianchi et al. 2006: 159–60).

The two German regions' weekly work hours differed more from the other countries, and from each other. Most individual characteristics predicted employed Germans worked fewer weekly hours than their US counterparts. The magnitude of effects was usually greatest in West Germany. As in Australia and the United Kingdom, employed Germans with less education worked fewer hours than similar US persons. The size of this low-education work hours penalty was greater for German men than similar men in the three English-speaking countries. The low-education penalty was also more acute in West Germany as compared with East Germany. The work hours penalty was greater among less-educated German women than men, and twice as great for West German women than East German women. But the hours penalty associated with less education did not indicate greater class inequality in work hours among German men because possessing a university degree also predicted fewer work hours. Compared with their employed US counterparts, less-educated employed East German men worked two fewer hours per week, whereas those with university degrees worked three fewer hours. The predicted effects were greater among West German men.

Effects were similar for employed West German women, although those with less education worked even fewer hours than less-educated West German men. Less-educated East German women worked more hours than similar West German women, but fewer than US women.

There was no significant difference between the weekly work hours of employed East German women with university degrees as compared with similar US women. Consequently, class differences in work hours were slightly greater among East German women than men, and as compared with either West German or US women.

Having a young child reduced East and West German women's weekly work hours, but not quite as much as it did in Australia or the United Kingdom, relative to the United States. In contrast to Australian and British fathers, German fathers did not work fewer hours. Partnership effects differed more dramatically across the two German regions and in comparison to the other countries. Only partnered East German men, not women, worked fewer hours. West German men and women with partners both worked significantly fewer hours compared with US partnered individuals, but the magnitude of the effect was twice as large among West German women as compared with West German men. So not only did partnership predict that West German women were less likely to be employed (Table 6.1), partnership also predicted that those who were employed worked almost 10 fewer hours per week than partnered US women. These differences put the East/West policy contrasts in sharp relief. The socialist policies diminished East German women's economic dependence on a male breadwinner but not their responsibilities as mothers. West German policies directly encouraged wives' dependency on their husbands in addition to their motherhood responsibilities (Ferree 1995).

Countervailing the substantial individual effects that reduced employed German's weekly work hours were the large and positive main country effects for each gender as compared with the United States. These greater average German work hours might seem counter-intuitive given the United States' long work-hours culture and the shorter weekly work hours of more coordinated economies (Hall and Soskice 2001). The LIS sample, however, included young adults from the age of 20. The stratified German schooling system has histori-cally been better at school-to-work transition because of the extensive vocational training (Cooke 2003). A separate analysis (not shown) found German young adults between the ages of 20 and 25 not still in school worked on average full-time, whereas this age group in the other countries was more likely to work part-time. Consequently, the main German country effect reflects the longer weekly work hours of German employees with post-secondary education,[8] who were very likely to have formal vocational qualifications.

As a whole, the country differences in how individual characteristics altered the weekly work hours of those in employment complemented those predicting the probability of employment. Women were less likely to be employed than men and those who were employed generally worked fewer hours than men. Educational differences in employment and work hours were greater among women than men in Australia, Spain, and the United Kingdom, indicating greater class differences in accumulated work experience among women than men in these countries.

Women also faced a specific care penalty in employment likelihood and/or work hours except in Spain, where far fewer women were likely to be employed at all. Care responsibilities also reduced Australian and British men's employment or work hours, albeit only slightly. Spain and West Germany continued to epitomize strong male breadwinner states, with partnered men more likely to be employed or work longer hours whereas partnered women exited employment or reduced their work hours. Consequently, the institutional equality frame shaped relative gender-class equality in employment likelihood as well as the working hours of those employed.

Gender-Class Wage Inequalities in Context

Under the human capital model, an individual's accumulated education and work experience predict his or her wages. But as shown throughout this book, there are group differences in education and experience that in turn predict group differences in wages. Blinder (1973) and Oaxaca (1973) were the first to "decompose" the US gender wage gap to illustrate that less than half of it could be explained by education or years of experience. More of the wage gap was explained, but did not disappear, when including detailed measures of gender differences such as educational major, actual work experience, occupation, industry, job characteristics, or family status (Stanley and Jarrell 1998). Even more but not all of the gender wage gap was explained when women and men were matched on individual characteristics such as educational major and occupation (Black et al. 2008; Weichselbaumer and Winter-Ebmer 2005).

Given the country differences in relative gender education and employment equality detailed here, it should not be surprising that the size of the gender wage gap varies across countries (Blau and Kahn 1996, 2003). Most cross-national comparisons have concluded the gender gap is smaller where class policies promote greater wage equality—what labor economists call greater "wage compression"—and/or where fewer women are employed (Blau and Kahn 2003; Katz and Murphy 1992; Pettit and Hook 2009). Blau and Kahn (2003: 106) argued that wage compression had an especially large effect. Others have found that wage compression policies might equally benefit less-skilled women and men, but lower the wages of highly skilled women more than the wages of highly skilled men (Mandel and Semyonov 2005). These findings suggest wage compression policies possibly reduce class inequality more among women than men, but because of the larger gender wage gap among more educated workers. In this section, the LIS data are used to explore these conclusions at a more detailed level, by comparing gender-class wage equality in each of the country cases.

Average wages of employed individuals are displayed in Table 6.2. In 2000, average hourly wages of both men and women were highest in the United States and lowest in Spain. West German men and women also had relatively high wages, with East German wages more similar to Spain's than the West German *Länder*. Australian wages were between the two extremes. British men's average wages were similar to West German men's, whereas British women's were similar to East German women's.

These averages can be used to provide snapshots of relative gender-class equality. Gender wage equality exists when the ratio of women's to men's wages equals 1. A ratio of less than 1 indicates a gender wage gap; a ratio of greater than 1 means women actually enjoy a wage advantage.

The ratio of women's to men's hourly wages is displayed in the third row of Table 6.2. These ratios reveal that greater class equality (wage compression) and lower female employment do not always lead to greater gender wage equality. Women in Australia and East Germany appeared to benefit from those countries' class equality policies. East German women, in fact, earned slightly more on average than East German men. Yet West German women earned on average only 86 percent of West German men's wages. Fewer Spanish women were employed, but those who were employed earned slightly more relative to men than their West German counterparts. US women earned 79 percent of men's average hourly wages, which reflected the greater class inequality of that liberal market. The additional gender penalties embedded in the British institutional equality frame were also apparent, as employed British women earned just 75 percent of British men's average hourly wages.

The configuration of class inequality within each gender is displayed in the fourth (men) and fifth (women) rows of Table 6.2. One straightforward measure of earnings inequality is the 90/10 ratio, which is the ratio of those who earn near the very top of the wage distribution (90th percentile) to those who are among the lowest-paid (10th percentile). The larger the ratio, the greater the wage (class) inequality. US men faced the greatest wage inequality. US men at the top of the wage distribution earned more than five times the wages of men at the bottom. Wage inequality among employed men was also fairly high in the two

Table 6.2 Unadjusted mean hourly wages and 90/10 ratio, employed men and women circa 2000; $US equivalents

	AUSTRALIA	UNITED KINGDOM	UNITED STATES	EAST GERMANY	WEST GERMANY	SPAIN
Men average	$13.17	15.14	18.82	10.90	16.00	7.74
Women average	$13.10	11.42	14.83	11.58	13.83	6.91
Women/Men	.99	.75	.79	1.06	.86	.89
Men 90/10	2.8	3.6	5.2	4.3	4.3	3.6
Women 90/10	2.6	3.4	4.8	4.4	4.9	4.6

Source: Author calculations of hourly wages (US$ Jan 2000 equivalents) by gender for individuals earning more than zero.

German regions, with employed men at the top earning four times the hourly wage of men at the bottom.[9] Australia's labor market policies minimized wage inequality among working men, with Australian men at the top end of the earnings distribution earning less than three times as much as men at the bottom. Wage inequality was slightly higher and similar among British and Spanish men.

Earnings equality among employed women differed somewhat from employed men's. East German men and women had similar 90/10 ratios, whereas the ratios for Australian and British women were slightly smaller than those for men. The 90/10 ratio among US women was the second largest, but smaller than US men's ratio. In contrast, class inequality among West German women was greater than among men and greater than in the other countries. Employed West German women at the top end of the distribution earned almost five times as much as women at the bottom. Class inequality among Spanish women was almost as great as in the United States. Spain also had the greatest gender difference in class inequality, reflecting the insider-outsider divides in the Spanish labor market that are greater for women than men.

These comparisons indicate that relative class equality varies for women and men within a country. A more detailed picture of the gender differences in class wage inequality is presented in Figure 6.3. This figure displays men's and women's predicted hourly wage premium associated with having a university degree across the wage distribution in each country, controlling for the country differences in each gender's likelihood of being employed and country effects of the individual characteristics (see technical appendix). A university degree should predict higher wages in all industrialized societies, and a greater premium in more liberal labor markets. A zero effect indicates that a university degree does not predict any wage premium. Points above the zero line indicate the percent wage advantage associated with a university degree; points below indicate if those with a university degree in fact face a wage penalty. Women's university returns are depicted with the dashed lines, whereas men's are solid lines. If there were no intersections of gender with class, then the returns to university should be the same for women as men.

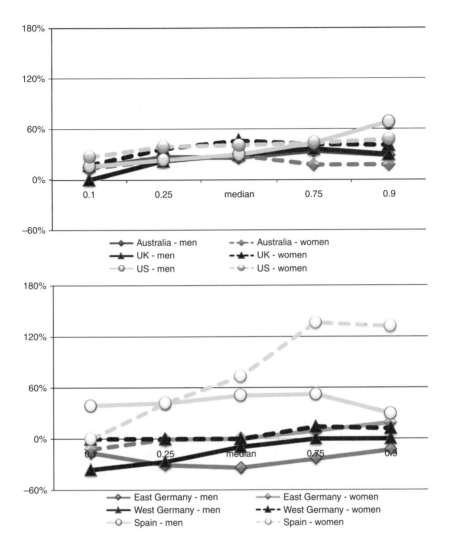

Source: Predicted university effect from a two-stage quantile regression model (see technical appendix).

Figure 6.3 Women's and men's predicted wage returns to a university degree across the wage distribution circa 2000 (see technical appendix)

As evident in the top panel of Figure 6.3, the returns to university education in the three English-speaking countries are more or less as expected. People with a university degree earn higher wages than those without a degree, and the differences in these returns between women and men are fairly small. The returns to a university degree are a bit greater for UK and US women than men across the lower half of the wage distribution. But also notice that Australian and US men's wage returns to a university degree exceed women's across the upper half of the distribution. These results confirm the average patterns noted above: that wage inequality among men in these labor markets is greater than wage inequality among women. Women at the lower end of the wage distribution get somewhat greater relative returns to a university degree than men, but men at the upper end of the wage distribution benefit more from a university degree than similar women.

Women's and men's returns to a university degree in the three continental European countries are displayed in the bottom panel of Figure 6.3, and reveal very different patterns than found in the English-speaking countries. A university degree did not significantly improve German men's hourly wages in 2000. This finding reflects the effects of the high regional unemployment at that time. During periods of high unemployment, persons with university degrees are more likely to have a job than people with less education, but the poor economic climate depresses the wages of all workers.[10] German women's returns to a university degree were somewhat greater than men's across the entire wage distribution. As in the English-speaking countries, however, this female premium for a university degree was greatest along the lower half of the wage distribution. Gender differences in returns to a university degree were greatest in Spain. Spanish men's returns to a university degree were greater than similar German men's, but of a similar magnitude across the wage distribution. In contrast, Spanish women's returns to a university degree increased sharply as hourly wages increased.

Class equality was therefore greatest in the two German regions in part because of the depressed economic conditions (see also Rosenfeld et al. 2004). Class inequality was greater in the English-speaking countries, although somewhat less among Australian women. Class inequality among women was greatest in Spain. These class comparisons within each gender group, however, do not necessarily determine the wage gap between women and men. If class inequality varies across the wage distribution for each gender, does the gender wage gap similarly vary?

The short answer to this question is not exactly. Figure 6.4 displays the adjusted gender wage gap in each country (see technical appendix and Table 6A.2). Perfect gender wage equality occurs when the gender wage gap equals zero along the entire wage distribution. Points above the line indicate women's percentage wage advantage as compared with men; points below the line indicate men's percentage wage advantage over women. As displayed in the top panel of Figure 6.4, there was little evidence of gender wage gap in the three English-speaking countries across the very bottom portion of the wage distribution. This could reflect the impact of minimum wage laws that forced employers to pay all workers no less than the legislated minimum. The gender wage gap quickly increased at higher wage levels in both the United Kingdom and United States. Consequently, the greater class gap between British and US men was reflected as well in a gender wage gap that increased at higher earnings.

Employed Australian women, in contrast, continued to benefit from the 1960s comparable worth policies in that they enjoyed a slight wage advantage over similar men across the upper half of the wage distribution. In general, employed Australians enjoyed relatively high class and gender wage equality. Australian women who worked full-time to command these excellent wages, however, have become a smaller group since the 1970s (Australian Bureau of Statistics 2005; Edwards and Magarey 1995). The Australian case lent some support for the argument that class-equality policies in conjunction with lower female employment rates coincide with greater gender wage equality (Katz and Murphy 1992; Pettit and Hook 2009).

The gender wage gaps for the three continental European countries are displayed in the bottom panel of Figure 6.4. Spanish women faced a gender wage gap along the entire wage distribution similar to that

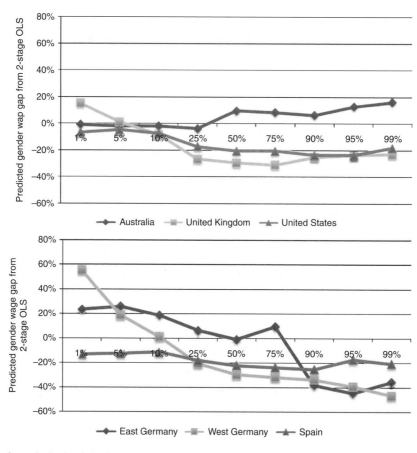

Source: Predicted gender hourly wage gap from a two-stage model (see technical appendix).

Figure 6.4 Adjusted gender wage gap across the wage distribution, circa 2000

faced by US women, despite the very different female employment rates in the two countries and the very different class wage patterns depicted in Figure 6.3. In contrast, employed German women enjoyed a wage advantage over men along the very bottom portion of the wage distribution. East German women sustained their relative wage advantage across most of the wage distribution, whereas the West German wage gap quickly favored men as wages increased. Among the highest earners, however, the East German gender wage gap was as large as the

West German gender wage gap. That said, East German women enjoyed greater wage equality than West German women. The high rate of employment among East German women as compared with West German women also did not lend support to the argument that gender wage equality is usually greater where fewer women are employed (Katz and Murphy 1992). The widening gender wage inequality in both regions, despite the relatively flat levels of German class wage equality, also did not lend support to the argument that greater gender wage equality results from greater class wage equality (Blau and Kahn 2003). Clearly, gender-class wage equality is more complexly structured than existing arguments imply (see also McCall 2001).

Summary: Employment Equality in Its Institutional Equality Frame

The elegance of the human capital model lies in its simplicity: an individual's accumulated education and work experience predicts his or her wages. Social life is not so simple. Each country's institutional equality frame reinforced systematic gender and other group differences in education, and its impact on the likelihood of being employed and the weekly work hours of those who were employed. Many Spanish women were not employed, but those who were generally worked full-time. East German and US women were most likely to be employed and also frequently worked full-time. Australian, British, and West German were more likely to be employed than Spanish women, but often in part-time jobs. In all of the countries, women with university degrees were more likely to be employed or work more hours. Employed women with less education generally worked fewer hours than either less-educated men or more-educated women. The educational differences among women were greater than those among men in all of the countries. Thus the educational component of human capital was a stronger predictor of employment for women as compared with men, indicative of greater class differences in employment among women.

But family was more important than education in reinforcing the gender employment divide. Partnered men were significantly more likely to be employed than single men in all of the countries. Employed partnered men also worked significantly more hours than employed single men except in West Germany. Partnered Australian, British, and East German women were also more likely to be employed, whereas partnership had no significant effect on US women's employment probability. These patterns attest to the partial erosion of the male breadwinner model where either the market or policies encouraged female employment. In contrast, partnered West German and Spanish women were significantly less likely to be employed. In these countries, "wife" and "breadwinner" were still important gender identities (see Ferree 1995).

The care role more universally affected women's employment, even in countries with either unpaid or poorly paid parental leave. With the exception of Spain and its already low female employment rate, women with young children were less likely to be employed and/or to work fewer hours if they were employed. A young child reduced US women's probability of employment the least, and employed British and German mothers' work hours the most. Encouragingly, however, there was also evidence of a "father-carer" identity emerging in Australia and the United Kingdom. Australian fathers with young children were less likely to be employed, whereas a young child reduced British fathers' predicted weekly work hours.

These country differences in men's and women's accumulated work experience in turn predict gender wage differences. The pattern of gender-class wage equality, however, also differed across the countries even after accounting for education and work hours. Others have suggested how different institutional settings systematically differ relative wage gaps. Class equality policies by definition minimize the wage difference between the highest and lowest earners. Blau and Kahn (2003) have argued class equality policies also reduce the gender wage gap. Others have noted that women enjoy higher relative wages where fewer women are employed (Katz and Murphy 1992; Pettit and Hook 2009). In countries with class equality policies and a high female employment rate, Mandel and Semyonov (2005) found that the gender wage gap was smaller among the less-skilled workers, but larger among the most highly skilled because women were segregated into lower-paying public sector positions (Mandel and Semyonov 2006).

The country-by-country gender-class wage comparisons conducted here indicate gender-class wage equality is more complexly structured than can be captured by such generalizations. In all of the case countries, gender wage equality was greater among the bottom quartile of earners. Some of this could be explained by minimum wage legislation, but others have found a narrowing of the wage gap at the lowest end of the US earnings distributions despite the deterioration in the real value of minimum wages (Autor et al. 2008). The effect of class equality policies on the gender wage gap also differed. The lowest-earning German women had a wage advantage over men that decreased rapidly as earnings increased, similar to the trade-off reported by Mandel and Semyonov (2005). But Australian women's wage advantage over men increased at higher wage levels. These differing effects suggest other policies that often exist where there is greater class equality determine the gender wage gap, not the class equality policies themselves. The likely culprit is policy reinforcement of women's unpaid work, which occurred in both regions of Germany despite their very different policies affecting female employment.

The analyses offered little support for the argument that lower female employment rates predict greater gender wage equality. Spanish women were the least likely to be employed, and those who were worked full-time. But across all wage levels, Spanish women faced a more or less constant gender wage gap. At the same time, class wage inequality among Spanish women was far greater than Spanish men's class wage inequality and greater than women's class inequality in the other countries. West German women were also less likely to be employed than women in many of the other countries, but they faced a larger gender wage gap than East German women, who were the most likely to be employed.

The Australian case offered the most encouraging results relating to gender-class equality. Paid work did not dominate the lives of Australian women or men to the same degree as in the other countries. The Australian institutional equality frame therefore opened up more space for everyone's participation in unpaid pursuits, be it care, housework, or leisure. Time spent in paid and unpaid work, however, is another decision that is not made in social isolation. We next explore how the institutional equality frame structured gender-class differences in household time allocations to unpaid versus paid work.

Technical Appendix

Wave 5.2 of the Luxembourg Income Study (LIS) contains data from 1999 for the United Kingdom, 2000 for the United States, Germany and Spain, and 2001 for Australia. To focus on prime working-age adults, the sample was restricted to individual respondents between the ages of 20 and 54 (inclusive). At the younger age, the least educated would already have begun employment. To separate out students who are likely to work in similar jobs for a finite period in their lives, those reporting they were still in schooling were excluded from the sample. The top age of 54 was chosen as countries have some public or private options for early retirement beginning at age 55.

Employment Hours

Figure 6.1 displays the frequency distributions of hours of employment among this sample of individuals in each country. The marginal effects displayed in Table 6.1 are the coefficients from a dprobit predicting employment status (1 = employed; 0 = out of the labor force) based on the individual's age, an indicator variable for those with a university degree, an indicator variable for those with a partner (cohabiting and legally married are not necessarily distinguished in each country dataset), an indicator for individuals with a child younger than 3 years of age, and the individual's total household income minus their own labor earnings.

The LIS country data were pooled, and a series of country indicator variables and country interaction terms added to a baseline model to predict the weekly employment hours of those in employment using ordinary least squares regression. For these analyses, educational human capital was measured with two variables to contrast penalties with benefits as proxies for class differences in employment hours. One variable indicated those individuals who had completed secondary schooling or less, whereas another indicated those with a university degree. The referent was individuals with some post-secondary education short of a bachelor's degree. Completing some post-secondary education could include vocational certification, but this information was not available in all of the datasets. Contextual effects were captured with country indicator variables against a US referent. Country effects on individual characteristics were measured with a series of interaction terms, again using the United States as the referent. The coefficients for each variable are listed in Table 6A.1.

Table 6A.1 Coefficients from pooled OLS regression predicting weekly employment hours, circa 2000

	MEN	WOMEN
N—EMPLOYED / TOTAL	48,187 / 57,046	42,907 / 61,225
Main effects		
Age	0.96***	0.39***
Age squared	−0.01***	−0.004***
Secondary education or less	−0.28	0.63***
University degree	2.26***	2.61***
Partner	2.21***	−1.84***
Child under 3	0.80***	−1.97***
Country effects		
Australia	−0.66	−3.64***
East Germany	7.85***	3.40***
West Germany	9.40***	6.50***
Spain	−1.88***	0.34
United Kingdom	3.17***	−2.54***
Australia*secondary education	−1.12**	−3.14***
East Germany*secondary education	−2.31***	−3.26***
West Germany*secondary education	−4.51***	−7.03***
Spain*secondary education	4.12***	−1.35*
UK*secondary education	−0.08	−3.62***
Australia*university	−1.31**	1.11
East Germany*university	−3.36***	−1.60
West Germany*university	−6.24***	−5.97***
Spain*university	−0.89	−2.65***
UK*university	−1.79***	4.14***
Australia*partner	−0.52	−0.47
East Germany*partner	−3.90***	−1.19
West Germany*partner	−4.70***	−9.85***
Spain*partner	0.27	−0.11
UK*partner	−0.21	−2.38***
Australia*child<3	−1.21*	−4.36***

(*Continued overleaf*)

Table 6A.1 (Continued)

	MEN	WOMEN
N—EMPLOYED / TOTAL	48,187 / 57,046	42,907 / 61,225
East Germany*child<3	0.42	−3.49*
West Germany*child<3	−0.31	−2.90**
Spain*child<3	−0.38	1.62
UK*child<3 −1.12***	−4.60***	
Constant	22.59***	29.85***
Adjusted R²	0.07	0.11

* $p <= 0.05$; ** $p <= 0.01$; *** $p <= 0.001$

Wages

For the wage calculations, only those wages greater than US$1 were included, per Fortin and Lemieux (1998). The imposed minimum excludes a very small number of employed individuals, at most 0.67 percent in the countries. To smooth out effects of extremes, wages were top-coded at the 99th percentile. The natural log of wages was taken to facilitate gender comparisons. The antilog of women's minus men's log of natural wages along the frequency distribution was used to display the gaps as percentages in Figures 6.3 and 6.4.

The adjusted gaps along the earnings distribution were derived from two-step procedures. The employment probability models (Table 6.1) were used to calculate an inverse Mill's ratio to correct for women's and men's likelihood of being employed (selection effects per Heckman 1979). Normally such a correction is applied to women's wage models under the assumption that men's employment varies less. Yet the probabilities displayed in Table 6.1 suggest men's employment probability does differ across the countries, even if not as much as women's. So the dprobit results were used to calculabe lambda (phi/PHI) for women and for men. This lambda was then included as a control in the second equations.

For Figure 6.3, the log of hourly wage was estimated using simultaneous quantile regression with bootstrap standard errors to allow effects to differ across the dependent variable. Independent variables included age, age squared, if the respondent had lower secondary or less education, if the respondent had a university degree, weekly employment hours, weekly employment hours squared, whether a partner resided in the household, the presence of children younger than three in the household, and the lambda computed from the dprobit models. What is displayed in Figure 6.3 is the predicted effect of having a university degree at each point in the wage distribution for each gender.

For Figure 6.4, ordinary least squares regression was used to predict log of hourly wages. Independent variables included age, age squared as a proxy for work experience, an indicator variable when the respondent had lower secondary education or less, an indicator when the respondent had a university degree, a continuous measure of weekly employment hours, a control of weekly employment hours squared (000), an indicator variable when the individual was partnered, and an indicator when there was a child aged 3 or younger in the household. The coefficients are listed in Table 6A.2. The predicted log of wages of women and of men based on these equations along the frequency distribution are displayed in Table 6A.3. The antilog of the women-minus-men difference in log of hourly wages at these points in the distribution was taken to display the gender gap as a percentage in Figure 6.4.

Table 6A.2 Predicting log of hourly wages controlling for selection into employment, circa 2000

	AUSTRALIA		UNITED KINGDOM		UNITED STATES	
	MEN	WOMEN	MEN	WOMEN	MEN	WOMEN
Age	0.03***	0.04***	0.07***	0.05***	0.07***	0.06***
Age-squared	−0.0003**	−0.0005***	−0.0007***	−0.0006***	−0.0008***	−0.0006***
Weekly work hours	−0.005	−0.02***	0.03***	0.02***	−0.00	−0.005***
Work hours squared	0.000	0.0002***	−0.0004***	−0.0002***	−0.0000***	0.000
Secondary or less	−0.07***	−0.09***	−0.24***	−0.23***	−0.21***	−0.24***
University	0.24***	0.22***	0.19***	0.33***	0.29***	0.34***
Partner	0.04	0.02	−0.12***	−0.05**	0.09***	0.04***
Child<3	0.03	0.24***	0.04**	0.22***	−0.00	0.06***
Lambda	−0.16***	−0.12	−0.89***	−0.24**	−0.47***	−0.24***
Constant	1.93***	1.97***	0.77***	0.98***	1.34***	1.52***
N	2915	2689	9269	9044	23411	21554
Adj R²	.14	.15	.26	.22	.25	.19

(*Continued overleaf*)

Table 6A.2 (Continued)

	EAST GERMANY		WEST GERMANY		SPAIN	
	MEN	WOMEN	MEN	WOMEN	MEN	WOMEN
Age	0.16***	0.11***	0.13***	0.10***	0.05***	0.05***
Age-squared	−0.002***	−0.001***	−0.001***	−0.001***	−0.0004**	−0.001*
Weekly work hours	−0.05***	−0.04***	−0.18***	0.007**	−0.004	0.007
Work hours squared	0.0003***	0.0003***	0.000	−0.0002***	−0.0001*	−0.0002**
Secondary or less	−0.15***	−0.23***	−0.13***	−0.16***	−0.22***	−0.29***
University	−0.25***	0.08	−0.11***	0.05	0.36***	0.51***
Partner	−0.35***	−0.08	−0.17***	0.09**	0.26	0.01
Child<3	0.09	0.86***	0.00	1.18***	0.12**	0.05
Lambda	−2.48***	−1.23***	−2.85***	−1.17***	0.53	0.25
Constant	1.29***	1.29***	1.21***	0.80***	0.79*	0.31
N	1131	1063	3909	3223	1426	950
Adj R²	.47	.30	.42	.15	.40	.38

* $p<=0.05$; ** $p<=0.01$; *** $p<=0.001$

Table 6A.3 Predicted log hourly wages from two-stage model (Table 6A.2)

	AUSTRALIA		UNITED KINGDOM		UNITED STATES	
	MEN	WOMEN	MEN	WOMEN	MEN	WOMEN
1%	2.1	2.09	1.46	1.6	1.99	1.92
5%	2.21	2.19	1.7	1.71	2.14	2.09
10%	2.28	2.26	1.85	1.76	2.26	2.18
25%	2.39	2.35	2.27	1.96	2.49	2.3
50%	2.49	2.58	2.51	2.16	2.71	2.48
75%	2.61	2.69	2.71	2.34	2.94	2.71
90%	2.75	2.81	2.93	2.64	3.19	2.92
95%	2.8	2.92	3.02	2.75	3.26	2.99
99%	2.94	3.09	3.07	2.81	3.31	3.11

Continued

	EAST GERMANY		WEST GERMANY		SPAIN	
	MEN	WOMEN	MEN	WOMEN	MEN	WOMEN
1%	1	1.21	1.13	1.57	1.18	1.04
5%	1.36	1.59	1.65	1.82	1.38	1.25
10%	1.62	1.79	1.94	1.95	1.51	1.39
25%	1.99	2.05	2.41	2.18	1.73	1.53
50%	2.31	2.3	2.7	2.35	1.96	1.71
75%	2.6	2.69	2.86	2.48	2.17	1.9
90%	3.54	3.06	3.03	2.62	2.4	2.11
95%	3.74	3.15	3.22	2.72	2.48	2.29
99%	3.93	3.49	3.49	2.86	2.65	2.42

Source: Log of US equivalent predicted hourly wages of employed 20–54-year-olds earning more than US$1, top-coded to 99th percentile.

7

GENDER-CLASS EQUALITY IN PAID AND UNPAID WORK

Introduction

Time spent in employment takes up just a portion of our daily lives, one activity among a choice of paid and unpaid ones. These choices, however, are not made in social isolation. The previous chapters outlined how the institutional equality frame structured the larger socio-economic context of paid and unpaid work. At a more intimate level, the institutional frame reinforces social expectations as to the gendered division of household labor within the "family" (Collins 2000; Fink 2001). This includes not only care work, but also the cooking, cleaning, laundry, and other activities necessary to maintain our bodies and homes. Gender-class differences in paid work interlink with gender-class differences in unpaid work.

Male breadwinner policies reinforced a gendered division of paid and unpaid work. Women's greater labor force participation therefore created practical questions as to who would perform a household's unpaid work. The time availability model predicted that the partner who spent fewer hours in paid work would perform more unpaid work (Coltrane 2000). Bargaining and social exchange models included the value of individual resources such as education or earnings in the household decision-making process (Blau 1960; Blood and Wolfe 1960).

Women tend to be employed fewer hours than men and earn lower wages, and so they have retained primary responsibility for unpaid work even when employed. Thus the gendered division of unpaid work perpetuated gender inequalities in paid work and vice versa, locking women and men in a seemingly vicious circle of inequality.

In this chapter, data from the 2002 International Social Survey Program (ISSP) are used to explore current gender-class configurations of unpaid work at the individual and household levels. One limitation of the ISSP dataset is that it contains measures of housework, but not child care. There are, however, two substantive reasons for limiting analyses to housework. First, only a subset of adults have child care demands. Second, the time availability and bargaining models assume unpaid tasks are unpleasant activities that the partner with fewer resources must perform (Ferree 1990). Such an assumption can be defended when assessing who cleans the bathroom, but seems inappropriate when ascertaining who bathes the children. Fathers as well as mothers have increased their time with children over the past few decades, regardless of employment status (Gauthier et al. 2004). Parents' greater time with their children is evident even after controlling for the decline in family sizes (Bianchi et al. 2006). Where possible, however, the potential impact of child care time reported in other studies will be noted.

The next section provides a summary of what we know about the gendered division of housework and paid work across affluent economies. This summary highlights that the institutional equality frame directly and indirectly shaped gender differences in unpaid work, just as it shaped gender differences in paid work. The frame altered the gendered effects of individual and family characteristics that predict unpaid work hours. The frame also varied the availability of market substitutes that reduce either gender's required time in housework. The intersection of these frame effects yielded somewhat different gender-class configurations of housework across the six country cases.

In the third and fourth sections, the 2002 ISSP data are used to explore the country differences in the housework of individual women and men. The first analysis explores the probability 20- to 54-year-old men and women engage in *any* housework. These comparisons offer little support for the dynamics purported by the time allocation or male breadwinner models. Instead, family and employment affect men's and women's housework participation the same way within each country. What differs is the magnitude of these effects across countries. Gender differences in the effects of individual and family characteristics are apparent when predicting housework *hours* too, as they were when predicting paid work hours. The pattern of individual effects on housework, however, bears little resemblance to those found for paid work. These findings suggest paid and unpaid work are not two ends of a single time dimension as implied by the individual-level models. Instead paid and unpaid represent distinct albeit intersecting dimensions of our individual and social lives. Thus the vicious circle of gender inequality cannot be broken simply by increasing women's employment hours or wages.

Households are a key site where gendered divisions of paid and unpaid labor are reinforced within institutional equality frames. In the fifth section, the ISSP and LIS data are used to illustrate the predicted gender-class configurations of total household time in paid and unpaid work. These highlight the equality wins and losses among couples within each institutional frame. Those who enjoy the greatest degree of equality in paid or unpaid work pay for this privilege with time and/or money. The final section summarizes the implications of these findings for gender equality in paid and unpaid work across social classes.

Housework Over Time and Across Countries

The individual-level models used to predict housework hours complement those that predict employment. Employment hours, education, and earnings are inputs or outcomes in both types of models. Employment hours affect the remaining time available for unpaid activities such as housework, child care, or leisure. Education and earnings are important individual resources in the bargaining or social exchange models that depict household divisions of paid and unpaid work as negotiated exchanges between adults in the household (Blau 1960; Blood and Wolfe 1960). As women attained higher levels of education and spent more hours in employment, men were predicted to spend commensurately more time in domestic tasks. During the 1960s and 1970s, feminists predicted these exchange dynamics would result in a revolution in the gendered division of unpaid work (Simpson and England 1981).

In 1989, Arlie Hochschild proclaimed the anticipated gender revolution had "stalled." Evidence from the United States revealed that regardless of their employment levels, women increased their housework hours when they moved in with a man, whereas men decreased their housework hours when they moved in with a woman (Gupta 1999; South and Spitz 1994). Employed women had therefore not attained equality with men, but instead carried a double burden of paid and unpaid work (Hochschild 1989). Subsequent evidence from other countries suggested these gendered patterns were fairly universal (see Cooke and Baxter 2010 for a review).

At the same time, the degree of gendering had changed over time and varied in context. Hook (2006) used time diary data for 20 countries and found that men had increased their time in household tasks by about six hours per week between 1960 and the late 1990s. Men spent more time in these tasks in countries where more women were employed, regardless of their partners' actual employment status (see also Cooke 2007a, 2007b; Davis and Greenstein 2004; Fuwa 2004). Others have found that in countries with higher rates of female employment, both partners spent less time performing housework (Knudsen and Waerness 2008; Stier and Lewin-Epstein 2007).

This cross-national evidence seems to suggest that greater employment equality over time can indeed encourage greater gender equality in unpaid work (Baxter 1997; Gershuny 2000). This greater gender equality, however, occurred in part because some of the unpaid work shifted to the market. For example, Hook (2010) found that women over the decades had "disinvested" in cooking-related time without men increasing theirs.[1] She interpreted this as evidence of more market substitution for food preparation. The policy context can also limit the effect of female employment on men's housework (Fuwa 2004). Women spent disproportionately more hours performing housework in countries with male breadwinner policies such as lengthy maternity leaves or those that promoted women's part-time employment (Hook 2010: 1512).

The shortcomings of the time availability and bargaining models when predicting gendered divisions of unpaid work gave rise to alternative explanations. Those who argued from a gender perspective claimed that household divisions of paid and unpaid work were more than time allocations, but in part how we "do" gender (Fenstermaker Berk 1985; West and Zimmerman 1987). "Doing" gender is a symbolic representation of gender difference that produces and reproduces gender hierarchies and associated power in social interactions across the life course (Connell 1987; Goffman 1977; West and Zimmerman 1987). How individuals "do" gender varies in context and reflects the aggregate level of relative gender equality (Cooke 2006b; Deutsch 2007).

The institutional equality frames structured these differences along class as well as gender lines. The frame structured the class effects that altered the total amount of household unpaid work, as well as gendered effects on its division. For example, greater class inequality as found in the United Kingdom and United States fostered development of the low-wage service sector that provided more market substitutes for housework such as restaurant meals and cleaning services (de Ruijter et al. 2005).[2] In the Spanish labor market, the informal or black markets frequently provided such substitutes in the form of domestic servants (Bettio et al. 2006; Kofman et al. 2000; Tobio 2001).

Market substitutes have not directly enhanced gender equality because they required no change in men's unpaid work. Instead, market substitutes made gender equality in housework a class privilege. Gupta and his colleagues (2010) found that women's higher wages predicted fewer household hours in unpaid tasks. This means affluent women use their personal resources to reduce the household's unpaid work hours. Less-educated women, ethnic minorities, and immigrants deliver the legal or illegal market substitutes (Williams 2004). These workers have fewer market alternatives for their own housework because of their more limited financial resources.

Greater class inequality therefore shifted unpaid work from the private to the public work spheres without fundamentally altering its gendered nature. Market substitution also perpetuated class differences in gender equality. Educated women could pay for greater equality in unpaid work, whereas less-educated women could not afford to do so even when employed full-time. These class dynamics among women would be most extreme in the bifurcated Spanish market.

Greater class equality as found in Australia and Germany, in contrast, limited the possibilities for shifting unpaid work to the market. A compressed wage structure blunted development of the low-wage service sector that provides market substitutes (Scharpf and Schmidt 2000). Wage equality policies also capped the relative affluence of university-educated workers, reducing the household income available to purchase market substitutes. Consequently, policies that supported greater wage equality sustained greater hours of unpaid work across all households.

The institutional equality frames also affected the gendered division of these unpaid work hours. Class-equality policies of the West German male breadwinner model reinforced women's responsibility for the greater unpaid work hours. Those West German women who were employed therefore shouldered a greater housework burden as compared with employed women in liberal markets. Women's double work burden would be most pronounced in East Germany. The East German dual-earner policies supported women's full-time employment with public child care provision, but no policies reduced women's responsibility for the remaining unpaid work. The low regional wages following reunification were seldom sufficient to purchase many market substitutes (Cooke 2007b). Thus, the greater gender equality in paid work in East Germany came at a cost of greater time poverty for employed women because of the remaining inequalities in unpaid work.[3]

Australia's wage policies also reduced the availability of market substitutes. Australian class initiatives, however, made work pay for both men and women. As revealed in the analyses of paid work, time outside of employment is an option desirable to both Australian men and women. Under a bargaining model, the greater wage equality and more equal gender preferences for unpaid time should result in a more egalitarian division of housework.

Next, the 2002 ISSP data are used to explore the institutional equality frames and gender-class divisions of housework in relation to paid work. These comparisons reveal that the context varies the effects of individual and family characteristics on men's and women's housework. At the same time, the effects on housework are distinct from those on paid work reported in the last chapter. Paid and unpaid work therefore do not appear to be two options along a continuum of "work" time, but rather intersecting work dimensions that sustain relative group equality within each institutional frame.

Who Does Any Housework in Context?

Education, partnership, and parenthood all mattered when predicting individual employment, although the size and at times direction of effects differed across the countries. If paid and unpaid work relate directly to one another as expected within the time availability or bargaining models, similar but opposite effects should be found when predicting unpaid work. For example, a university degree increased men's and women's probability of employment (Table 6.1) as well as predicted employment hours (Figure 6.2). Only the magnitude of this effect differed between the genders and across the countries. If paid and unpaid are time trade-offs along a single work continuum, then a university degree should similarly lower each gender's probability of housework and/or predicted housework hours in each country.

To test whether paid and unpaid work are time trade-offs, a sample of adults between the ages of 20 and 54 in the six countries was drawn from the 2002 International Social Survey Program data (see the technical appendix to this chapter). These data were used to conduct similar analyses to those in the last chapter that predicted employment probabilities and paid work hours among employed individuals. The first is an analysis of the marginal effects of individual and family characteristics on men's and women's housework participation. The predicted probabilities men and women in each country performed any housework are displayed in the first row of the two panels of Table 7.1. As anticipated under a gendered division of labor, women in each country were more likely to do housework than men, just as men had been more likely to

Table 7.1 Marginal effects of individual characteristics on likelihood of performing any housework, men and women aged 20 to 54 in 2002

	AUSTRALIA		UNITED KINGDOM		UNITED STATES	
	MEN	WOMEN	MEN	WOMEN	MEN	WOMEN
Probability of doing any housework	*83 %*	*93 %*	*53 %*	*67 %*	*63 %*	*72 %*
Age	0.02	0.01	0.02	0.03	−0.01	−0.01
Age squared (00)	−0.03	−0.02	−0.03	−0.03	0.00	−0.00
Secondary education or less	−0.04	0.01	−0.11*	−0.02	−0.11	−0.10
University degree	−0.03	0.02	−0.04	−0.05	−0.12**	−0.10*
Partner	0.25***	0.20***	0.80***	0.88***	0.67***	0.69***
Employed part-time	0.01	0.03	0.08	0.15*	−0.05	−0.11
Employed full-time	0.08*	0.03	0.23***	0.15**	0.05	−0.07
Children < 17 in household	−0.04	0.03	−0.03	−0.10	−0.03	0.02
N	*827*	*827*	*1155*	*1155*	*801*	*801*

	EAST GERMANY		WEST GERMANY		SPAIN	
	MEN	WOMEN	MEN	WOMEN	MEN	WOMEN
Probability of doing any housework	*70 %*	*86 %*	*69 %*	*83 %*	*53 %*	*70 %*
Age	−0.03	0.01	0.04*	0.02	0.04**	0.02
Age squared (00)	0.04	−0.02	−0.06*	−0.03	−0.05**	−0.03
Secondary education or less	0.05	−0.05	−0.04	−0.04	−0.09**	−0.01
University degree	0.14	−0.05	0.11	0.05	−0.01	0.01
Partner	0.49***	0.57***	0.56***	0.61***	0.66***	0.76***
Employed part-time	0.17	0.04	0.20**	0.19***	0.15**	0.05
Employed full-time	0.33***	0.21**	0.19***	0.14**	0.19***	0.05
Children < 17 in household	0.07	0.10	−0.02	0.01	−0.03	−0.02
N	*240*	*240*	*554*	*554*	*1467*	*1467*

* *p<=0.05;* ** *p<=0.01;* *** *p<=0.001*
Source: Sample of individuals from 2002 ISSP aged 20 to 54 not still in school.

be employed than women (Table 6.1). Only half of British and Spanish men were predicted to perform any housework, as compared with 83 percent of Australian men. The dispersion in women's probabilities across the countries was almost as great. British women were the least likely to do any housework (67 percent), whereas Australian women were the most likely (93 percent). In short, British men *and* women were the least likely to do any housework (followed closely by the Spanish), whereas Australian men *and* women were most likely. These trends highlight the importance of the cultural context to men's or women's performance of housework (Baxter et al. 2009; Pfau-Effinger 1998, 2010).

British and US men *and* women had greater probabilities of employment than housework. The differences in the employment and housework probabilities among the women were quite small, but the differences among the men were large. British and US men's probability of being employed was almost 90 percent (Table 6.1). In contrast, only half of British men and two-thirds of US men were predicted to do any housework. These paid-versus-unpaid-work probabilities highlight that unregulated markets encourage employment and discourage unpaid work regardless of gender. Australians' probability of doing housework, however, was greater than either gender's probability of being employed (Table 6.1). This is further evidence that the Australian institutional equality frame created more space for women's and men's unpaid activities than in the other countries.

The German patterns differed. More than 80 percent of East and West German women were predicted to do housework, as were about 70 percent of East and West German men. Australian and German men and women were thus more likely to do housework than British, Spanish, or US men and women. These relatively high probabilities indicate that the greater class equality of Australia and Germany did not preclude men's unpaid work participation. There might instead be some pride in any type of work for both genders within these contexts, a proposition that cannot be tested with existing data.

The marginal effects of individual characteristics on the probability of doing housework did not generally support any of the market-based models. Relative resource effects were apparent only in the United States. Having a university degree reduced US women's and men's probability of doing any housework by a similar amount (10 percentage points for women, 12 points for men). In Spain and the United Kingdom, however, a man's lack of education had a similar effect.

Having secondary education or less reduced the probability British and Spanish men would do any housework by 11 and 9 percentage points, respectively.[4] So education does not denote similar individual propensities across country contexts as predicted by bargaining models (see also Cooke and Baxter 2010).

Partnership and employment effects on the probability of doing housework ran counter to the male breadwinner and time availability models. Having a partner significantly increased, not decreased, men's probability of doing some housework. The magnitude of the partnership effect was similar for each gender in each country, although it differed across the countries. Being employed part- or full-time increased, not decreased, the probability Australian, British, German, and Spanish men performed some housework. The same was true of British and German women, but the magnitude of the employment effect was greater among men.

Thus the individual and family characteristics that altered women's and men's employment probabilities did not similarly predict housework probabilities. Children had no impact whatsoever on either gender's probability of performing some housework. Employed and partnered individuals were more, not less likely to participate in housework. The magnitude of effects differed across countries, but differed less between men and women within each country. These findings hint that what matters are some unmeasured selection effects, not negotiated time trade-offs. People with characteristics that make them more likely to have a partner or a job are also more likely to spend some time doing unpaid work. As with employment, however, the gendered division of unpaid work becomes more pronounced when comparing actual weekly hours of housework.

Predicting Individual Housework Hours in Context

The ISSP sample of individuals who did some housework was analyzed similar to the analysis of employment hours described in the fourth section of Chapter 6. The factors that significantly altered individual men's and women's predicted 2002 weekly housework hours are displayed in the panels of Figure 7.1 (see Table 7A.1 for the full model results).

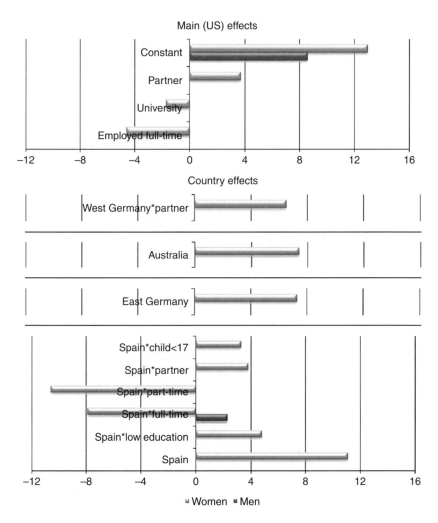

Source: Statistically significant coefficients when predicting weekly housework hours using the 2002 International Social Survey Program data for respondents aged 20 to 54 not still in school. See technical appendix, Chapter 7.

Figure 7.1 Main and country predictors of men's and women's weekly housework hours among those performing any housework, 2002

The top panel displays the significant US results. The constant term signifies that in 2002, a single, unemployed, 20-year-old US woman with some post-secondary education did 13 hours of housework each week, about four hours more than a similar US man. US women who were employed full-time, however, reduced their weekly housework by more than four hours. Employed US men did not. US women with a university degree reduced their housework hours by the same amount they had increased their employment hours (Figure 6.2). A university degree had no such effect on US men's housework hours even though it had predicted a slight increase in their weekly employment hours. Children had no effect on either gender's housework hours. These results indicate that single US men and women employed full-time spent similar amounts of time doing housework (see also Gupta 1999).

Partnership status was the only individual characteristic that predicted a US gender difference in housework. Partnered US women increased their housework hours twice as much as they had decreased their paid work hours. This, however, represented only two additional housework hours per week. The small increment in partnered women's domestic activities could reflect expressions of love rather than negotiated necessity (Ferree 1990), such as taking the time to prepare fresh meals rather than frozen dinners. In any event, these results fall far short of Hochschild's (1989) claim that employed US women worked a "second shift" of unpaid work.

Neither did British women. In the employment analyses (Figure 6.2), most of the individual and family characteristics predicted British women worked fewer weekly paid hours than US women. British women's and men's predicted housework hours, in contrast, did not differ from their US counterparts (i.e. no country or interaction terms were statistically significant). These findings suggest British men carried more of a double burden of paid and unpaid work than women. British women's time advantage, however, might erode with motherhood. Bianchi and her colleagues (2006: table 9.2) found that British mothers with preschool children spent on average 16 hours per week in child care, as compared with 7 hours per week for fathers. This compares with the 15 and 9 hours per week US mothers and fathers, respectively, spent with preschool children (Bianchi et al. 2006).

Women in the remaining countries, regardless of employment, generally performed more housework than men. Partnered West German women did six more hours of housework each week than US women. All Australian and East German women spent on average seven more hours doing housework each week than US women. A large proportion of Australian and German men had been likely to do some housework (Table 7.1), but their actual weekly housework hours did not differ significantly from US men's. Australian men spent on average two more hours per week doing housework as compared with German men (Table 7A.1), but with enough variation among them such that the effect was not statistically significant.[5] Thus, all three of the more class-equal contexts increased the amount of unpaid work as anticipated, which remained more gendered than in the United Kingdom or United States. Child care responsibilities would further enlarge these gendered divisions (Bianchi et al. 2006; Cooke 2007b).

The Spanish results highlight the significant inequalities among women as well as between women and men. The country effect displayed in the bottom panel of Figure 7.1 indicates that net of the individual factors, Spanish women spent almost 12 more hours doing housework than US women. This country effect was virtually eliminated when Spanish women were employed either part- or full-time. Spanish men had been less likely to do any housework (Table 7.1) and those that did performed no more housework than US men. Having less education or a partner or children further increased Spanish women's, but not men's, housework hours. Smith and Williams (2007) found that the hours and gender differences in child care were also greater in Mediterranean countries. Consequently, the gendered division of unpaid labor is extreme and time-consuming in Spain, even among many women employed full-time.

The institutional equality frames thus structured gender-class configurations of paid and unpaid work that share only part of a single time continuum. Greater class equality increased the unpaid work hours, which remained gendered irrespective of women's employment. Class inequality shifted some of the unpaid work to the market where it became the low-wage employment of less-skilled women, ethnic minorities, and immigrants. Despite these persistent gender-class inequalities, there was little evidence that women on average carried Hochschild's (1989) double burden of paid and unpaid work. Yet partnered women do "pay" for greater employment equality. What varies in each institutional equality frame is the nature of the payment.

Couple Time in Paid and Unpaid Work in Context

The institutional equality frame coordinated the paid and unpaid work of industrial societies. The juxtaposition of gender and class within each frame reinforced how couples were expected to organize total household labor. Figure 2.1 presented these as stylized distinctions between the gender specialization of a male breadwinner model versus the gender equality of a dual-earner/dual-carer model. Both models were assumed to be time-equitable, in that each gender spent a similar amount of total time in the different types of "work." This assumption undergirds the time availability model used to predict who does what in couple households.

As illustrated thus far, the reality is more complicated. Policies that directly or indirectly affected class equality affected average paid work hours, its gendered division, relative wages, and also total household unpaid work. Other policy spokes of the institutional equality frame further gendered the different types of work and their relative returns or value. As a result, each frame yielded the gender-class differences in the individual characteristics that predict paid and unpaid. These in turn yield national variations on the stylized household production diagrams of Figure 2.1, which are presented in Figure 7.2. Spheres on the left depict household production among couples with secondary education or less, whereas spheres on the right depict household production for those with university degrees.[6] These serve to highlight the class differences in gendered household production in each country. Women's average hours span the top half of each household sphere, with men's average hours displayed on the bottom half. The striped circles within the household sphere denote paid work hours. The gray-shaded circles denote the household's housework hours. Work circles positioned more above the line indicate that women spend more time in these activities than men; circles positioned below the line indicate that men perform more of this type of work. The predicted hours from the data used to construct these circles are displayed in Table 7A.2.

Two general patterns are immediately apparent in all of the countries. All households devoted more time to paid work than housework. This confirms that the lures or pressures of the market over time erode even strong male breadwinner policies that discouraged female employment (McDonald 2000). Second, highly educated couples spent considerably more time in paid work than less-educated couples, whereas class differences in housework were usually more modest. These patterns reflect the time/money trade-offs faced by all households. Greater gender employment equality among couples provides greater economic security for the household and each member therein. The economic security comes at a cost of what I call "time poverty" because full-time dual-earner couples spend more total hours in paid and unpaid work.[7]

Figure 7.2 shows that the gender-class time allocations differed across countries. The space the Australian institutional equality frame created for unpaid time is apparent. Australian couples, regardless of educational attainment, spent less time in both types of work than similar households in the other countries. The class-equality policies had increased households' housework as compared with the other two English-speaking countries, but this was counter-balanced by the substantially fewer hours Australian couples spent in paid work. Australian women's high relative wages revealed in the last chapter, however, had not shifted the gendered division of labor within households. Less-educated Australian women contributed about one-third of the household's paid labor, whereas their partners contributed about one-third of the household's housework. University-educated Australian women spent a few more hours in paid work, but without a commensurate reduction in their housework hours. University-educated Australian men also spent more hours in paid work than less-educated men without a reduction in their housework. The net result was a persistent but equitable gendered division of paid and unpaid labor that was somewhat more egalitarian among highly educated Australian couples. Adding any child care would widen the gendered division. Australian parents spent appreciably more time in child care than British or US parents,

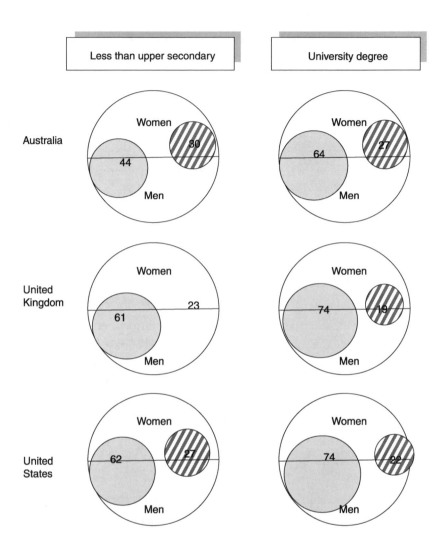

Source: Author calculations of average weekly hours spent by each gender on paid employment and unpaid housework, excluding child care, partnered individuals age 20 to 54. Employment hours are calculated from Luxembourg Income Study Wave 5.2 data (1999 for the United Kingdom, 2000 for the United States, Germany and Spain, and 2001 for Australia); housework hours are calculated from the 2002 International Social Survey Program data. Paid work hours are the gray shaded circles; unpaid are the striped circles. For actual hours, see Table 7A.2. The relative size of the circles is calculated as the square root of the total work hours average/π, divided by 2.

Figure 7.2 Partnered women and men's predicted weekly household hours in employment and housework by educational attainment, circa 2001

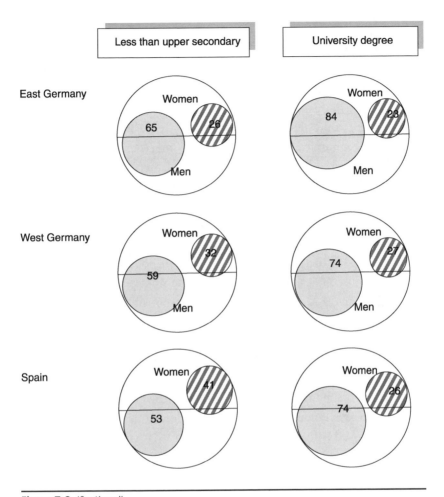

Figure 7.2 (Continued)

but Australian mothers devoted far more time to child care than fathers (Bianchi et al. 2006: 159–60).

Less-educated British women also contributed about one-third to household paid work and a slightly greater *share* of housework as compared with Australian women. What differed across the two countries was the total time in each type of work. British households spent more total hours in employment but fewer hours doing housework. The British gendered division of labor in couple households also provided women with more leisure time than men. Less-educated British women contributed 36 total hours to the household as compared with their partners' 46-hour contribution. A similar but smaller female time advantage occurred among highly educated couples as paid work hours increased for both partners. Including child care would not close the British gender time gap (Bianchi et al. 2006: 163). British women therefore traded economic equality for more free time (see also Warren 2004).

Some partnered West German women also enjoyed a relative time advantage but in the context of a more pronounced gendered division of paid and unpaid work. In part this was due to the industriousness of West German men. Less-educated West German men spent more hours in paid work than similar partnered men in any other country. They also spent the same amount of time in housework as partnered US men. But couples' total housework time was appreciably greater in West Germany and remained women's responsibility. Less-educated West German women spent more hours doing housework (25 hours) than paid work (18 hours). University-educated West German women increased their employment by 10 hours per week, but reduced their weekly housework time by only five hours. Their partners also increased their paid work hours with no reduction in their housework. The net result of these gendered divisions was that less-educated West German women enjoyed a five-hour time advantage that shrank to two hours among the highly educated. In contrast to the United Kingdom, however, parenthood would tip the West German couple free time balance back in men's favor (Cooke 2007b; Rosenfeld et al. 2004).

Spanish couples' households displayed more extreme gendered class patterns, but time equity within households. Spanish couples with less education spent almost as many hours in housework as in paid work, with women responsible for more than 80 percent of the unpaid hours. Highly educated Spanish women increased their employment hours twice as much as similar West German women, but this was balanced by a greater decrease in housework. Affluent Spanish couples reduced the excessive housework burden by employing low-wage legal and illegal domestic servants (Anderson 2000; Tobio 2001). Thus, highly educated Spanish couples had gendered divisions of labor similar to highly educated West German couples. What differed across the two countries was the extremity of the housework burden among less-educated Spanish couples.

Less-educated US couples had greater equality in paid work hours than similar couples in Australia, Spain, West Germany, or the United Kingdom. At the same time, housework hours among less-educated US couples remained as gendered as in the other two English-speaking countries. University-educated US women spent a further six hours in employment, balanced by a similar decrease in housework hours. Partnered US university-educated men also worked more paid hours than their less-educated counterparts, but with no significant reduction in their housework hours. Proportionately, then, the US gendered division of household labor was similar to that in the United Kingdom. US women's leisure advantage, however, increased rather than decreased with education. Less-educated US women had the unenviable position of needing to be employed more hours but at wages that limited their ability to purchase market substitutes for housework.

East German partnered women faced similar challenges to a slightly greater degree. Less-educated East German women worked more paid hours than their US counterparts, but performed a similar amount of housework. Highly educated East German women increased their paid work hours far more than similar US women but without the same market options for reducing housework hours. University-educated East German men also spent more time in paid work, with the result that educated East German couples were the most pressed for free time among the countries here. Educated East German women carried the greater total time burden, however, and were the only group of women to spend more time in paid and unpaid work than their partners. But educated East German women's time disadvantage was smaller than that of British men, although it would widen further among parents (Cooke 2007b: 947). These persistent time burdens for East German women illustrate that policy supports for maternal employment such as public child care do not on their own eliminate the gendered division of unpaid labor.

The panels of Figure 7.2 show the persistence of a gendered division of household paid and unpaid labor that varied across classes and countries. In all countries, the gendered division was more extreme among less-educated couples, but in exchange for more free time as compared with highly educated couples. Greater equality among more highly educated couples was paid for with both time and money. These couples spent more hours in employment and used some of their earnings to reduce the unpaid housework. This possibility remained more limited in contexts with greater class equality, and in turn increased the unpaid work that remained women's responsibility. Class equality therefore structured gender equality trade-offs not only in paid work (Pettit and Hook 2009), but also unpaid work.

Equality Exchanges in Their Institutional Frames

Gendered divisions of paid and unpaid work reflect more complex processes than can be depicted with time availability or bargaining models. Those models consider paid and unpaid work to be two ends of a single time continuum, with an increase in one type of work balanced by an equal reduction in the other. In couple households, the household time in paid and unpaid work is theoretically redistributed via negotiation based on the relative value of each partner's time. Paid work, by definition, has greater value than unpaid work, at least under bargaining parameters of market exchange. As a result, these models predicted that women's greater employment hours and wages would directly increase gender equality in the household division of unpaid work.

The evidence in this chapter showed that this was true to a point, but not in the way predicted. Employed women did spend less time doing housework than women who were out of the labor force. But employed women's reduction in housework hours was just a fraction of their increase in employment hours. In couple households, little if any additional housework was taken up by the partners of employed women. Instead, some housework shifted to the market in the form of restaurant meals, laundry services, domestic servants, and other market substitutes for domestic work. Purchasing such domestic substitutes required no increase in men's unpaid work.

In short, the growth in women's employment created new paid jobs to replace some of the unpaid work, and women retained primary responsibility for whatever unpaid work remained. The new jobs were frequently performed by less-educated, ethnic, or immigrant women. Domestic work thus remained gendered and under-valued, but more of it was now in the public sphere of the labor market. A "gender revolution" has not occurred between women and men, but among women along class lines, and between women and ethnic or immigrant groups.

Each country's institutional equality frame structured the gender, class, and other group exchanges. Class-related policies affected group differences in paid work hours and earnings, and also unpaid housework and child care time. Wage inequality fueled development of the service sector, which provided the market substitutes for housework and child care. The greater class inequality found in Spain, the United Kingdom, and the United States therefore allowed affluent households to shift more unpaid work to the low-wage service sector. The greater income equality in Australia and the two German regions limited the possibilities for market substitution. Even affluent households in more class-equal societies faced greater unpaid work burdens.

At the same time, Australian and German women *and* men were far more likely to do some unpaid work as compared with adults in the other three countries. Greater class equality seemed to create a sense of pride or obligation to unpaid as well as paid work even if the hours spent in each type of work remained gendered. British and US men and women, in contrast, were more likely to be employed than do any housework. This suggests that the self-interest rewarded in unregulated markets erodes the societal value of unpaid time for both genders. In other words, paid work crowds out the unpaid tasks that foster family solidarity. The high divorce rates that plague both the United Kingdom and United States might be one effect when market time trumps family time. Indeed, recent evidence has found that husbands' greater domestic participation reduced the divorce risk in both countries (Cooke 2006b; Sigle-Rushton 2010).

Class dynamics also resulted in a more gendered division of paid and unpaid work among less-educated couples. Less-educated Spanish and West German couples faced the greatest housework burden, as well as the most gendered division of paid and unpaid work. Australian class policies increased the leisure time for less-educated women and men, but the greater gender wage equality had not narrowed the gendered division of any type of work. Less-educated British women faced a gendered division of labor similar to Australian women, but gained the most leisure time by simply not doing much housework. Less-educated US women spent a few more hours in employment than British women, but also enjoyed a slight leisure advantage over their partners. Similar East German women enjoyed the greatest employment equality with their partners, but spent more hours doing housework than either British or US women. Overall, less-educated couples exchanged greater gender equality for more free time as compared with more educated couples.

In contrast, highly educated couples enjoyed greater equality in paid and unpaid work, but in exchange for both time and money. Highly educated women or men have always been more likely to be employed and to work more hours than less-educated individuals. The wage inequality of British and US markets allowed educated couples to purchase more market substitutes for domestic tasks, because relative earnings were high and the cost of market substitutes was low. The nature of wage inequality in the Spanish labor market required more employment hours to purchase a similar degree of market substitution in the form of legal or illegal domestic servants. In all three countries, educated women's equality gains in unpaid work were therefore not negotiated with their partners, but directly or indirectly with less-advantaged women via the market.

Greater wage equality in Australia and the two German regions limited market substitution of unpaid work even among highly educated couples. The relatively high wage equality among educated Australian women and men modestly narrowed the gendered division of this unpaid labor, and both genders enjoyed more leisure time than similar German couples. Educated, partnered German women also retained responsibility for the greater housework hours, but spent more hours in employment than Australian women. This time pressure on affluent German households extended their search for market substitutes across national borders (Misra et al. 2006). For example, a growing number of German couples utilize black market *Buelgelfrauen*, "ironing board women," and *Putzfrauen*, "cleaning women," from Eastern Europe who are paid far lower wages than permissible in the formal German labor market (Cooke 2007b). Because of the lower wages in the East *Länder*, only the highest-paid East German women can afford to purchase these services (Cooke 2007b). In fact, educated East German women enjoyed the greatest employment equality with their partners but endured the greatest time poverty because of their unpaid work burden. This was the only group of women studied here that contributed more total hours to the household than their partners.

East German women's time penalty for employment equality, however, fell far short of Hochschild's (1989) "second shift." In the remaining countries, couples' total time allocations between employment and housework were equitable or women had some leisure time advantage. Men still retained their economic advantage by spending more hours in paid work than their partners. But many men have also increased their time in housework and child care over the past few decades (Hook 2006). The evidence provided here indicated that employed and partnered men were more rather than less likely to do some housework than unemployed or single men. In contrast to women, men did not usually reduce their already modest housework hours when they were employed for more hours. The gendered division of paid and unpaid labor has therefore narrowed, particularly among educated couples, with little evidence that most women shoulder a greater time burden in exchange for this greater equality. Recent research in fact suggested US fathers now struggle as much as mothers in finding work-family balance (Galinsky et al. 2009).

In summary, the vicious circle of gender inequality cannot be made a virtuous one by promoting women's greater employment equality. The time poverty faced by educated East German women highlighted that public provision of child care did not eliminate all barriers to gender equality within households. The market substitution that allowed affluent women to reduce their unpaid work hours did so by exacerbating gender-class inequalities for other groups. Given the zero-sum exchanges within each institutional equality frame, can any policies enhance group equality without countervailing group costs?

Technical Appendix

The International Social Survey Program (ISSP) is a continuing annual program of cross-national research collaboration that utilizes existing national social science projects and coordinates research goals in numerous countries.[8] The 2002 module was the third devoted to Family and Changing Gender Roles, with earlier ones conducted in 1988 and 1994. Only the 2002 module contained estimates of actual housework hours, excluding child care and leisure activities, rather than questions asking who "usually does" several domestic tasks. The ISSP surveys only one adult member of a household, so partnered men and women supply information for their spouses. Such self and spousal estimates have proven to be somewhat inaccurate (Coltrane 2000). Yet the nature and extremity of the self-reports as well as spousal estimates differs in context (Cooke 2006a).

A sample of individuals between the ages of 20 and 54 who were not still in school was selected from the ISSP dataset, a sample commensurate to that used for the LIS analyses. Not all available independent measures were identical to those in the LIS data. Although earnings are an important relative resource, the ISSP information on individual earnings could not always be differentiated from total family income in dual-earner households. This was particularly problematic with the Australia data. Ethnicity or immigrant status could not be clearly differentiated, either, because the ISSP question asked only the country of origin of a respondent's ancestors. The ISSP data relating to the age and number of children contained substantial missing values, particularly the question as to the number of children in the household younger than 5 or 6, which would have been most commensurate with the LIS measure. Consequently, the measure indicating the total number of children younger than 17 was used.

As with the LIS analyses, education was differentiated as those completing lower secondary or less (high school degree in the United States) and those with a university degree. The referent was individuals with some post-secondary education. Part-time employment was defined as working 10–29 hours per week, except in Spain. In Spain part-time work was that between 15 and 35 hours per week. Full-time work was defined as working 30 or more hours per week, except in Spain where it was defined as working more than 35 hours per week.

Probability of and Hours Doing Housework

The marginal effects displayed in Table 7.1 are the coefficients from a dprobit predicting whether the respondent performs any housework in a given week (1 = yes; 0 = no) based on the individual's age, age-squared to control for the fact that older cohorts tend to have more gendered divisions of labor than younger cohorts (Coltrane 2000), an indicator variable for those with lower secondary (high school) education or less, an indicator for those with a university degree, an indicator for those with a partner (cohabiting and legally married are not necessarily distinguished in each country dataset), indicators for whether the respondent was employed part-time or full-time, and the number of children younger than 17 in the household.

The country data were pooled and a series of country indicator variables and country interaction terms added to a baseline model to predict the weekly housework hours of those doing any, using ordinary least squares regression. Because of the smaller sample sizes than with the LIS data, a more parsimonious model needed to be used. The ISSP data do not provide continuous measures of paid work hours, so employment status was used instead: part- or full-time employment as compared with being out of the labor force. Two educational measures were used as rough proxies for social class. One measure indicated those with secondary education or less, whereas a second indicated those with a university degree. Family measures included when individuals were married or cohabiting, and another for any children in the household younger than 17.[9] Country indicator variables and country-individual interactions terms against a US referent were included to compare effects across the institutional equality frames. The age variables did not provide further information or change the size of other coefficients and so were excluded. Neither could country interaction terms with both high and low education be included. The one using the country*low education interaction term proved a slightly better fit than the one using the country*university interaction terms. Results are presented in Table 7A.1.

Table 7A.1 Coefficients from pooled OLS regression predicting weekly housework hours 2002

	MEN	WOMEN
N	*3,053*	*3,403*
Main effects		
Secondary education or less	0.91	2.85
University degree	−0.61	−1.71**
Employed part-time	−2.33+	−3.44+
Employed full-time	−0.91	−4.59**
Partner	−0.98	3.72**
Children < 17 in household	0.93	2.01
Country effects		
Australia	2.23	7.41***
East Germany	−0.95	7.33+
West Germany	−1.44	−2.91
Spain	−1.36	11.06***
United Kingdom	−0.88	−3.30
Australia* secondary education	−0.56	−1.16
East Germany*secondary education	−0.83	−2.16
West Germany*secondary education	−0.49	1.56
Spain*secondary education	−0.67	4.78*
UK*secondary education	−0.56	−1.45
Australia*employed part-time	0.77	−3.25
East Germany* employed part-time	−1.12	−6.31
West Germany* employed part-time	2.02	−0.80
Spain* employed part-time	2.88+	−10.63***
UK* employed part-time	0.82	1.14
Australia*employed full-time	0.16	−2.03
East Germany* employed full-time	−1.60	−2.88
West Germany*employed full-time	0.25	2.68
Spain*employed full-time	2.34*	−7.91***
UK*employed full-time	0.42	3.38
Australia*partner	1.52	0.74
East Germany*partner	1.89	−3.04
West Germany*partner	1.11	6.47**
Spain*partner	0.67	3.80*
UK*partner	0.04	−0.92
Australia*children<17	−1.19	1.89
East Germany*children<17	−0.19	1.48
West Germany*children<17	−1.72	1.31
Spain*children<17	0.83	3.27*
UK*children<17	−0.37	2.50
Constant	*8.58****	*12.99****
Adjusted R²	*0.04*	*0.27*

*+ p<=0.10; * p<=0.05; **p<=0.01; ***p<=0.001*

Couple Time Allocations to Paid and Unpaid Work

A subsample of partnered individuals was taken from the main LIS and
ISSP 20–54-year-old samples described above and in the first section
of the appendix to Chapter 6. These subsamples were used to estimate
the weekly employment hours (LIS) and housework hours (ISSP)
among partnered individuals by the two educational categories. The
estimates are presented in Table 7A.2. The size of the spheres depicted
in Figure 7.2 was based on calculating the radius assuming total hours
represented the circle area (Area = π × radius²).

Table 7A.2 Partnered women and men's predicted weekly hours in paid and unpaid work by
educational attainment, circa 2001

	LESS THAN UPPER SECONDARY				UNIVERSITY DEGREE			
	HOUSEWORK		EMPLOYMENT		HOUSEWORK		EMPLOYMENT	
	WOMEN	MEN	WOMEN	MEN	WOMEN	MEN	WOMEN	MEN
Australia	23.3	10.2	15.4	29.4	18	10.1	26.6	37.4
United Kingdom	14.6	5.6	21.1	40.4	11.5	5.4	31.3	45
United States	17.8	7	23.7	37.6	12.9	6.4	29.8	44
East Germany	18.1	6.8	25.9	38.5	16.5	5.9	38.7	45.3
West Germany	24.9	6.9	18.1	41.3	20	6.2	28.6	45.1
Spain	34.3	6.8	12.4	40.9	19.1	7.1	31.2	42.6

TOTAL HOUSEHOLD HOURS

	LESS THAN UPPER SECONDARY			UNIVERSITY DEGREE		
	WOMEN	MEN	TOTAL	WOMEN	MEN	TOTAL
Australia	39	40	**78**	45	48	**92**
United Kingdom	36	46	**82**	43	50	**93**
United States	42	45	**86**	43	50	**93**
East Germany	44	45	**89**	55	51	**106**
West Germany	43	48	**91**	49	51	**100**
Spain	47	48	**94**	50	50	**100**

8

SUSTAINABLE POLICY FOR GREATER EQUALITY

The Resilience of Complex Inequality

Sociologists have long regarded the state as holding the silver bullet for eliminating the inequalities of industrial markets. Marx (1967 [1848]) argued market mechanisms would cause a worldwide worker revolt that would hand the reins of production over to the state. Polanyi (1944) claimed it was the state's minimum obligation to ease the most deleterious individual consequences of market exchange. Wedderburn (1965) suggested the role of the welfare state was to actively structure social equality. Esping-Andersen (1990) pointed out that only social-democratic welfare regimes shared a goal of greater social equality, whereas most welfare regimes actively reinforced social and material hierarchies.

These musings focused primarily on the role of the state in attenuating class differences among workers. Some economists have suggested that policies supporting greater class equality also narrow the gender wage gap (Blau and Kahn 2003). Yet others have found more trade-offs between class and gender employment equality (Bertola et al. 2007). Cross-national evidence reveals that where more women are employed in conjunction with greater class equality, they encounter high occupational segregation (Mandel and Semyonov 2006), often into part-time public sector jobs (Gornick and Jacobs 1998). Where class-equality policies instead limit women's labor force participation, those women who are employed generally endure less segregation and enjoy greater wage equality (Katz and Murphy 1992; Pettit and Hook 2009). Class inequality is associated with greater female employment rates, but in the context of large gender wage gaps (Blau and Kahn 2003). Pettit and Hook (2009: 168) concluded it is therefore necessary to look at all components of paid work—employment rates, hours worked, and wages—as well as the household and societal factors that structure relative gender equality.

Here I conducted a comprehensive examination across six states and also over historical time to unveil why relative group inequalities persist. I traced the role of early state policies in Australia, East and West Germany, Spain, the United Kingdom, and the United States in institutionalizing gender-class inequalities in the components of paid and unpaid work across the life course. Population policies reinforced the state's desired class and ethnic mix, along with women's responsibility to bear children. Compulsory schooling reinforced class and other group differences in the education and skills related to later careers. The expansion of compulsory schooling also created a "care void" overwhelmingly assumed by women, which widened gender employment differences. Employment regulations and social security benefits reinforced group differences in time allocations between market and family that in turn shaped group differences in accumulated work experience and wages.

The resultant institutional equality frame reinforced by these policies allocated the paid and unpaid work of industrial economies among social groups. Class policies created insider-outsider groups of workers, which were complemented by gender and ethnic divides contained in population and education policies. The privileged core group of workers enjoyed greater employment continuity and wage equality in private sector positions, whereas the outsider groups had a more tenuous attachment to the labor force and/or worked fewer hours. In all countries, White male workers comprised the core group of privileged workers; women, ethnic minorities, and immigrants were invariably the outsiders. Outsider groups were allocated society's domestic work, whether paid or unpaid. Women retained responsibility for any unpaid work. These group divisions of paid and unpaid work sustained each country's group equilibrium within its institutional equality frame.

An individual's place within each institutional equality frame, however, cannot be determined by a single characteristic such as class or gender, but by the intersection of group memberships (Collins 2000; Crenshaw 1989). The gender-class intersections noted throughout this volume highlight that the relative equality in paid and unpaid work experienced by highly educated women differs, at times dramatically, from that experienced by less-educated women. In all of the countries compared here, women with university degrees were more likely to be employed or work more hours. Employed women with less education generally worked fewer hours than either less-educated men or more-educated women. The educational differences among women were therefore greater than those among men in all of the countries, indicating greater class employment inequality among women than men.

Relative gender returns to employment differed yet again across classes and countries. In the three English-speaking countries, there was slightly greater wage inequality among men than women, although the absolute level differed across the countries. In the two German regions and Spain, class wage inequality was substantially greater among women than men. In general, lower-earning women enjoyed greater relative wage equality than high-earning women regardless of the aggregate degree of wage equality or women's relative employment rate. The gender wage gap among high-earners also differed across the countries regardless of aggregate class equality. These findings indicate there is a less direct relationship between class and gender wage equality than argued to date. What matters is how gender-class material relations were structured within each country's institutional equality frame.

I found that class also structured the gendered division of paid and unpaid work within households. Common to all of the countries was that less-educated households faced a more extreme gendered division in both types of work, whereas highly educated couples enjoyed greater equality in both. In the context of greater gender inequality, however, less-educated couples enjoyed more leisure time than highly educated couples. Highly educated couples paid for greater gender equality in paid and unpaid work with both time and money. These couples spent more hours in employment and used some of their earnings to reduce the unpaid housework. This possibility remained more limited in countries with greater class equality, as the resultant wage compression inhibited development of the low-wage service sector to which domestic tasks might be commodified. Consequently, employed women in more class-equal societies shouldered a greater burden of unpaid work than employed women in class-unequal societies. This burden was most acute among highly educated East German women, who enjoyed greater employment hours equality than the women in the remaining countries, but also spent more total hours in paid and unpaid work than their partners. Class equality therefore structured gender equality trade-offs not only in paid work (Pettit and Hook 2009), but also unpaid work.

Despite the complexity of gender-class equality in its institutional context, it must be noted that women do *not* bear a double-burden of paid and unpaid labor as once suggested by Arlie Hochschild (1989). Countries and classes differed in how much time the household and each gender spent in paid and unpaid work, but with the exception of highly educated East German women, the time division within the home was equitable. Less-educated British women in fact enjoyed significantly more leisure time than their partners. But highly educated households spent more hours in paid work and only slightly fewer hours in unpaid work despite purchasing more market substitutes than less affluent households. Highly educated women spent more hours in paid work, but so, too, did highly educated men. Highly educated mothers as well as fathers also spend more time in child care (Bianchi et al. 2006). As a result, highly educated dual-earner couples have greater economic resources, but this advantage is offset by having less leisure time to enjoy them. The individual time poverty associated with carrying a double burden of paid and unpaid labor is therefore more a class than gender phenomenon.

These complex trade-offs among social groups and types of work are what make inequalities so resilient even in the aftermath of equal opportunity and affirmative action policies. Such policies enabled some women and ethnic minorities to complete higher levels of education and pursue better jobs, but widened class differences among them. Policy support for female employment also increased class differences in unpaid work as more of it became commodified. Less-educated women and immigrant workers performed the domestic work of affluent households but could not afford to purchase an equal amount of domestic relief for themselves. In short, gender-class inequality persists because advances for one group require a counter-balance within a country's institutional equality frame. The gains and losses can be exchanged among social groups, and/or among the individual components of paid and unpaid work. For example, advances for women in employment hours are offset by losses in other dimensions (e.g. wages or unpaid work) or for some other group (e.g. immigrants). In addition, women retain responsibility for domestic tasks, whether they are the new service sector paid work, public care positions, or the remaining unpaid work in the home. Equal opportunity and affirmative action policies were not silver bullets that eliminated group inequalities, but merely reshuffled inequalities within each frame.

Finding a policy silver bullet is all the more difficult because gender, class, and other group intersections of inequality are differently structured in each of the countries. The six country cases represented four combinations of relative class equality (as measured by the Gini coefficient) and the relative gender employment gap depicted in Figure 1.1. Comparing the more detailed gender gaps in paid work hours, wages, and unpaid work hours revealed even greater diversity across the six countries, such that each represented a unique case (Table 5.2). To see whether this uniqueness was coincidental or more typical of the national institutional framing of relative equality, I expanded these aggregate comparisons with an additional 11 countries as shown in Table 8.1. This exercise confirmed the diversity in gender-class equality frames. For example, the structure of gender-class equality in paid and unpaid work differed in the transitional economies of the Czech Republic and Poland, and the structure of each differed from that in East Germany. The structure of gender-class equality in paid and unpaid work in Italy differed from nearby Spain (Cooke 2009). The three Nordic countries

Table 8.1 Relative class and gender equality, circa 2000

COUNTRY	GINI COEFFICIENT[1] 2000	GENDER EMPLOYMENT GAP (MALE-FEMALE) 2000	GENDER WAGE RATIO 2000	GENDER GAP PART-TIME EMPLOYMENT (FEMALE-MALE) 2000	MEN'S SHARE HOUSE-WORK 2002	WOMEN'S AVERAGE WEEKLY HOUSE- WORK HOURS, 2002*
East Germany	A (.28)	A (6)	A (91)	A (20)	B (30)	= (12)
West Germany	A (.28)	B (30)	B (77)	B (32)	B (28)	B (15)
Australia	B (.32)	B (25)	A (90)	B (32)	A (35)	B (19)
Spain	B (.34)	B (31)	B (82)	A (13)	B (33)	B (17)
United Kingdom	B (.35)	A (16)	B (76)	B (35)	A (38)	A (8)
United States	B (.37)	A (16)	B (76)	A (12)	A (39)	A (9)
Average 17 countries	**0.29**	**17**	**83**	**21**	**34 %**	**12 hours**
Canada	B	A	B	A	A	A
Finland	A	A	B	A	=	A
Norway	A	A	A	B	A	A

Sweden	A	A	=	A	A
Netherlands	A	B	B	B	A
Austria	A	B	B	B	B
Belgium	A	B	A	=	B
France	A	A	A	A	A
Czech Republic	A	A	B	B	A
Poland	=	A	A	A	B
Italy	B	B	A	B	B

Source: Gini coefficients are from Luxembourg Income Study Key Figures accessed 10 September 2009 (http://www.lisproject.org/php/kf/kf.php#kf). Australia and US employment and unadjusted median wage gaps between all employed women and men aged 25 to 64 are from OECD *Employment Outlook 2002*; these data for the other countries are from Eurostat: http://epp.eurostat.ec.europa.eu/portal/page/portal/labour_market/earnings/main_tables, accessed 15 January 2010. The wage information is for 2006 and represents the difference between women's and men's average gross hourly earnings of among all paid employees in enterprises with 10 or more employees. The East German wage gap is from Rosenfeld et al. (2004); East German part-time gender gap is from Matysiak and Steinmetz (2008: 333). Housework share and hours based on author calculations of the 2002 International Social Survey Program data, with the exception of Canada and Italy, which are based on estimates of 1994 International Social Survey Program data. "A" indicates the country is above average in gender equality on this indicator; "B" indicates the country is below average. For the housework hours measure, greater equality means women spend fewer hours performing housework than average, whereas less equality means they spend more hours.

also differed from one another as well as the remaining countries (Hiilamo and Kangas 2006; Sainsbury 2001). Sweden offered individuals the greatest degree of class and gender equality in paid and unpaid work, being above average on all of the measures. Being above average, however, does not mean Sweden has achieved a perfect gender-class equality equilibrium. Swedish women still faced a gender wage gap, responsibility for the majority of unpaid work, and high occupational segregation (Evertsson and Nermo 2004, 2007; Johansson et al. 2005; Lewis and Astrom 1992).

Thus, as observed by researchers studying class mobility, hierarchies in market economies are amazingly resilient across time (Sorokin 1927), although the specific structure of these varies across countries (Erikson and Goldthorpe 1992; Featherman et al. 1975). Members of some groups might subsequently enjoy an increase in their absolute level of equality, but advances toward greater equality for one group or in one dimension extract a social cost in another. Relative group positions within each institutional equality frame are therefore maintained. This suggests there is no single policy silver bullet that can eliminate group inequalities across all contexts. So should we abandon the search for a policy solution to group material inequalities in free market economies? After all, don't markets work best with inequality and minimal state intervention? Before answering the first question, let us consider some evidence pertaining to the second.

The Inefficiency of Market Inequalities

Economic models have strongly influenced the extent and nature of state policies, but they are based on synthetic assumptions that deserve further scrutiny. The first assumption lies at the heart of the liberal tenets that guide many governments: markets function most efficiently without policy intervention (Friedman 1962). This efficiency comes at a cost of income inequality among workers, but such inequality was predicted to provide work incentives necessary for economic growth. Kuznets (1963), in fact, argued that increasing inequality was just a temporary phenomenon within the industrialization process. He hypothesized that income inequality would initially increase as countries shifted from agrarian to industrial economies, but then decrease as industrialization advanced. This pattern was evident in the United States and other OECD countries through the 1970s (Aghion et al. 1999). In the past two decades, however, income inequality has again increased in most advanced industrial economies (Brandolini and Smeeding 2009).

Does this increasing income inequality mark a period of greater economic growth? A growing body of cross-national empirical studies provides a mixed answer to this question. In general, the positive effects of inequality on economic growth occur when the inequality is within the top portion of the earnings distribution. More detrimental effects result from greater inequality across the bottom end of the earnings distribution, or when overall inequality is greater (Voitchovsky 2009). When comparing inequality in "assets" such as land or human capital, the evidence overwhelming indicates that such inequality is inversely related to economic growth (Voitchovsky 2009). This evidence offers little support for *laissez-faire* policy approaches that allow inequalities, particularly those in human capital, to perpetuate under free market mechanisms. Clearly, people's human capital is a unique "good" in market exchange, and individuals as well as economies benefit from greater public investment in it.

The benefits of individual investment in human capital are, of course, part of the classic labor market model (Becker 1993; Mincer 1974). Indeed, class inequalities had been predicted to decrease as children from any background obtained the education necessary to enter the most desirable occupations (Erikson and Goldthorpe 1992). As detailed here, however, most compulsory schooling systems reinforced and magnified class, gender, and other group inequalities. Class educational inequalities were sustained through a stratified vocational tracking system in Germany, rural-urban divides in Australia and Spain, public-private schooling divisions in Australia and the United Kingdom, and local school financing in the United States. The public educational systems also reinforced gender inequalities by creating a care void in the years prior to the start of compulsory schooling and in schooling schedules. Among the countries here, only the East German educational system provided comprehensive childhood care provision that enabled mothers to pursue full-time employment. In the United States, private care filled some of the care void, whereas a spotty mix of public and private care filled some of the void in Australia, Spain, West Germany, and the United Kingdom. The specific public-private care mix institutionalized varying class differences in mothers' access to employment in each country. Children's future educational success varies with the quality of their preschool environment, which also differs across social classes (Cunha and Heckman 2010; Lareau 2000). Educational human capital is therefore an individual investment that is greatly influenced by the institutional context, which has thus far muted rather than harnessed education's potential to minimize group inequalities in life chances.

Economic models also put forth that education along with accumulated work experience and on-the-job training determine individual wages. The institutional context, however, structured systematic group differences in employment probability and work hours. Women's probability of employment was always lower than men's, but the probability each gender was employed varied across the countries. Having a university degree increased women's probability of employment more than men's, indicating that employed women were a select group of varying size in all of the countries. Less-educated Australian and British women worked fewer hours than less-educated US women, but educated British women worked appreciably more hours than educated Australian or US women. Employed Germans with less education also worked fewer hours than similar US persons. This low-education work hours penalty was greater in West Germany as compared with East Germany, and twice as great for West German women than East German women. Thus, there are gender differences in the impact of education on employment that vary considerably across institutional contexts.

The largest gender differences in employment, however, derived from family, not education. For example, partnered men in all of the case countries were significantly more likely to be employed and worked more hours than single men. Only in Spain and West Germany were partnered women significantly *less* likely to be employed, highlighting the continuing importance of "wife" and "breadwinner" identities in those two countries. Women with young children in all of the countries were less likely to be employed and/or to work fewer hours if they were employed. A young child reduced US women's probability of employment the least, and employed British and German mothers' work hours the most. At the same time, there was evidence of a "father-carer" identity in Australia and the United Kingdom. Australian fathers with young children were less likely to be employed, whereas a young child reduced British fathers' predicted weekly work hours.

Under the human capital model, any gender differences in education and accumulated work experience would in turn predict gender wage differences. A gender wage gap remained, however, after controlling for education, age, employment hours, partnership status, and children. But as noted above, the country patterns of gender wage equality across the earnings distribution differed substantially. The institutional equality frame therefore structures gender-class differences in the educational and work-experience components of human capital, and gender-class differences in the effect of human capital on wages.

Economic models also assume individual and couple time allocations between paid and unpaid work are two possibilities along a single time continuum. The mix of the two types of work selected by single men and women was quite similar across these countries, with both genders spending more time in paid work and much less time doing unpaid tasks. The division of paid and unpaid work was more gendered in couple households. Bargaining models suggest these divisions result from partner negotiations based on relative educational and economic resources. As men tend to be employed more hours and earn higher wages, these models predict that partnered women would do more housework. As illustrated here, however, individual resources did not fully explain the gendered division of household paid and unpaid work, and it varied across social classes as well as the institutional contexts. In all of the countries, partnered individuals and those in employment were more likely to perform some housework than single or unemployed persons. The size of these effects differed across the countries but not between men and women within each country. Another intriguing finding is that in the countries with greater class equality—Australia and the two German regions—women *and* men were far more likely to do some unpaid work as compared with adults in the other three countries. British and US men and women, in contrast, were more likely to be employed than do any housework. These effects might be explained in part by the extent to which greater class inequality allows households in these countries to purchase more market substitutes for domestic tasks. But these effects also suggest that the self-interest rewarded in markets erodes the societal value of unpaid time for both genders. The draw of market forces also explains the dominance of dual-earner households in all of the countries.

Economic theory, however, predicts rather deleterious consequences for dual-earner households. In *The New Home Economics*, Nobel Prize-winning economist Gary Becker (1981) argued that the gendered division of paid and unpaid work is the most efficient household arrangement. Each partner specializes in either paid or unpaid work, and then trades the fruits of that specialization with the other, a process that Becker argued fosters mutual interdependence. If instead a partnered woman is employed, her wages represent an "opportunity cost" that would reduce her likelihood of having children. A woman's wages also provide her with the economic independence to leave the marriage, and so would increase the risk of divorce.

The institutional context varies these hypothesized effects as well. Until the 1990s, for example, there was a negative relationship between a country's female employment and total fertility rates as predicted by Becker's theory (Brewster and Rindfuss 2000). Across affluent economies, however, recent fertility levels were higher where female employment rates were higher and lowest in countries such as Spain and West Germany where married women were less likely to be employed (Dalla Zuanna and Micheli 2004). Some have argued public child care and similar supports for maternal employment, as found in the Scandinavian countries, have sustained fertility levels simultaneous with high female employment (McDonald 2000). But fertility rates were higher still in the United States, a country that offers no universal policy supports for maternal employment (Brewster and Rindfuss 2000) and where married women were likely to be employed and to work full-time (Blau et al. 2002).

Country variation has also been found in the relationship between partnered women's employment and relationship dissolution. For example, Liefbroer and Dourleijn (2006) found a partnered woman's employment significantly *increased* the risk of dissolution among couples in Austria, Finland, Italy, Lithuania, Poland, and West Germany; *decreased* dissolution risk in France and Latvia; and had no significant effect in the Czech Republic, East Germany, Flanders, Hungary, Norway, Slovenia, Spain, and Sweden. The countries within each grouping differ substantially in institutional support for partnered women's employment, as well as the female employment rate, women's average weekly work hours, and the size of the gender wage gap. Another research program in which I am involved is assessing how the institutional context of men's as well as women's employment alters the effects of a given individual's employment on dissolution risk (cf. Cooke and Gash, 2010). In any event, Becker's hypothesized family-level dynamics are not universal; the institutional context varies the size and even direction of effects.

The family context also alters the hypothesized dynamics. In particular, tensions created by a partnered woman's employment might be eased by her partner's greater participation in unpaid tasks (Cooke 2004). For example, Mills and her colleagues (2008) found that a more unequal distribution of household labor lowered fertility intentions among couples in Italy and the Netherlands. Hungarian and US couples with more egalitarian divisions of housework were more likely to have a second child (Oláh 2003; Torr and Short 2004). Swedish couples where fathers took parental leave following the first birth were also more likely to have additional children (Oláh 2003), as were German (Cooke 2004) and Italian (Cooke 2009) couples where the father spent more time in child care. Men's domestic behavior also affects divorce risk. Husbands' greater time in unpaid work countervailed the increase in divorce risk associated with wives' employment in Australia (Craig and Sawrikar 2007), the United Kingdom (Sigle-Rushton 2010), and the United States (Cooke 2006b). But the institutional context can vary these family-level effects, too. For example, in West Germany with its historical support for a male breadwinner model, a husband's greater participation in housework increased the divorce risk regardless of his wife's employment (Cooke 2006b).

Thus, many of the economic assumptions that justified group inequalities in free market economies have not stood the test of time. Allowing the least advantaged to lose further educational or economic ground stymies rather than spurs economic growth. Policies have contributed to an institutional equality frame that alters the dynamics of the individual-level economic models predicting labor supply and demand, which generally reinforced rather than narrowed group inequalities. The institutional equality frame also structured gendered divisions of paid and unpaid work across social classes that carry repercussions for family fertility and stability. Lower fertility and greater relationship instability associated with higher rates of female employment also have negative consequences for the state. High female employment contributes to current tax revenues, but lower fertility predicts lower tax revenues in the future. Mothers' employment is the best assurance against child poverty (Kamerman et al. 2003), but if it increases the risk of divorce, more children will experience the poverty of single-parent households (Heuveline and Weinshenker 2008; Rainwater and Smeeding 2004). Single-mother households are also far more reliant on state transfers than two-parent households (Daly and Rake 2003). So the market and post-war policy merged in a vicious circle of group inequalities, rather than the virtuous circle initially envisioned by economists and sociologists. Consequently, breaking the life course and intergenerational chain of gender-class inequalities is in the best interests of individuals, market economies, as well as the state.

Social Investment Strategies

The vicious circle of inequality continued because even the most generous state safety net for employed adults did not alter the risk individuals would need it, and the risks were changing over time (Taylor-Gooby 2004). The intergenerational mobility models of the post-war decades predicted that children were likely to end up in similar occupations to their fathers—boys via their employment and girls via marriage (Erikson and Goldthorpe 1992). As good jobs for low-skilled

men evaporated in the shift from industrial to post-industrial production, and the number of female heads of households increased under the
second demographic transition, the nature of intergenerational transfers
and risks changed. For example, McLanahan (2004) noted the "diverging
destinies" of children depended on their mothers' educational attainment, not their fathers' occupation. Mothers' education predicts at what
age a woman is likely to have her first child, whether that child will be
born in or out of wedlock, and the likelihood the child will be raised
in poverty and/or a subsequent single-parent household (Sobotka
2008). Each of these factors affects the child's cognitive development
and future educational attainment, transition into employment, and
their own family formation patterns (Duncan and Brooks-Gunn
1997; Heuveline and Weinshenker 2008; Hout and DiPrete 2006; Pong
et al. 2003).

The new risks and growing awareness of accumulated disadvantage
encouraged many European and Latin American states to move away
from a strictly interventionist welfare approach, and instead implement
preventive measures under a "social investment" approach (Esping-
Andersen et al. 2002; Goodin et al. 1999; Jenson 2004, 2009). In market
economies, poverty is the primary condition that sets the trajectory of
children's destinies (Bergh 2005; OECD 2009b). Poverty carries the
greatest future penalty when experienced during a child's first five years
of life, which are also the years children are most at risk of being poor
(Duncan and Brooks-Gunn 1997; Gornick and Jäntti 2009). Maternal
employment has been found to greatly reduce the risk of child poverty
(Kamerman et al. 2003), which was one reason for the EU's female
employment targets in the 2000 Lisbon Treaty and subsequent work—
family reconciliation policies (Plantenga and Remery 2005).

An important policy support for maternal employment was the
expansion of public early childhood education. From a social investment perspective, high-quality care also enhances the cognitive abilities
and subsequent academic success of children from the most disadvantaged households (Bergh 2005; Esping-Andersen 2004; Heckman and
Masterov 2007; Scarr and Eisenberg 1993). Research has found that
ability gaps between children of different socioeconomic groups open

up at early ages, gaps which can be accounted for by family background factors like parental education (Carneiro and Heckman 2003). The risks of unemployment and welfare receipt later in the life course can therefore be greatly reduced by greater investment in children's earliest home and educational environments. Policies that reduce the economic and educational constraints during children's first five years also turn out to be less costly than remedial measures later in the life course (Carneiro and Heckman 2003).

At the same time, subsequent public investments along the life course complement earlier ones. For example, Currie and Thomas (1995) found that the benefits of Head Start for minority participants began to erode after students left the program and returned to disadvantaged environments. Students who dropped out of secondary school faced further difficulties transitioning to the next productive phase of life (Rumberger and Lamb 1998). Investment-oriented educational policy must therefore ensure young people at each stage of schooling attain the skills necessary for future academic and economic success (Machin 2009). Public investments in individual human capital not only reduce future social costs such as unemployment and crime (Cunha and Heckman 2010), but also narrow the societal inequality in human capital that has been shown to impede economic growth (Aghion et al. 1999; Voitchovsky 2009).

As highlighted here, each country's schooling system would face different challenges to reduce group educational inequalities. The German system had the greatest gender and immigrant educational inequalities, and the German government is exploring ways to reduce the "educational poverty" evident in the dispersion of academic competence across social groups (Allmendinger and Leibfried 2003; OECD 2010). The expansion of public preschool across the European Union also bodes well for narrowing future group educational inequalities (Eurydice 2009). In contrast, the lack of universal preschool in Australia and the United States sets the stage for greater future class educational inequalities, but the Australian compulsory schooling system yielded less subsequent class inequalities in educational performance than the US system. The United States educational system in general resulted in sharp class disparities. A large proportion of the adult population had some post-secondary education, but also a large percentage of high school drop-outs (Rumberger and Lamb 1998). Of the countries here, the United States remains staunchly and uniquely neoliberal in its rejection of universal early childhood education (Gornick and Meyers 2003). Only time will tell if this ideological stubbornness will ultimately cost the country its economic dominance.

One reason a social investment strategy is more sustainable than earlier welfare strategies is that it narrows the economic outcomes of group differences, in particular bringing up the bottom, but without challenging the underlying social hierarchy that could cause reforms to lose voter support. For example, universal early childhood education improves the educational outcomes of less-advantaged children without taking away the most privileged classes' access to the best higher education. In fact, Pettit and Hook (2009) found that public provision of child care was an important predictor of highly educated women's employment. Such policies that also benefit the middle class tend to garner broader political support (Gornick and Jäntti 2009; Kenworthy 2008). In contrast, affirmative action approaches that instead compensate for rather than minimize group disadvantage in education or employment trigger a political or legal revolt among the advantaged groups that lose out (Behning and Pascual 2001; McGlynn 2001).

The combination of universal preschool, smaller group differences in subsequent stages of compulsory education, and a stratified higher education system also supports that distribution of inequality equated with stronger economic growth. Stronger economic growth provides the taxes for further public investment. The rhetoric of social investment notwithstanding, however, country funding strategies do not yet reflect the necessary initial investment. Governments in affluent economies currently spend less than 4 percent of gross domestic product (GDP) on primary, secondary, and non-tertiary post-secondary education, and a further 1 percent on tertiary education.[1] In contrast, just over one-half of one percent of GDP is spent on all pre-primary education.[2] Public funding needs to align with the processes and goals of social investment (see also Esping-Andersen 2009).

Policy and Sustainable Unpaid Time

Despite their advantages, current social investment strategies will not result in gender equality. They are child-focused, with policy support for maternal employment intended to reduce child poverty and welfare transfers to families (Jenson 2009). Policies that encourage girls to remain longer in education do not alter gender differences in subject areas or subsequent gender differences in occupations that these predict. As illustrated here, the impact of women's education on the likelihood of employment, paid work hours, and relative wages differed within each institutional equality frame, but never mirrored the impact of education on men's employment.

In any event, the evidence here lent no support to Esping-Andersen's (2009) assertion that policies enhancing gender employment equality would complete the gender revolution in unpaid work. The example of East Germany illustrated that public child care and other supports for maternal employment enabled East German women to enjoy the greatest equality in paid work hours and even a wage premium across much of the earnings distribution. But East German women "paid" for this greater equality in paid work by having more total hours of paid plus unpaid work than women in the other countries. In highly educated East German couples' households, women spent more total hours in paid plus unpaid work than their partners.

In countries with greater class inequality such as Spain, the United Kingdom, or the United States, highly educated women enjoyed greater equality in paid work hours by shifting more unpaid work to the low-wage service sector, not their partners. The penalty of this strategy was borne by less-educated partnered women, who had a more extreme gendered division of household labor. In addition, carework provided by the private sector in more class-unequal societies remained more gendered and incurred a greater wage penalty (Budig and Misra, 2010).

So as women spent more time in employment, they "bargained" any reduction in unpaid work with either the state or the market, not their partners. All partnered women retained primary responsibility for any remaining unpaid work in the household. Yet as noted earlier, partnered men who contributed more time to unpaid tasks buoyed both family fertility and stability in dual-earner households. Clearly greater gender equality in unpaid work has significant benefits for families and, in turn, the state. Nurturing these benefits requires a more fundamental change in policy approach.

Early state policies attempted to allocate the paid work of markets and the unpaid work of the society without undermining the market's inherent employment incentives. Free market mechanisms, however, are self-perpetuating. Free markets encourage consumption, which leads to greater production, which draws more people into employment. These market mechanisms trumped even the West German male breadwinner policies that attempted to exclude women from employment. The power of unregulated markets was most evident in the United Kingdom and United States, where both women and men were more likely to spend some time in employment and the least doing housework.

An ever-increasing contribution of societal time to paid work crowds out the unpaid time necessary to sustain families and communities. One symptom of this could be the high British and US divorce rates (Cooke and Baxter 2010; Sigle-Rushton 2010). Not surprisingly, today's women *and* men report greater difficulty in balancing work and family (Galinsky et al. 2009; Jacobs and Gerson 2004). The ill-effects spill over into other areas. Andersen and his colleagues (2006) found that US women's time in civic activities has decreased since the 1960s and more sharply after 1975, even after controlling for the time spent in employment and child care. The individualization reinforced by the market seems to crowd out community obligations beyond the direct effect of time constraints from employment.

Defining gender equality around market parameters only magnifies these problems, and further inhibits the ability to achieve gender equality in unpaid work as it becomes increasingly devalued. Policies instead need to ease the extent to which market mechanisms crowd out the value and availability of unpaid time. The case of Australia offered evidence that the institutional frame can create more unpaid time for both women and men. High wages for both genders have allowed Australians to enjoy more time outside of paid work, an option that is desirable to both men and women. Australian men and women had a lower overall probability of employment and a much higher probability of doing some unpaid work. Bianchi and her colleagues (2006) reported that Australian parents also spent more time in child care than British or US parents. Gender equality remains elusive in Australia, however, because of policies that continue to reinforce gender differences in paid work.

Together the evidence suggests that society would benefit from a two-prong policy approach. First, in addition to the social investment policies minimizing group differences in human capital, policies should not inhibit the employment participation of members of any social group. These policies should be complemented, however, with policies that constrain "excess" employment that crowds out the value of unpaid time for both women and men. Constraints could include limits to weekly work hours as well as a return to more progressive high-end taxation. Marginal tax rates for the highest earners have fallen dramatically since the 1960s.[3] This trend has coincided with the increased concentration of wealth from financial derivatives in the upper percentiles, a wealth that is more gendered than labor earnings (Walby 2010).

Curbing the returns to financial speculation would in general be a more prudent and fair taxation policy. Men benefited most from the wealth accumulation, but women are expected to shoulder the long-term costs of the 2008 financial crisis (Walby 2010). For example, a study conducted by the UK House of Commons Library estimated that more than 70 percent of the revenue raised by proposed tax and benefit changes to reduce the state debt resulting from the bailouts would come from female taxpayers.[4] In his detailed discussion of various policies for supporting employment growth and equality, Kenworthy (2008) raised concerns about the ability to raise tax rates because of the mobility of capital. Yet he acknowledged that there is room for tax increases in countries such as the United Kingdom and United States, where tax revenue was less than 40 percent of GDP (2008: 289).

In summary, free markets are self-sufficient systems that require no further incentives from the state. Policies that restrict certain groups' access to the labor market perpetuate material inequalities and inefficiencies in both paid and unpaid work. At the same time, the warp of the social fabric unravels when states prioritize the functioning of markets over the needs of people. Through social investment strategies, the state can narrow group material inequalities that impede economic growth. Policy must also minimize the social costs of market excesses that impede group equality. Markets can be made to work for people, not just the other way around.

NOTES

1 Gender-Class Equality Over Time

1. Examples include Pedersen's (1993) comparison of France and the United Kingdom during the nineteenth century, or Bock and Thane's (1991) and Wikander et al.'s (1995) historical cross-country comparisons, and Linda Gordon's (1990, 1994) analyses of gender in the US welfare state. These are complemented by post-war policy comparisons (cf. Lewis 1992b or Moeller 1993). The volume of more recent policy comparisons has exploded, with many cross-national policy comparisons available from the Organisation for Economic Co-operation and Development (www.oecd.org).

2. Early comparisons of the relationship between women's employment and housework include Kalleberg and Rosenfeld (1990) and Baxter (1997), with later comparisons summarized in Cooke and Baxter (2010). Blau and Kahn (1996) conducted one of the first international comparisons of the gender wage gap, whereas Jaumotte (2003) and more recently Pettit and Hook (2009) provide cross-national comparisons of gender differences in employment, work hours, wages, and occupations vis-à-vis support for maternal employment. See also Mandel and Semyonov (2005, 2006), and the Luxembourg Income Study working paper series, www.lisproject.org/php/wp/wp.php.

3. Reported in Michael Förster and Marco Mira d'Ercole, (2005). *Income Distribution and Poverty in OECD Countries in the Second Half of the 1990s*. OECD Working Paper no. 22, 10/03/2005. Paris: OECD.

4. Social class is differentiated as well by other employment and non-employment factors (Erikson and Goldthorpe 1992; Wright 2005), but these were beyond the scope of the book and the datasets.

5. Many recent comparisons of policy effects on gender and class include countries from what Esping-Andersen (1990) termed "social-democratic" regimes of Scandinavia. Yet these comprise a third set of countries and would require comparisons among them. They have similarly greater market equality (Gini coefficients of about 0.25) and a below-average gender employment gap as in East Germany, but still differ in historical policies. For example, Norway initially promoted a male breadwinner model, Sweden

the dual-earner (Sainsbury 2001), and Finland women's right to choose (Hiilamo and Kangas 2006). Including three additional country cases would make the historical comparison far too unwieldy without necessarily offering additional insight into the processes and outcomes theorized here.

6. A classic example of path dependence is the order of the letters QWERTY on the standard English-language typewriter patented by Christopher Sholes in 1867 (David 1985). Through several years of trial and error, this letter ordering was selected to ensure sufficiently slow typing so as to not jam the mechanical keys. QWERTY persists under subsequent advances in typewriter and keyboard technology, despite the greater inefficiency inherent in the ordering.

7. California (1997), Washington State (1998), and Nebraska (2008). It has been contested in at least some venues in Colorado (2008), Florida (2000), Kentucky (2006), and Michigan (2000).

8. Sweden and Denmark, representatives of Esping-Andersen's (1990) "social-democratic" regimes, also introduced more supports for women's employment during this period, although policies in Finland and Norway were more mixed (Hiilamo and Kangas 2006; Sainsbury 2001).

9. In the intersectionality literature, the bimodal category for gender is contested (Fraser 1997; McCall 2005; Yuval-Davis 2006), but the datasets offer no other option.

2 Paid and Unpaid Work in Context

1. The International Student Assessment (PISA) at www.pisa.oecd.org/ provides information on relative literacy, and the Trends in International Math and Science Study tracks relative performance in these subjects at different grade levels (http://timss.bc.edu/).

2. Recent labor force statistics can be downloaded from the Organisation for Economic Co-operation website, www.oecd.org/document/23/0,3343,en_2649_33935_36225815_1_1_1_1,00.html

3. The problem of human commodification lay at the heart of Karl Marx's (1967) class analysis.

4. In his 1904–5 essays, Max Weber (2009) argued a similar dismantling of kinship ties was brought about by the rationalization inherent in capitalism.

5. Marshall (1950) considered state provision of welfare a "social right," at the end of a universal progression from civil to political to social rights of citizenship in democratic market economies. His hypothesized progression has been criticized, however, for not being universal. For example, women were granted social rights in some countries before gaining the right to vote. Some immigrants have the right to vote in some elections but are not entitled to welfare benefits (Lister 2003; Williams 1989).

6. The concept of "de-commodification" refers to the extent to which the welfare state minimizes people's vulnerability vis-à-vis the market to reduce their need to compete with one another by selling their labor for the lowest wage.

7. Only in Australia (1901), Finland (1907) and Canada (1920) were women granted the right to vote the same year as working-class men (Pierson 1998: 106).

8. Bock (1991) suggested some state intervention in men's sexuality during Germany's Third Reich, but the extremity of that government serves to make the general point.

9. *Muller v. Oregon*, 208 US 412 (1908).

10. For example, see the Australian Institute for Health and Welfare (2005) or the US briefing by the National Center for Children in Poverty, http://nccp.org/publications/pub_628.html, accessed March 15, 2010.

11. OECD Labour Force Data, http://stats.oecd.org/index.aspx?DatasetCode=KEI.
Accessed July 21, 2009.

3 Population Policies and Group Divides

1. This is the estimate reported by Sobotka (2005) based on data for 17 countries from a
variety of sources (vital statistics, census records, large-scale family surveys, and population registers); the US Census Bureau (2003 CB03–166) reported 18 percent of US
women aged 40–44 in 2002 had no children.
2. Tronto (1993) notes how during the Scottish Enlightenment, men were presumed to
have a sense of connection and attachment to others. The philosophy of men as rational
and detached developed later, under Kant's notion of rational actors in industrialized
market economies. This reflects the same sort of objective market exchange assumptions
applied to human decisions embedded in the individual, household, and welfare state
theories discussed in the last chapter.
3. One measure of the relative balance is the proportion of people too young and too old to
work (those under 15 and those 64 or older) divided by the population age 15–64. The
greater this "dependency ratio," the greater the strain on social security systems.
4. Some credit the Great Fire of 1666 with stopping the Great Plague of London, because
it killed off those persons weak with illness and in its aftermath, London was recon-
structed with improved sewage drainage.
5. The first edition in 1798 was published anonymously. The 1803 edition was the first in
which Malthus's authorship was acknowledged.
6. The specifics for France and Sweden are from Borrie et al. (1946), and relate to what has
been termed the first demographic transition associated with industrialization, a concept
suggested by Thompson (1929).
7. Historians debate the exact definition of maternalism, with Sklar (1993) arguing it anal-
ogous to paternalism but reflecting women's assumptions as to women's nature, whereas
Gordon (1994) argues it is rooted in the subordination of women.
8. Orloff (1996) overviews the research in this area, including Koven and Michel's (1990)
summary of the work on maternalist movements in France, Germany, the UK and
United States. Bock and Thane's (1991) edited volume includes these efforts in several
European countries, whereas Pedersen (1993) contrasts the movements in France and
Britain. Sklar (1993) highlights these activities in the United States.
9. Gilligan (1996) ignored the social construction of the milieux, in contrast to Nancy
Chodorow (1978), who argued women's socially assigned roles as mothers sexually reproduced the role. Joan Tronto (1993) offers an excellent critique of the concept generally
and Gilligan specifically, noting how it disempowers women. Gordon (1976), too, argues
that offering women responsibility for "morality" was an empty trade for status and power.
10. "Quickening" refers to the point at which the mother can feel the fetus move. This
usually occurs at the end of the first trimester, a distinction persisting in many current
abortion laws and on-going political debates.
11. Bradlaugh and Besant republished an 1832 pamphlet on birth control in order to challenge the sentencing of a Bristol bookseller for having done the same. They were
convicted, won on appeal, and in doing so had "brought contraception to the forefront
of public discussion" (Francome 1984: 36–37).
12. Across the nineteenth century, the number of Catholics in the United States increased
from about 5 percent to about 12 percent of the population (Finke and Stark 1992).
13. See Francome (1984) and Gordon (1976).
14. See Leibfried and Ostner (1991), Ostner (1992) and Moeller (1993, 1997) for more
detailed discussions.

15. Only the Nazis imposed any restrictions on men (Bock 1991).
16. These estimates are cobbled together from a range of sources (including Borrie et al. 1946; Borrie 1948), the Australian Bureau of Statistics website (www.abs.gov.au/), US Census Bureau website (www.census.gov/), Bacci (1968) for Spain, Francome (1984) for Great Britain, and the *International Historical Statistics, Europe, 1750–1993, 4th Edition*.
17. The United States timeline and migration numbers come from Harvard University's Open Collections Program, available online at: http://ocp.hul.harvard.edu/immigration/dates.html (accessed June 24, 2008).
18. See Tataki (1990) for a discussion of Asian immigrants in general, and Mink (1986) for the interface between immigrants and the US labor movement.
19. Despite the penalties, US companies hired Irish and Chinese immigrants to construct the first transcontinental railroad (Arnesen 2007).
20. Harvard University's Open Collections Program: http://ocp.hul.harvard.edu/immigration/dates.html (accessed June 24, 2008).
21. Borrie et al. (1946) and Borrie (1948) offer a history of the demography of early Australia, and Sutcliffe (1963) provides a history of the population structure on the Australian trade union movement. The Australian immigration office also provides information on historical policy in Fact Sheet 8, available at www.immi.gov.au/media/fact-sheets/08abolition.htm (accessed June 25, 2008).
22. See www.abc.net.au/federation/fedstory/ep2/ep2_immigration.htm, accessed June 27, 2009.
23. This recommendation built on pioneering social research conducted by Seebohm Rowntree in Britain during the 1930s, wherein he found that many poor were not idle, but working poor (Glennerster 1995). This revelation increased trade union demands for a "family wage," yet Rowntree subsequently reported that the majority of British workers had no dependent children (Pedersen 1993). Keynes argued that in this circumstance, increasing wages would trigger inflation without reducing child poverty (Timmins 1995).
24. With the Social Security Act of 1935, the US federal government supplied matching grants to states for two means-tested programs: Aid to Dependent Children under the age of 16 (Title IV), and Maternal and Child Welfare (Title V). States needed to comply with general federal directives, but also retained considerable discretion in setting eligibility criteria, access, benefit amount, and duration.
25. Yet the US tax system sends mixed signals in this regard, as married couples are taxed at a higher rate than two single earners making the same amount of money.
26. This was an old and recurring British debate, beginning with the 1911 introduction of maternity allowance for working men's wives. Many British politicians, from the left as well as the right, argued that paying a benefit directly to the mother undermined marriage. See Pat Thane's (1996) history of the British welfare state development 1870–1945, and Land (1976), Pedersen (1993), Pascall (1997). See also Bennett (2002) for a repeat of the debate with the 1999 Working Families Tax Credit.
27. An unpaid maternity leave had been introduced in Germany before the war.
28. For discussions and details of West German policies highlighted here, see Kolbe (1999), Moeller (1993, 1997), Ostner (1992, 1993) and Zimmerman (1993).
29. In the early 1950s, divorcees or widows headed nearly 5 million out of the 15 million West German households (Moeller 1997).
30. The five were Brandenburg, Mecklenburg, Saxony, Saxony-Anhalt, and Thuringia.
31. See Einhorn (1993), Gerhard (1992), Harsch (1997), Münz and Ulrich (1995), Trappe (2000).
32. These descriptive statistics are supported by empirical analyses that suggest little relationship between population or family policies and fertility in the long run (Gauthier and

Hatzius 1997). Legge and Alford (1986) and Monnier (1990) found aggressive socialist pro-natalist policies at most altered timing of birth rather than completed fertility rates.

33. The Irish Republican Army and subsequent splinter groups, however, posed a significant terrorist threat to England throughout the latter half of the twentieth century.

34. In Germany, citizenship is based on *jus sanguinis* (Latin for "right of blood"). Citizenship rights might derive from residency (*jus domicile*) as in Sweden, or where one is born (*jus soli*) as in the United States. Lister (2003) discusses citizenship in detail, and Sainsbury (2006) discusses implications for immigrants under the different legal definitions vis-à-vis access to welfare.

35. The exact meaning of the term "globalization" remains contested, as do the implications for changes contained under the rubric (Guillén 2001). For a discussion of the framing and sensemaking, see Fiss and Hirsch (2005). For specific trends affecting the welfare state, see Esping-Andersen et al. (2002) or Taylor-Gooby (2004). For analyses of the recent trends on different life transitions, see the output from Hans-Peter Blossfeld's GlobaLife project, www.soziologie-blossfeld.de/globalife/

36. For example, the Washington Consensus of 1989 contained ten recommendations to be applied to any IMF or World Bank aid to Latin America, including redirection of public spending to pro-growth services, market-determined interest rates, competitive exchange rates, liberalization of trade as well as foreign direct investment, privatization of state enterprises, and deregulation.

37. For a comparison of the discourse on abortion in the United States and Germany that highlights how important national differences remain, see Ferree et al. (2002).

38. See www.telegraph.co.uk/news/uknews/1582539/The-Human-Fertilisation-and-Embryology-Bill.html, accessed June 27, 2009.

39. See O'Connor et al. (1999) contrasting legal precedence and relative abortion rights across Australia, Canada, the UK and US.

40. See Stetson (2001) for a summary of the US political debates during this period, in her volume that includes similar overviews for several countries. Also Luker (1984) and Jenson (1987) for the process of the political debate.

41. *Roe v. Wade* 410 US 113 (1973).

42. *Harris v. McRae* 448 US 297, 308 (1980).

43. Glendon (1987) claims only in the United States has a profit-making industry grown up around abortion.

44. *Rust v. Sullivan* 500 US 173 (1991).

45. *Webster v. Reproductive Health Services* (492 US 490 (1989)) and *Planned Parenthood v. Casey* (505 US 833 (1992).

46. See also Gonzales et al. (2000).

47. Abortion was common in the socialist countries because the state would pay for termination but did not provide contraception (Henshaw 1986).

48. The lack of unanimity would recur, however, in the vote for reunification with West Germany.

49. The figures for Britain and West Germany are also from Kiernan (2004a); US figures are from Raley (2000) and Australian are from de Vaus (2004). See also Nazio (2008) for analyses of the diffusion of cohabitation across societies.

4 Educational Foundations of Equality

1. Thanks are due to Katie Hoffman for gathering information on current child care provisions in each of the countries.

2. In the welfare state literature, however, education was considered a key mechanism for reinforcing class inequalities (Wilensky 1975).

3. Similar sentiments about reproducing social hierarchies were found across Europe during the mass schooling debates (see Boyd 1997; Müller et al. 1987; Ringer 1979).

4. Prussia passed a law limiting child labor in 1839, and Australia passed the 1873 Victoria Factory and Shop Act based on the British statutes. In the United States, individual states had some rarely enforced restrictions on child labor by the end of the nineteenth century. Reformers established the National Child Labor Committee in 1904 to lobby for federal legislation, leading to passage of the Keating-Owen Act in 1916 banning the sale of items produced by child labor. As with many US legislative attempts to mediate market mechanisms, the Owen-Keating Act was subsequently overturned when the US Supreme Court ruled it unconstitutional in *Hammer v. Dagenhart* 247 US 251 (1918).

5. Trow (1973) described the rapid expansion of post-secondary education after World War II, using a three-category classification based on gross enrollment ratios, calculated as the percentage of the applicable age group enrolled in higher education. He categorized systems as elitist when the gross enrollment ratio was less than 15 percent; mass with ratios between 15 and 50 percent, and universal when ratios exceeded 50 percent.

6. See Mazon (2003) for a history of German women's access to higher education between 1865 and World War I, and Ringer (2000) for Germany in comparative European perspective in this regard.

7. The Catholic Church objected to the initial legal requirement that children attend public schools, with parents' freedom to choose a private school ultimately supported by a 1925 US Supreme Court ruling, *Pierce v. Society of Sisters of the Holy Names of Jesus and Mary*, 268 US 510 (1925).

8. This is Goldin's (2001) estimate as of the 1920s.

9. *Plessy v. Ferguson*, 163 US 537 (1896). See King (1995) for an analysis of how the US federal government further enabled racial segregation.

10. Cited in Australian National Co-operating Body for Education (1951: 16).

11. *Schools, Australia, 1960.*

12. See Australian Bureau of Statistics, *Year Book Australia, 1955*, or *Schools, Australia, 1960.* www.abs.gov.au/AUSSTATS/abs@.nsf/allprimarymainfeatures/090AA9E828B55329 CA2573AE00046015?opendocument, last accessed March 5, 2009.

13. Ireland and Scotland had separate compulsory educational systems from the English and Welsh.

14. Even English socialists Sidney and Beatrice Webb lobbied for the elitist tripartite system before World War II, with the proviso that the most able working-class youths be granted access (Glennerster 1995; Timmins 1995).

15. The percentage varied, with children of lower socioeconomic classes less likely to go on to grammar school than middle- and upper-class children (Floud et al. 1956).

16. Ferrera (1996) argued this commitment to education is typical of the Mediterranean welfare states and further differentiates them from northern European ones.

17. Quoted in Castilliejo (1937: 76). See also Valiente (2002).

18. Kagan (1974) documents the popularity of university education in Spain in the early modern period, a popularity which had waned by the time of the Moyano Law.

19. Only Jesuit *colegios* were closed.

20. See Meyer et al. (1977) and Trow (1973).

21. OECD *Employment Outlook 1990*, table 5.2, updated with Eurybase for the European Countries, http://eacea.ec.europa.eu/portal/page/portal/Eurydice/, accessed March 2, 2009; Australia from Australian Bureau of Statistics. With the exception of Great Britain, compulsory schooling is under the jurisdiction of regional governments, so exact schedules for individual states, *Länder*, or autonomous regions differ.

22. It has been discussed at different times in different countries, but financial constraints, objections from experts claiming full-day education would be too exhausting for young

children, and/or public objection to granting states too much control over children's ideas and values have prevented it from occurring. Some programs added on to existing public education might, however, contain pedagogical elements, whereas others focus more on leisure activities for children.

23. A similar state commitment can be found in the social democratic countries of Scandinavia. For summary comparisons see Eurydice (2009) or Kamerman (2000).
24. This perspective was based on Bowlby's (1997) contentious attachment theory about maternal deprivation.
25. Pub.L. 88–452, 78 Stat. 508, 42 USC. § 2701.
26. For a timeline of the different changes to Head Start, see the history page at www. ilheadstart.org/historical.html (accessed March 8, 2009).
27. www.acf.hhs.gov/programs/ohs/about/index.html#mission (accessed March 13, 2009).
28. www.acf.hhs.gov/programs/ohs/about/fy2008.html
29. See Grimmett and Garrett (1989) for an initial review of evidence, and analyses of different US longitudinal datasets revealing some positive benefits for both White and Black children who had attended relative to their peers (Currie and Thomas 1995; Garces et al. 2002).
30. From Doherty (2002), as reported in Gornick and Meyers (2003: 188).
31. US families can deduct 20–35 percent of child care costs from their federal tax bill based on a sliding income scale, up to a maximum amount.
32. *Education Week* provides an annual report of state-level efforts, with the 2007 edition used for comparable preschool enrollment figures: www.edweek.org/ew/toc/2007/01/04/index.html (accessed March 8, 2009).
33. These figures are from different sources, with the child care spaces estimated by Bryson (1995), and the demand estimated by Edwards and Magarey (1995). The Australian Institute for Health and Welfare (2005) acknowledged the lack of nationally comparable information on Australian preschool services, which they hoped to rectify in ensuing years.
34. Allocation of funding to different types of care programs was detailed in the report published by Australia's Office of the Status of Women (2003), subsequently made the Office for Women within the Department of Families, Housing, Community Services and Indigenous Affairs.
35. Only in the Northern Territory and Queensland do regional governments run preschools.
36. Long-day care programs might offer educational programs (Australian Institute for Health and Welfare 2005).
37. See Australian Institute for Health and Welfare (2005).
38. Ibid., page 66. The proportion of 3- to 4-year-old children in very remote parts was 43 percent as compared with 58 percent in cities; among indigenous 46 percent as compared with 57 percent for other children; among lowest income households 48.5 percent as compared with 65.9 percent in households with the highest incomes.
39. Shortly after its election, New Labour accepted the 1993 Maastricht Treaty social charter that Thatcher had rejected.
40. Since 1998, UK parents can claim a tax credit for 70 percent of child care costs, up to a weekly maximum depending on number of children.
41. See www.ukchild care.ca/policy/strategy.shtml. For discussion of the effects of New Labour's child care policies, see Wincott (2006).
42. The lack of full-time spaces is exceptional among European countries (EU Memo/08/592). http://europa.eu/rapid/pressReleasesAction.do?reference=MEMO/08/592& format=HTML&aged=0&language=EN&guiLanguage=en
43. Eurydice (2009) offers an comprehensive review of the most current Early Childhood Education and Care arrangements in 30 European countries.

44. See Caprile and Escobedo (2003), Jurado Guerrero and Naldini (1996) or Tobio (2001).
45. The wage used was the gross earnings of an average production worker. Manufacturing wages tend to be higher than average wages in the service sector dominated by women.
46. See www.unesco.org/education/information/nfsunesco/doc/isced_1997.htm
47. *Ministerio de Educacion y Ciencia* (1990).
48. *Brown v. Board of Education of Topeka*, 347 US483 (1954).
49. *Swann v. Charlotte-Mecklenburg Board of Education*, 402 US 1 (1971).
50. US Department of Education, National Center for Education Statistics (2008). *The Condition of Education 2008* (NCES 2008–31).
51. *Parents Involved in Community Schools v. Seattle School District No. 1*, 551 U.S. 701 (2007).
52. Committee on Higher Education. 1963. *Robbins Report*. London: HMSO.
53. This was the conversion process Thatcher hoped to thwart by expanding preschool (Timmins 1995).
54. For example, one-third of private Australian schools remained sex-segregated and some co-educational schools offered sex-segregated classes as of 2005. Sex-segregation is slightly more prevalent for females: 19 percent females-only versus 15 percent boys-only (from data provided by Caroline Miller of the Independent Schools Council of Australia, which includes enrollments at Catholic independent schools that are not included in Australian Bureau of Statistics data). An on-going debate within Australian education is whether gender segregation enhances girls' educational achievement (Gill 2004). Proponents of single-sex education argue that the social pressures of co-educational environments can reinforce gender learning stereotypes (Gill 2004).
55. In 2001, Commonwealth grants comprised over 40 percent of all private and 50 percent of Catholic school per student income (Australian Bureau of Statistics 2001: table 26).
56. In England, religious secondary schools comprise just 16 percent of the total according to data provided by the Department of Education and Skills (SFR 42/2005).
57. See www.pisa.oecd.org/pages/0,3417,en_32252351_32235907_1_1_1_1_1,00.html, accessed June 30, 2009. The UK data contain information on all of the educational systems (England, Scotland and Wales). A survey was conducted in 2006, but does not contain the problem-solving section, and the US reading assessment scores. Given the importance of gender and immigrant differentials in reading, the 2003 dataset has been used here for most comparisons.
58. Using father's education provides a conservative estimate of class differences, as members of upper classes generally attain higher occupational positions regardless of their educational performance (Goldthorpe 2006).
59. Private school differentials in Australia and England would also reflect class differences, and these were substantial in England (17 percent greater). But the Australian data did not allow for comparisons between private and public schools, based on "long-standing agreements between the states and federal government not to release achievement data by sector" (personal communication with the Australian Council for Educational Research, July 2, 2009). And although only a small percentage of German students attend private school, the performance differential of those students is commensurate with the English private school differential.
60. As of 2000, the majority of Italians who migrated to Australia, Turks who migrated to Germany, Moroccans who migrated to Spain, Pakistanis who migrated to the United Kingdom, and Mexicans who migrated to the United States had completed only primary education (OECD 2008a: table 3.2). In contrast, one-fifth or more of British who migrated to Australia, Romanians who migrated to Germany, Germans who migrated to Spain, Indians who migrated to the United Kingdom, and Chinese who migrated to the United States as of 2000 had completed some post-secondary education (OECD 2008a: table 3.2).

61. The OECD has begun an analytic review of the policies that improve educational outcomes of immigrant children, but the frame does not incorporate the heterogeneity of migrant groups (www.oecd.org/document/17/0,3343,en_2649_39263294_39887569 _1_1_1_1,00.html).

62. This is a term used by the OECD to classify vocationally based post-secondary education, to be contrasted with tertiary type-A, which is general theory-based higher education leading to a degree (OECD 2007).

63. Tertiary type-A education is the theoretical post-secondary education associated with universities, but in some countries it is available at other institutions (OECD 2007).

64. www.gibill.va.gov/GI_Bill_Info/history.htm, accessed April 14, 2010.

65. As of 2009, there were almost 1,200 community and technical colleges (American Association of Community Colleges, www.aacc.nche.edu/AboutCC/Pages/fastfacts. aspx).

66. www.aacc.nche.edu/AboutCC/Pages/fastfacts.aspx

67. According to the College Board (*Trends in College Pricing*, 2009), published tuition fees for 2009/2010 at US public four-year universities were approximately $7,000, while those for similar private universities were $26,000. These figures exclude books and living expenses.

68. See also www.trends-collegeboard.com/student_aid/pdf/2009_Trends_Student_Aid.pdf for more details on US student financing.

69. The British government upgraded Exeter, Nottingham, and Southampton, and newly sanctioned Sussex, East Anglia, York, Essex, Lancaster, Kent, and Warwick.

70. Since 1985, the number of public universities in Spain increased from 30 to 50, whereas the number of private universities increased from 4 to 25 (OECD 2009a: table 3.1).

71. A few Australian university students paid fees, which the Whitlam government abolished in 1974.

72. As of 2004, the cost charged a student was approximately $500 per credit unit, with most semester courses worth two units. The student is to begin paying the total once they make a minimum annual salary of A$35,000.

73. Labour Party Conference, Bournemouth, UK, September 28, 1999. Full text published by the BBC online: http://news.bbc.co.uk/1/hi/uk_politics/460009.stm, accessed April 16, 2010.

74. The US equivalent in 2002 was $522 to $609.

75. The seven *Länder* introducing fees 2007–8 were Baden-Württemberg, Bavaria, Hamburg, Hesse, Lower Saxony, North Rhine-Westphalia, and Saarland.

76. In the United States, ethnic differences also narrowed. By 1990, 25 percent of Black youth and 16 percent of Hispanic American youth were enrolled in college (Lazerson 1998: 66).

5 Policy Foundations of Gender-Class Employment Equality

1. This vulnerability for women in public sector positions can occur in countries with few policies supporting greater income equality. For example, the UK government announced significant public spending cuts in June 2010 to reduce the public debt that accumulated from the 2008 bank bailout. A story in the *Guardian* newspaper reported that a study conducted by the House of Commons Library estimated that the cuts will disproportionately hurt women, who make up the majority of the UK's public sector workforce (see www.guardian.co.uk/politics/2010/jul/04/women-budget-cuts-yvette-cooper).

2. The relative union density rates between Australia and the United States have persisted over time, whereas it has declined more sharply in the United Kingdom. In the 1990s, 80 percent of Australian, 45 percent of British and less than 20 percent of US wage

earners were covered by collective bargaining or conciliated agreements (O'Connor et al. 1999: 89–90).

3. English women's work days were limited under the 1844 Factory Act (Lewis and Rose 1995).

4. *Lochner v. New York*, 198 US 45 (1905).

5. *Muller v. Oregon*, 208 US 412 (1908).

6. Australian states introduced other equal opportunity policies during this period, but they had much less effect than the union-won comparable worth policies. Individual states introduced complaint-based sex discrimination legislation in the late 1970s and 1980s, followed by the Commonwealth in 1984 (Baldock 1988). In 1984 and 1986, Australia introduced affirmative action policies that required larger private sector employers to set goals and timetables for achieving a representative workforce (Edwards and Magarey 1995). Less than half of Australian employers had the requisite number of workers, however, and the penalties for non-compliance were negligible (O'Connor et al. 1999). Through 1992, it was naming in Parliament. After 1992, non-compliant companies were ineligible for Commonwealth contracts (O'Connor et al. 1999).

7. This is a moniker the EEOC applied to itself in its 35th history website, accessed January 8, 2009: www.eeoc.gov/abouteeoc/35th/1965–71/index.html

8. See www.eeoc.gov/abouteeoc/35th/milestones/1974.html, accessed January 6, 2008.

9. *General Electric Company v. Gilbert*, 429 US 125 (1976).

10. *Nashville Gas v. Satty*, 434 US 136 (1977).

11. The "European Union" was not formally established until signing of the Maastricht Treaty in 1992.

12. For an article in *Woman's Own* magazine published October 31, 1987 (pp. 8–10), journalist Douglas Keay quotes Thatcher as saying: "I think we've been through a period where too many people have been given to understand that if they have a problem, it's the government's job to cope with it . . . They're casting their problem on society. And, you know, there is no such thing as society." (Margaret Thatcher Foundation, www.margaretthatcher.org/speeches/displaydocument.asp?docid=106689, accessed July 19, 2009).

13. *Kalanke v. Freie Hansestadt Bremen* Case C-450/93 [1995] ECR I-3051.

14. *Marschall v. Land Nordrhein-Westfalen* Case C-409/95 [1997] ECR I-6363. For a detailed history of the legal framework of equal treatment for men and women in the European Court of Justice rulings up to this time, see Arnull (1999: chapter 13).

15. The unemployment rate in the East *Länder* averaged 17 percent across the 1990s, as compared with 11 percent in the West *Länder* (Cooke 2007b: 939).

16. "Delivering on Gender Equality: A Progress Report on the Gender Equality Public Service Agreement 2003–6," Women and Equality Unit, March 2005.

17. In 2003, 27 percent of employed women and 18 percent of employed men reported working under some kind of flexibility arrangement (Women and Equality Unit, March 2005).

18. See www.db-decision.de/GenderMainstreaming/germany.html, accessed July 19, 2009.

19. Ibid.

20. Ibid.

21. http://aspe.hhs.gov/hsp/abbrev/prwora96.htm, accessed May 7, 2010.

22. Ibid.

6   Current Gender-Class Employment Equality

1. The analyses presented in this chapter were possible with funding from the UK ESRC research grant RES-000–22–2819, and the research assistance provided by Pierre Walthery.

2. The data are from wave 5.2, which are 1999 data for the United Kingdom, 2000 data for the United States, Germany and Spain, and 2001 data for Australia.
3. I do not analyze occupational segregation because the occupational structure is another institution that supports group inequalities, not an outcome of inequalities. For example, occupational segregation tends to be lower where fewer women are employed (Katz and Murphy 1992; Pettit and Hook 2009). Occupational segregation is greater in the Scandinavian countries, where it supports greater but not absolute gender employment and wage equality through high-quality public sector employment (Gornick and Jacobs 1998; Mandel and Semyonov 2006; Pettit and Hook 2009). In other countries like the United Kingdom, occupational segregation channels women into lower-paid "female" jobs (Charles and Grusky 2004). The group differences reinforced by the occupational structure therefore manifest as group differences in relative employment hours and/or wages (Goedicke and Trappe 2005; Stanley and Jarrell 1998).
4. In 2000, the unemployment rate in the East *Länder* exceeded 18 percent (Cooke 2007b).
5. See OECD Labour Force Data at http://stats.oecd.org/index.aspx?DatasetCode=KEI
6. The "Black" populations in the Australian and Spanish LIS data could not be differentiated and there were too few in Germany and the United Kingdom to yield meaningful comparisons.
7. Computing actual work hours requires adding significant main, country, and interaction effects together.
8. Because measures accounted for those with lower secondary or less and those with a university degree, effects of the middle range of education are reflected in each country term.
9. The high wage inequality among German men illustrates the importance of that country's welfare and tax policies, not the wage structure, in reducing relative class inequality among some workers.
10. This explanation is supported by the fact that a university degree did predict a wage premium for both genders before controlling for selection into employment (see technical appendix to chapter 6).

7 Gender-Class Equality in Paid and Unpaid Work

1. The cooking measure included time spent preparing food, setting the table, and washing and putting away dishes.
2. Morgan (2005, 2006) has argued the same applies to child care provision.
3. Persistent inequalities in unpaid work despite greater employment equality have been found in other transitional economies (Batalova and Cohen 2002; Fuwa 2004).
4. These did not appear to be income effects related to educational attainment, based on an additional analysis (not shown) using the smaller samples that included family income data.
5. Other analyses (not shown) suggest that Australian men who live in one of the urban centers perform significantly more housework than men living in more rural locations.
6. These are based on individual data of partnered respondents (60 percent of the total sample in each dataset) and assume educational homogamy within couples.
7. Jacobs and Gerson (2004) referred to this as the "time divide" faced by US dual-earner couples, but this term does not reflect the time cost involved.
8. See www.issp.org
9. The ISSP data included a question as to the number of children in the household younger than 5 or 6, but there was more missing information on this question than on the question asking total number of children younger than 17.

8 Sustainable Policy for Greater Equality

1. OECD education statistics accessed September 13, 2009; see Indicator B4 at www. oecd.org/document/24/0,3343,en_2649_39263238_43586328_1_1_1_37455,00. html#4
2. OECD family database accessed July 27, 2010; see Indicator PF3.1, www.oecd.org/ document/4/0,3343,en_2649_34819_37836996_1_1_1_37419,00.html
3. For the United States, see www.truthandpolitics.org/top-rates.php
4. As reported in the *Guardian*, July 4, 2010: www.guardian.co.uk/politics/2010/jul/04/ women-budget-cuts-yvette-cooper

BIBLIOGRAPHY

Adler, Marina. 2004. "Child-free and Unmarried: Changes in the Life Planning of Young East German Women." *Journal of Marriage and Family* 66: 1170–79.

Adsera, A. 2003. "Labor Market Performance and the Timing of Births: A Comparative Analysis across European Countries." University of Chicago Population Research Center Working Paper: www.src.uchicago.edu/prc/pdfs/adsera03.pdf

Aghion, Philippe, Eve Caroli and Cecilia García-Peñalosa. 1999. "Inequality and Economic Growth: The Perspective of the New Growth Theories." *Journal of Economic Literature* XXXVII: 1615–60.

Ahnert, Lieselotte and Michael E. Lamb. 2001. "The East German Child Care System: Associations with Caretaking and Caretaking Beliefs, and Children's Early Attachment and Adjustment." *American Behavioral Scientist* 44: 1843–63.

Aisenbrey, Silke, Marie Evertsson and Daniela Grunow. 2009. "Is There a Career Penalty for Mothers' Time Out? Germany, Sweden, and the US Compared." *Social Forces* 88: 573–606.

Allen, Sarah M. and Alan J. Hawkins. 1999. "Maternal Gatekeeping: Mothers' Beliefs and Behaviors That Inhibit Greater Father Involvement in Family Work." *Journal of Marriage and Family* 61: 199–212.

Allmendinger, Jutta and Stephan Leibfried. 2003. "Education and the Welfare State: The Four Worlds of Competence Production." *Journal of European Social Policy* 13: 63–81.

Altonji, Joseph G. and Rebecca M. Blank. 1999. "Gender and Race in the Labor Market," pp. 3143–259 in Orley Ashenfelter and David Card (Eds.), *Handbook of Labor Economics, Volume 3*. New York: Elsevier Science Press.

Andersen, Robert, James Curtis and Edward Grabb. 2006. "Trends in Civil Association Activity in Four Democracies: The Special Case of Women in the United States." *American Sociological Review* 71: 376–400.

Anderson, Bridget. 2000. *Doing the Dirty Work? The Global Politics of Domestic Labour*. London: Zed.

Anderson, Perry. 1974. *Lineages of the Absolutist State*. London: Verso.

Andersson, G. 2003. "Dissolution of Unions in Europe: A Comparative Overview." Working paper 2003–4. Rostock, Germany: Max Planck Institute for Demographic Research.

Anker, Richard. 1998. *Gender and Jobs: Sex Segregation of Occupations in the World.* Geneva: International Labour Organization.

Ariza, Alfredo, Sara de la Rica and Arantza Ugidos. 2003. "The Effect of Working Hours Flexibility on Fertility: A Comparative Analysis of Selected European Countries." WP 2003–5 DFAEII, Universidad del Pais Vasco. www.ehu.es/SaradelaRica/docs/parttime.pdf

Arnesen, Eric. 2007. *Encyclopedia of US Labor and Working-class History.* New York: Routledge.

Arnull, Anthony. 1999. *The European Union and its Court of Justice.* Oxford: Oxford University Press.

Arrow, Kenneth. 1976. "Economic Dimensions of Occupational Segregation: Comment I." *Signs* 1: 233–37.

Austin, A. G. 1961. *Australian Education, 1788–1900. Church, State and Public Education in Colonial Australia.* Melbourne: Sir Isaac Pitman and Sons.

Australian Bureau of Statistics. 2005. *Year Book Australia 2005.* Canberra: Commonwealth of Australia.

—— 2002. *Year Book Australia 2002.* Canberra: Commonwealth of Australia.

—— 2001. *Australian Schools in 2001.* Canberra: Commonwealth of Australia.

—— 1997. *Australian Social Trends 1997.* Canberra: Commonwealth of Australia.

—— 1996. *Housing Australia: A Statistical Overview.* Canberra: Commonwealth of Australia.

Australian Institute for Health and Welfare. 2005. *A Picture of Australia's Children.* Canberra: Commonwealth of Australia. Accessed 5 March 2009: www.aihw.gov.au/publications/phe/apoac/apoac.pdf

Australian National Co-Operating Body for Education. 1951. *Compulsory Education in Australia.* Paris: UNESCO.

Autor, David H., Lawrence F. Katz and Melissa S. Kearney. 2008. "Trends in U.S. Wage Inequality: Revising the Revisionists." *The Review of Economics and Statistics* 90: 300–23.

Bacci, Massimo Livi. 1968a. "Fertility and Nuptiality Changes in Spain from the Late 18th to the Early 20th Century: Part I." *Population Studies* 22: 83–102.

—— 1968b. "Fertility and Nuptiality Changes in Spain from the Late 18th to the Early 20th Century: Part II." *Population Studies* 22: 211–34.

Bade, Klaus J. and Myron Weiner (Eds.). 1997. *Migration Past, Migration Future: Germany and the United States.* Oxford: Berghahn Books.

Bagnall, Nigel F. 2000. "The Balance Between Vocational Secondary and General Secondary Schooling in France and Australia." *Comparative Education* 36: 459–75.

Baker, Maureen. 2001. *Families, Labour and Love.* Sydney: Allen and Unwin.

Baldock, Cora V. 1988. "Public Policies and the Paid Work of Women," pp. 20–53 in Cora V. Baldock and Bettina Cass (Eds.), *Women, Social Welfare and the State in Australia.* Sydney: Allen and Unwin.

Banaszak, Lee Ann. 1998. "East-West Differences in German Abortion Opinion." *The Public Opinion Quarterly* 62: 545–82.

Barbera, Marzia and Tiziana Vettor. 2001. "The Case of Italy," pp. 283–320 in Ute Behning and Amparo Serrano Pascual (Eds.), *Gender Mainstreaming in the European Employment Strategy.* Brussels: European Trade Union Institute.

Bardasi, Elena and Janet C. Gornick. 2008. "Working for Less? Women's Part-time Wage Penalties Across Countries." *Feminist Economics* 14: 37–72.

Barron, D. A., J. M. Black and M. A. Loewenstein. 1993. "Gender Differences in Training, Capital and Wages." *Journal of Human Resources* 28: 343–55.

Bassett, George W. 1970. "Australian Education," pp. 21–37 in Frederick M. Katz and Ronald K. Browne (Eds.), *Sociology of Education: A Book of Readings Pertinent to the Australian Education System.* Sydney: Macmillan.

Batalova, Jeanne A. and Philip N. Cohen. 2002. "Premarital Cohabitation and Housework: Couples in Cross-National Perspective." *Journal of Marriage and Family* 64: 743–55.

Baxter, Janeen. 1997. "Gender Equality and Participation in Housework: A Cross-national Perspective." *Journal of Comparative Family Studies* 28: 220–47.

Baxter, Janeen, Belinda Hewitt and Michelle Haynes. 2008. "Life Course Transitions and Housework: Marriage, Parenthood, and Time on Housework." *Journal of Marriage and Family* 70: 259–72.

Baxter, Janeen, Belinda Hewitt and Mark Western. 2009. "Domestic Outsourcing: Choice and Constraint in Hiring Household Help." *Feminist Economics* 15: 1–26.

Beck, Ulrich. 1992. *Risk Society: Towards a New Modernity.* London: Sage.

Becker, Gary S. 1993. *Human Capital: A Theoretical and Empirical Analysis, with Special Reference to Education.* Chicago: University of Chicago Press.

—— 1985. "Human Capital, Effort, and the Sexual Division of Labor." *Journal of Labor Economics* 3, Part 2: S33–S58.

—— 1981. *A Treatise on the Family.* Cambridge, MA: Harvard University Press.

—— 1971. *The Economics of Discrimination, 2nd Edition.* Chicago: University of Chicago Press.

Behning, Ute and Amparo Serrano Pascual (Eds.). 2001. *Gender Mainstreaming in the European Employment Strategy.* Brussels: European Trade Union Institute.

Beisel, Nicola and Tamara Kay. 2004. "Abortion, Race, and Gender in Nineteenth-Century America." *American Sociological Review* 69: 498–518.

Bennett, Fran. 2002. "Gender Implications of Current Social Security Reforms." *Fiscal Studies* 23: 559–84.

Bergh, Andreas. 2005. "On the Counterfactual Problem of Welfare State Research: How Can We Measure Redistribution?" *European Sociological Review* 21: 345–57.

Bertola, Giuseppe, Francine D. Blau and Lawrence M. Kahn. 2007. "Labor Market Institutions and Demographic Employment Patterns." *Journal of Population Economics* 20: 833–67.

Besemeres, J. F. 1980. *Socialist Population Politics.* White Plains, NY: Sharpe.

Bettio, F., A. Simonazzi and P. Villa. 2006. "Change in Care Regimes and Female Migration." *Journal of European Social Policy* 16: 271–85.

Beveridge, William. 1942. *Social Insurance and Allied Services.* London: HMSO.

Bianchi, Suzanne M., Melissa A. Milkie, Liana C. Sayer and John P. Robinson. 2000. "Is Anyone Doing the Housework? Trends in the Gender Division of Household Labor." *Social Forces* 79.1: 191–228.

Bianchi, Suzanne M., John P. Robinson and Melissa A. Milkie. 2006. *Changing Rhythms of American Family Life.* New York: Russell Sage Foundation.

Bielby, William T. and Denise D. Bielby. 2002. "Telling Stories about Gender and Effort: Social Science Narratives About Who Works Hard for the Money," pp. 193–217 in Mauro F. Guillen, Randal Collins, Paula England and Marshall Meyer (Eds.), *The New Economic Sociology: Developments in an Emerging Field.* New York: Russell Sage Foundation.

Bielby, Denise D. and William T. Bielby. 1988. "She Works Hard for the Money: Household Responsibilities and the Allocation of Work Effort." *American Journal of Sociology* 93: 1031–59.

Bittman, Michael, Paula England, Nancy Folbre, Liana C. Sayer and George Matheson. 2003. "When Does Gender Trump Money? Bargaining and Time in Household Work." *American Journal of Sociology* 109(1): 186–214.

Black, Dan A., Amelia M. Haviland, Seth G. Sanders and Lowell J. Taylor. 2008. "Gender Wage Disparities Among the Highly Educated." *Journal of Human Resources* XLIII: 630–59.

Blanden, Jo and Stephen J. Machin. 2004. "Educational Equality and the Expansion of UK Higher Education." *Scottish Journal of Political Economy* 51: 230–49.

Blank, Rebecca. 2007. "Improving the Safety Net for Single Mothers Who Face Serious Barriers to Work." *The Future of Children* 17: 183–97.

Blau, Francine D. 1998. "Trends in the Well-Being of American Women, 1970–95." *Journal of Economic Literature* 36: 112–65.

Blau, Francine D., Marianne A. Ferber and Anne E. Winkler. 2002. *The Economics of Women, Men and Work, 4th Edition.* Englewood Cliffs, NJ: Prentice Hall.

Blau, Francine D. and Lawrence M. Kahn. 2003. "Understanding International Differences in the Gender Wage Gap." *Journal of Labor Economics* 21: 106–44.

—— 1997. "Swimming Upstream: Trends in the Gender Wage Differential in the 1980s." *Journal of Labor Economics* 15(1, Part 1): 1–42.

—— 1996. "Wage Structure and Gender Earnings Differentials: An International Comparison." *Economica* New Series 63(250): S29–S62.

—— 1992. "The Gender Earnings Gap: Learning from International Comparisons." *American Economic Review* 82: 533–38.

Blau, Peter. 1960. *Exchange and Power in Social Life.* New York: John Wiley and Sons.

Blinder, Alan S. 1973. "Wage Discrimination: Reduced Form and Structural Estimates." *Journal of Human Resources* 8: 436–55.

Blood, Robert O. and Donald M. Wolfe. 1960. *Husbands and Wives.* New York: Free Press.

Blossfeld, Hans-Peter and Sonja Drobnič. 2001. *A Cross-National Comparative Approach to Couples' Careers.* Oxford: Oxford University Press.

Blossfeld, Hans-Peter and Andreas Timm. 2003. *Who Marries Whom? Educational Systems as Marriage Markets in Modern Societies.* European Studies of Population Series. Dordrecht, Netherlands: Kluwer Academic Publishers.

Blossfeld, Hans-Peter, Melinda Mills, Erik Klijzing and Katrin Kurz (Eds.), 2005. *Globalization, Uncertainty and Youth in Society.* London: Routledge.

Boarini, Romina and Hubert Strauss. 2007. "The Private Internal Rates of Return to Tertiary Education: New Estimates for 21 OECD Countries." *Economics Department Working Paper 591* (2007/51). Paris: OECD.

Bock, Gisela. 1991. "Antinatalism, Maternity and Paternity in National Socialist Racism," pp. 233–55 in Gisela Bock and Pat Thane (Eds.), *Maternity and Gender Policies: Women and the Rise of the European Welfare States 1880s–1950s.* London: Routledge.

Bock, Gisela and Pat Thane (Eds.). 1991. *Maternity and Gender Policies: Women and the Rise of the European Welfare States 1880s–1950s.* London: Routledge.

Boris, Eileen. 1993. "The Power of Motherhood: Black and White Activist Women Redefine the 'Political,'" pp. 213–45 in Seth Koven and Sonya Michel (Eds.), *Mothers of a New World: Maternalist Politics and the Origins of Welfare States.* London: Routledge.

Borra Marcos, Cristina. 2006. *Female Labour Participation and Child Care Choices in Spain.* Seville, Spain: Fundación Centro de Estudios Adaluces.

Borrie, W. D. 1948. *Population Trends and Policies: A Study in Australian and World Demography.* Sydney: Australasian Publishing.

Borrie, W. D., G. Cuthbert, G. L. Wood, H. L. Harris and A. P. Elkin. 1946. *A White Australia: Australia's Population Problem.* Sydney: Australasian Publishing.

Bourdieu, Pierre. 1977. *Reproduction in Education, Society, Culture.* Beverly Hills, CA: Sage.

Bowlby, John. 1997. *Attachment and Loss, vol. 1, 2nd edition.* London: Pimlico.

Boyd, Carolyn P. 1997. *Historia Patria: Politics, History, and National Identity in Spain, 1875–1975.* Princeton, NJ: Princeton University Press.

Boyd, William L. 1987. "Balancing Public and Private Schools," pp. 163–83 in William L. Boyd and Don Smart (Eds.), *Educational Policy in Australia and America: Comparative Perspectives*. New York: Falmer.

Bradley, Robert H., B. Caldwell and Stephen L. Rock. 1988. "Home Environment and School Performance: A Ten-Year Follow-up and Examination of Three Models of Environmental Action." *Child Development* 59: 852–67.

Brady, David, Jason Beckfield and Martin Seeleib-Kaiser. 2005. "Economic Globalization and the Welfare State in Affluent Democracies, 1975–2001." *American Sociological Review* 70: 921–48.

Brandolini, Andrea and Timothy M. Smeeding. 2009. "Income Inequality in Richer and OECD Countries," pp. 71–100 in Wiemer Salverda, Brian Nolan and Timothy M. Smeeding (Eds.), *The Oxford Handbook of Economic Inequality*. Oxford: Oxford University Press.

Breen, Richard and Lynn Prince Cooke. 2005. "The Persistence of the Gendered Division of Domestic Labour." *European Sociological Review* 21: 43–57.

Breen, Richard and Cecilia García-Peñalosa. 2002. "Bayesian Learning and Gender Segregation." *Journal of Labor Economics* 20: 899–922.

Breen, Richard and John H. Goldthorpe. 1997. "Explaining Educational Differentials: Towards a Formal Rational Action Theory." *Rationality and Society* 9: 275–305.

Breen, Richard and Jan O. Jonsson. 2005. "Inequality of Opportunity in Comparative Perspective: Recent Research on Educational Attainment and Social Mobility." *Annual Review of Sociology* 31: 223–43.

Breen, Richard and Ruud Luijkx. 2004. *Social Mobility in Europe*. Oxford: Oxford University Press.

Breen, Richard, Ruud Luijkx, Walter Müller and Reinhard Pollak. 2010. "Long-Term Trends in Educational Inequality in Europe: Class Inequalities and Gender Differences." *European Sociological Review* 26: 31–48.

Brewster, Karin L. and Ronald R. Rindfuss. 2000. "Fertility and Women's Employment in Industrialized Nations." *Annual Review of Sociology* 26: 271–96.

Brines, Julie. 1994. "Economic Dependency, Gender and the Division of Labor at Home." *American Journal of Sociology* 100: 652–88.

Brint, Steven G. 2006. *Schools and Societies, 2nd edition*. Stanford, CA: Stanford University Press.

Bryceson, Deborah. F. and Ulla Vuorela. 2002. *The Transnational Family: New European Frontiers and Global Networks*. Oxford: Berg.

Bryson, Lois. 1995. "Two Welfare States: One for Women, One for Men," pp. 60–76 in Anne Edwards and Susan Magarey (Eds.), *Women in a Restructuring Australia: Work and Welfare*. Sydney: Allen and Unwin.

Buchmann, Marlis and Maria Charles. 1995. "Organizational and Institutional Factors in the Process of Gender Stratification: Comparing Social Arrangements in Six European Countries." *International Journal of Sociology* 25: 66–95.

Budde, Gunilla-Friederike. 1999. "Women's Policies in the GDR in the 1960s/70s: Between State Control and Societal Reaction," pp. 199–217 in Rolf Torstendahl (Ed.), *State Policy and Gender System in the Two German States and Sweden 1945–1989*. Lund, Sweden: Bloms i Lund Tryckeri AB.

Budig, Michelle J. and Paul England. 2001. "The Wage Penalty for Motherhood." *American Sociological Review* 66: 204–25.

Budig, Michelle J. and Joya Misra. 2010. "How Carework Employment Shapes Earnings in a Cross-National Perspective." *International Labour Review*. 149(4), December 2010.

Butz, William P. and Michael P. Ward. 1979. "The Emergence of Counter Cyclical US Fertility." *American Economic Review* 69: 318–28.

Caprile, Maria and Anna Escobedo. 2003. "Overcoming Barriers to Equal Pay in Spain: Monitoring Gender Mainstreaming," pp. 199–246 in Lars Magnusson, Lilja Mosesdottir and Amparo Serrano Pascual (Eds.), *Equal Pay and Gender Mainstreaming in the European Employment Strategy*. Brussels: European Trade Union Institute.

Card, David and Alan Krueger. 1992a. "Does School Quality Matter? Returns to Education and the Characteristics of Public Schools in the United States." *Journal of Political Economy* 100: 1–40.

—— 1992b. "School Quality and Black-White Relative Earnings: A Direct Assessment." *Quarterly Journal of Economics* 107: 151–52(X).

Carneiro, Pedro and James J. Heckman. 2003. "Human Capital Policy," pp. 77–239 in J. J. Heckman, A. B. Krueger and B. M. Friedman (Eds.), *Inequality in America: What Role for Human Capital Policies?* Cambridge, MA: MIT Press.

Cass, Bettina. 1995. "Gender in Australia's Restructuring Labour Market and Welfare State," pp. 38–59 in Anne Edwards and Susan Magarey (Eds.), *Women in a Restructuring Australia: Work and Welfare*. Sydney: Allen and Unwin.

—— 1994. "Citizenship, Work, and Welfare: The Dilemma for Australian Women." *Social Politics* 1: 106–24.

—— 1988. "Redistribution of Children and to Mothers: A History of Child Endowment and Family Allowances," pp. 54–88 in Cora V. Baldock and Bettina Cass (Eds.), *Women, Social Welfare and the State in Australia*. Sydney: Allen-Unwin.

Castilliejo, Jose. 1937. *Wars of Ideas in Spain*. London: William Clowes & Sons.

Castles, Francis G. 1985. *The Working Class and Welfare: Reflections on the Political Development of the Welfare State in Australia and New Zealand 1890–1980*. London: Allen and Unwin.

Castles, Francis G. and Deborah Mitchell. 1992. "Identifying Welfare State Regimes: The Links Between Politics, Instruments, and Outcomes." *Governance* 5: 1–26.

Castles, Stephen. 1985. "The Guests Who Stayed: The Debate on 'Foreigners Policy' in the German Federal Republic." *International Migration Review* 19: 517–34.

Castles, Stephen and Mark J. Miller. 2003. *Age of Migration: International Population Movements in the Modern World*. Basingstoke: Palgrave Macmillan.

Chafetz, Janet Saltzman. 1986. *Female Revolt: Women's Movements in World and Historical Perspective*. Lanham, MD: Rowman and Littlefield.

Charles, Maria. 2005. "National Skill Regimes, Postindustrialism, and Sex Segregation." *Social Politics* 12: 289–316.

Charles, Maria and David Grusky. 2004. *Occupational Ghettos: The Worldwide Segregation of Women and Men*. Stanford, CA: Stanford University Press.

Chodorow, Nancy. 1978. *The Reproduction of Mothering: Psychoanalysis and the Sociology of Gender*. Berkeley: University of California Press.

Christopher, Karen, Paula England, Timothy M. Smeeding and Katherin Ross Phillips. 2002. "The Gender Gap in Poverty in Modern Nations: Single Motherhood, the Market, and the State." *Sociological Perspectives* 45: 219–42.

Coleman, James S. 1988. "Social Capital in the Creation of Human Capital." *American Journal of Sociology* 94: S95–S120.

Coleman, Karen. 1988. "The Politics of Abortion in Australia: Freedom, Church and State." *Feminist Review* 29: 75–97.

Collier, Ruth Berins and David Collier. 1991. *Shaping the Political Arena: Critical Junctures, the Labor Movement and Regime Dynamics in Latin America*. Princeton, NJ: Princeton University Press.

Collins, Patricia Hill. 2000. "It's All in the Family: Intersections of Gender, Race, and Nation," pp. 156–76 in Uma Narayan and Sandra Harding (Eds.), *Decentering the Center: Philosophy for a Multicultural, Post-colonial, and Feminist World*. Bloomington: Indiana University Press.

—— 1990. *Black Feminist Thought*. Boston: Unwin Hyman.

Coltrane, Scott. 2000. "Research on Household Labor: Modeling and Measuring the Social Embeddedness of Routine Family Work." *Journal of Marriage and Family* 62: 1208–33.

Commission of the European Communities. 1997. *Proposal for Guidelines for Member States' Employment Policies, 1998*. COM(97) 497 final. Brussels: European Commission.

Commonwealth Bureau of Census and Statistics. 1969. *Child Care*. Ref. 17–2. Canberra: Commonwealth Bureau of Census and Statistics.

Connell, R. W. 1987. *Gender and Power: Society, The Person and Sexual Politics*. Stanford, CA: Stanford University Press.

Connell, R. W., Dean J. Ashenden, Sandra Kessler and Gary W. Dowsett. 1982. *Making the Difference: Schools, Families and Social Division*. Sydney: Allen and Unwin.

Connolly, Sara and Mary Gregory. 2008. "Moving Down: Women's Part-Time Work and Occupational Change in Britain 1991–2001." *Economic Journal* 118: F52–F76, 02.

Cooke, Lynn Prince. 2010. "The Politics of Housework," pp. 59–78 in Judith Treas and Sonja Drobnič (Eds.), *Dividing the Domestic: Men, Women, and Household Work in Cross-National Perspective*. Stanford, CA: Stanford University Press.

—— 2009. "Gender Equity and Fertility in Italy and Spain." *Journal of Social Policy* 38: 123–40.

—— 2007a. "Policy Pathways to Gender Power: State-Level Effects on the Division of Housework." *Journal of Social Policy* 36(2): 239–60.

—— 2007b. "Persistent Policy Effects on Gender Equity in the Home: The Division of Domestic Tasks in Reunified Germany." *Journal of Marriage and Family* 69: 930–50.

—— 2006a. "Policy, Preferences and Patriarchy: The Division of Domestic Labor in East Germany, West Germany and the United States." *Social Politics* 13(1): 1–27.

—— 2006b. "'Doing Gender' in Context: Household Bargaining and the Risk of Divorce in Germany and the United States." *American Journal of Sociology* 112(2): 442–72.

—— 2004. "The Gendered Division of Labor and Family Outcomes in Germany." *Journal of Marriage and Family* 66: 1246–59.

—— 2003. "A Comparison of Initial and Early Life Course Earnings of the German Secondary Education and Training System." *Economics of Education Review* 22: 79–88.

Cooke, Lynn Prince and Janeen Baxter. 2010. "'Families' in International Context: Comparing Institutional Effects across Western Societies." *Journal of Marriage and Family* 72: 516–36.

Cooke, Lynn Prince and Vanessa Gash. 2010. "Wives' Part-time Employment and Marital Stability in Great Britain, West Germany and the United States." *Sociology* 44(6).

Costain, Anne N. and W. Douglas Costain. 1987. "Strategy and Tactics of the Women's Movement in the United States: The Role of Political Parties," pp. 196–214 in Mary Fainsod Katzenstein and Carol McClurg Mueller (Eds.), *The Women's Movements of the United States and Western Europe*. Philadelphia: Temple Press.

Cox, Eva. 1988. "Pater-Patria: Child-rearing and the State," pp. 190–204 in Cora V. Baldock and Bettina Cass (Eds.), *Women, Social Welfare and the State in Australia*. Sydney: Allen and Unwin.

Craig, Lynn and P. Sawrikar. 2007. *The Effect of (Dis)satisfaction with the Division of Domestic Labour on Relationship Survival*. Report for the Department of Families, Housing, Community Services and Indigenous Affairs. Canberra, Australia: Australian Federal Government.

Crenshaw, Kimberlé. 1989. "Demarginalizing the Intersection of Race and Sex: A Black Feminist Critique of Antidiscrimination Doctrine, Feminist Theory and Antiracist Politics." *University of Chicago Legal Forum* 1989: 139–67.

Crompton, Rosemary. 1999. *Restructuring Gender Relations and Employment: The Decline of the Male Breadwinner*. Oxford: Oxford University Press.

—— 1993. *Class and Stratification: An Introduction to Current Debates.* Cambridge, UK: Polity Press.

Cunha, Flavio and James J. Heckman. 2010. "Investing in Our Young People." NBER Working Paper #16,201. Cambridge, MA: National Bureau of Economic Research.

Currie, Janet and Duncan Thomas. 1995. "Does Head Start Make a Difference?" *American Economic Review* 85(3): 341–64.

Cutright, Phillips. 1965. "Political Structure, Economic Development, and National Social Security Programs." *American Journal of Sociology* 70: 537–50.

Dale, Angela, Joanne Lindley and Shirley Dex. 2006. "A Life-Course Perspective on Ethnic Differences in Women's Economic Activity in Britain." *European Sociological Review* 22: 459–476.

Dalla Costa, M. 1972. "Women and the Subversion of the Community." *Radical America* 6: 67–102.

Dalla Zuanna, Gianpiero and Giuseppe A. Micheli. (Eds.). 2004. *Strong Family and Low Fertility: A Paradox? European Studies of Population, vol. 14.* Dordrecht, Netherlands: Kluwer Academic Publishers.

Daly, Mary and Katherine Rake. 2003. *Gender and the Welfare State: Care, Work and Welfare in Europe and the USA.* Cambridge: Polity Press.

Danziger, Sandra, Elizabeth Oltmans Ananat and Kimberly G. Browning. 2004. "Child Care Subsidies and Transition from Welfare to Work." *Family Relations* 53: 219–28.

Danziger, Sheldon, Colleen M. Heflin, Mary E. Corcoran, Elizabeth Oltmans and Hui-Chen Wang. 2002. "Does it Pay to Move from Welfare to Work?" *Journal of Policy Analysis and Management* 21: 671–692.

Darwin, Charles. 1874. *The Descent of Man, and Selection in Relation to Sex, 2nd Ed.* London: John Murray.

David, Miriam. 1980. *The State, the Family and Education.* London: Routledge and Kegan Paul.

David, Paul A. 1985. "Clio and the Economics of QWERTY." *The American Economic Review* 75: 332–37.

Davis, Kathy. 2008. "Intersectionality as Buzzword: A Sociology of Science Perspective on What Makes a Feminist Theory Successful." *Feminist Theory* 9: 67–85.

Davis, Sue N. and Theodore N. Greenstein. 2004. "Cross-national Variations in the Division of Household Labor." *Journal of Marriage and Family* 66: 1260–271.

De Beauvoir, Simone. 1973. *The Second Sex.* New York: Vintage.

de la Rica, Sara and Amaia Iza. 2003. *Career Planning in Spain: Do Temporary Contracts Delay Marriage and Motherhood ?* WP 2003–8 DFAEII, Universidad del Pais Vasco (Spain). www.ehu.es/SaradelRica/docs/reho.pdf

de Ruijter, Esther, Judith Treas and Philip N. Cohen. 2005. "Outsourcing the Gender Factory: Living Arrangements and Service Expenditures on Female and Male Tasks." *Social Forces* 84: 306–22.

de Vaus, D. 2004. *Diversity and Change in Australian Families. Statistical Profiles.* Melbourne: Australian Institute of Family Studies, Commonwealth of Australia.

Deutsch, Francine M. 2007. "Undoing Gender." *Gender and Society* 21: 106–27.

Dewhurst, J. Frederic, John O. Coppock, P. Lamartine Yates and Associates. 1961. *Europe's Needs and Resources: Trends and Prospects in Eighteen Countries.* New York: Macmillan.

Dex, Shirley and Lois B. Shaw. 1986. *British and American Women at Work: Do Equal Opportunity Policies Matter?* London: Macmillan Press.

DiPrete, Thomas A. and Claudia Buchmann. 2006. "Gender-Specific Trends in the Value of Education and the Emerging Gender Gap in College Completion." *Demography* 43: 1–24.

DiPrete, Thomas A. and Gregory M. Eirich. 2005. "Cumulative Advantage as a Mechanism for Inequality: A Review of Theoretical and Empirical Developments." *Annual Review of Sociology* 32: 271–97.

Douglass, John Aubrey. 2005. "The Carnegie Commission and Council on Higher Education: A Retrospective." *University of California—Berkeley Center for Studies in Higher Education Research and Occasional Paper Series* CSHE.14.05.

Drobnič, Sonja, Hans-Peter Blossfeld and G. Rohwer. 1999. "Dynamics of Women's Employment Patterns over the Family Life Course: A Comparison of the United States and Germany." *Journal of Marriage and Family* 61: 133–46.

Dumont, Louis. 1977. *From Mandeville to Marx: The Genesis and Triumph of Economic Ideology.* Chicago: University of Chicago Press.

Duncan, Greg J. and Jeanne Brooks-Gunn (Eds.). 1997. *The Consequences of Growing Up Poor.* New York: Russell Sage Foundation.

Ebbinghaus, Bernhard and Jelle Visser. 1999. "When Institutions Matter: Union Growth and Decline in Western Europe 1950–95." *European Sociological Review* 15(2): 135–58.

Edwards, Anne and Susan Magarey. 1995. *Women in a Restructuring Australia: Work and Welfare.* Sydney: Allen and Unwin.

Ehrenreich, Barbara and Arlie Hochschild. 2003. *Global Woman: Nannies, Maids and Sex Workers in the New Economy.* London: Granta.

Einhorn, Barbara. 1993. *Cinderella Goes to Market: Citizenship, Gender and Women's Movements in East Central Europe.* London: Verso.

Equal Employment Opportunity Commission. 2000. "35 Years of Ensuring the Promise of Opportunity." Washington, DC: Equal Employment Opportunity Commission, at www.eeoc.gov/35th/

Erikson, Robert and John H. Goldthorpe. 1992. *The Constant Flux: A Study of Class Mobility in Industrial Societies.* Oxford: Clarendon Press.

Escobedo, Anna. 2001. "The Case of Spain," pp. 251–82 in Ute Behning and Amparo Serrano Pascual (Eds.), *Gender Mainstreaming in the European Employment Strategy.* Brussels: European Trade Union Institute.

Esping-Andersen, Gøsta. 2009. *The Incomplete Revolution: Adapting to Women's New Roles.* Cambridge: Polity Press.

—— 2004. "Unequal Opportunities and Mechanisms of Social Inheritance," pp. 289–314 in Miles Corak (Ed.), *Generational Income Mobility in North American and Europe.* Cambridge: Cambridge University Press.

—— 1999. *Social Foundations of Postindustrial Economies.* New York: Oxford University Press.

—— 1996. *Welfare States in Transition: National Adaptations in Global Economies.* London: Sage.

—— 1990. *The Three Worlds of Welfare Capitalism.* Princeton, NJ: Princeton University Press.

—— 1987. "The Comparison of Policy Regimes: An Introduction," pp. 3–13 in Martin Rein, Gøsta Esping-Andersen and Lee Rainwater (Eds.), *Stagnation and Renewal in Social Policy. The Rise and Fall of Policy Regimes.* Armonk, NY: Sharpe.

Esping-Andersen, Gøsta, Duncan Gallie, Anton Hemerijck and John Myles. (Eds), 2002. *Why We Need a New Welfare State.* Oxford: Oxford University Press.

Estevez-Abe, Margarita, Torben Iversen and David Soskice. 2001. "Social Protection and the Formation of Skills: A Reinterpretation of the Welfare State," pp. 145–83 in Peter Hall and David Soskice (Eds.), *Varieties of Capitalism: The Institutional Foundations of Comparative Advantage.* New York: Oxford University Press.

Eurostat. 2007. *Demographic Outlook: National Reports on the Demographic Developments in 2005.* Luxembourg: Office for the Official Publications of the European Communities.

Eurydice. 2009. *Early Childhood Education and Care in Europe: Tackling Social and Cultural Inequalities*. Brussels: European Commission. Accessed 3 March 2009: http://eacea.ec. europa.eu/ressources/eurydice/pdf/0_integral/098EN.pdf

Evans, Peter B., Dietrich Rueschemeyer and Theda Skocpol. 1985. *Bringing the State Back In*. Cambridge, UK: Cambridge University Press.

Evers, Aldabert, Jane Lewis and Birgit Riedel. 2005. "Developing Child-Care Provision in England and Germany: Problems of Governance." *Journal of European Social Policy* 15: 195–209.

Evertsson, Marie. 2004. "Formal On-the-Job Training: A Gender-Typed Experience and Wage-Related Advantage?" *European Sociological Review* 20: 79–94.

Evertsson, Marie and Magnus Nermo. 2007. "Changing Resources and the Division of Housework: A Longitudinal Study of Swedish Couples," *European Sociological Review* 23: 455–70.

——— 2004. "Dependence within Families and the Household Division of Labor—Comparing Sweden and the United States." *Journal of Marriage and Family* 66: 1272–86.

Fagan, Collette and Pierre Walthery. 2007. "The Role and Effectiveness of Time Policies for Reconciliation of Care Responsibilities." Directorate for Employment, Labour and Social Affairs Working Paper DELSA/ELSA/WP1(2007). Paris: Organization for Economic Co-operation and Development.

Fassmann, Heinz and Rainer Münz. 1992. "Patterns and Trends of International Migration in Western Europe." *Population and Development Review* 18: 457–80.

Featherman, David L., F. L. Jones and Robert M. Hauser. 1975. "Assumptions of Social Mobility Research in the US: The Case of Occupational Status." *Social Science Research* 4: 329–60.

Fenstermaker Berk, Sarah. 1985. *The Gender Factory: The Apportionment of Work in American Households*. New York: Plenum Press.

Ferree, Myra Marx. 2010. "Filling the Glass: Gender Perspectives on Families." *Journal of Marriage and Family* 72: 420–39.

——— 1995. "Patriarchies and Feminisms: The Two Women's Movements of Post-Unification Germany." *Social Politics* 2: 10–24.

——— 1993. "The Rise and Fall of 'Mommy Politics': Feminism and Unification in (East) Germany." *Feminist Studies* 19: 89–115.

——— 1992. "Institutionalizing Gender Equality: Feminist Politics and Equality Offices." *German Politics and Society* 24 and 25: 53–65.

——— 1990. "Beyond Separate Spheres: Feminism and Family Research." *Journal of Marriage and Family* 52: 866–84.

Ferree, Myra Marx, William Anthony Gamson, Jürgen Gerhards, and Dieter Rucht. 2002. *Shaping Abortion Discourse: Democracy and the Public Sphere in Germany and the United States*. Cambridge, UK: Cambridge University Press.

Ferrera, Maurizio. 2005. *Welfare State Reform in Southern Europe*. London: Routledge.

——— 2004. "Democratization and Social Policy in Southern Europe: From Expansion to 'Recalibration.'" Discussion paper for UNSRID's program on Social Policy in a Developmental Context.

——— 1996. "The 'Southern Model' of Welfare in Social Europe." *Journal of European Social Policy* 6: 17–37.

Fink, Janet. 2001. "Silence, Absence and Elision in Analyses of 'The Family' in European Social Policy," pp. 163–79 in Janet Fink, Gail Lewis and John Clarke (Eds.), *Rethinking European Welfare: Transformations of Europe and Social Policy*. London: Sage.

Finke, Roger and Rodney Stark. 1992. *The Churching of America 1776–1990: Winners and Losers in Our Religious Economy*. New Brunswick, NJ: Rutgers University Press.

Firestone, S. 1974. *The Dialectic of Sex: The Case for Feminist Revolution*. New York: Morrow.

Fisher, H. 1993. *Anatomie de liebe* [Anatomy of Love]. Munich: Droemer Knaur.

Fiss, Peer C. and Paul M. Hirsch. 2005. "The Discourse of Globalization: Framing and Sensemaking of an Emerging Concept." *American Sociological Review* 70: 29–52.

Floud, Jean E., A. H. Halsey and F. Martin. 1956. *Social Class and Educational Opportunity*. London: Heinemann.

Förster, Michael and Marco Mira d'Ercole. 2005. "Income Distribution and Poverty in OECD Countries in the Second Half of the 1990s." OECD Social, Employment and Migration Working Paper 22. Paris: Organization for Economic Co-operation and Development. Available at www.oecd.org/dataoecd/48/9/34483698.pdf, accessed 15 March 2010.

Fortin, Nicole M. and Thomas Lemieux. 1998. "Rank Regressions, Wage Distributions, and the Gender Gap." *Journal of Human Resources* 33: 610–43.

Franco, A. and Winqvist, K. 2002. "Women and Men Reconciling Work and Family Life." EUROSTAT *Population and Social Conditions*, Theme 3–9/2002.

Francome, Colin. 1984. *Abortion Freedom: A Worldwide Movement*. London: Allen and Unwin.

Francome, Colin and Edward Freeman. 2000. "British General Practitioners' Attitudes toward Abortion." *Family Planning Perspectives* 32: 189–91.

Fraser, Nancy. 1997. *Justice Interruptus: Critical Reflections on the "Post-Socialist" Condition*. New York: Routledge.

—— 1994. "After the Family Wage: Gender Equity and the Welfare State." *Political Theory* 22: 591–618.

Freeden, Michael. 1978. *The New Liberalism: An Ideology of Social Reform*. Oxford: Clarendon Press.

Freeman, Gary P. 1995. "Modes of Immigration Politics in Liberal Democratic States." *International Migration Review* 29: 881–902.

Freeman, Gary P. and Bob Birrell. 2001. "Divergent Paths of Immigration Politics in the United States and Australia." *Population and Development Review* 27: 525–51.

Freeman, Richard B. 1988. "Labour Markets." *Economic Policy* 3: 63–80.

Frevert, Ute. 1989. *Women in German History: From Bourgeois Emancipation to Sexual Liberation*. Oxford: Berg.

Friedman, Milton. 1962. *Capitalism and Freedom*. Chicago: University of Chicago Press.

Fuwa, Makiko. 2004. "Macro-level Gender Inequality and the Division of Household Labor in 22 Countries." *American Sociological Review* 69: 751–67.

Galinsky, Ellen, Kirsten Aumann and James T. Bond. 2009. *The Times They Are A-Changing: Gender and Generation at Work and at Home*. New York: Families and Work Institute. Available on-line at: http://familiesandwork.org/site/research/reports/Times_Are_Changing.pdf

Garces, Eliana, Duncan Thomas and Janet Currie. 2002. "Longer-Term Effects of Head Start." *The American Economic Review* 92(4): 999–1012.

Gauthier, Anne H. 2005. "Trends in Policies for Family-Friendly Societies," pp. 95–110 in Miroslav Macura, Alphonse L. MacDonald and Werner Haug (Eds.), *The New Demographic Regimes: Population Challenges and Policy Responses*. New York: United Nations.

Gauthier, Anne H. and Jan Hatzius. 1997. "Family Benefits and Fertility: An Econometric Analysis." *Population Studies* 51: 295–306.

Gauthier, Anne H., Timothy M. Smeeding and Frank Furstenberg. 2004. "Are Parents Investing Less Time in Children? Trends in Selected Industrialized Countries." *Population and Development Review* 30: 647–71.

Geddes, Andrew. 2008. *Immigration and European Integration: Beyond Fortress Europe?* Manchester, UK: Manchester University Press.

Geertz, Clifford. 1994. "Thick Description: Toward an Interpretive Theory of Culture," pp. 213–32 in Michael Martin and Lee C. McIntyre (Eds.), *Readings in the Philosophy of Social Science*. Cambridge, MA: MIT Press.

Gerhard, Ute. 1992. "German Women and the Social Costs of Unification." *German Politics and Society* 24 and 25: 16–33.

Gershuny, Jonathan. 2000. *Changing Times: Work and Leisure in Postindustrial Society*. Oxford: Oxford University Press.

Gershuny, Jonathan, Michael Bittman and J. Brice. 2005. "Exit, Voice, and Suffering: Do Couples Adapt to Changing Employment Patterns?" *Journal of Marriage and Family* 67: 656–65.

Geschka, Otti. 1991. "Participation and Disadvantage: Women in the Educational System," pp. 189–98 in Eva Kolinksy (Ed.), *The Federal Republic of Germany*. Oxford: Berg.

Gill, Judith. 2004. *Beyond the Great Divide: Single Sex or Coeducation?* Sydney: University of New South Wales Press.

Gilligan, Carol. 1996. *In a Different Voice: Psychology Theory and Women's Development*. Cambridge, MA: Harvard University Press.

Glass, David V. 1967. *Population: Policies and Movements in Europe, 2nd edition*. London: Frank Cass.

Glendon, Mary Ann. 1987. *Abortion and Divorce in Western Law*. Cambridge, MA: Harvard University Press.

Glenn, Evelyn Nakano. 1992. "From Servitude to Service Work: Historical Continuity in the Racial Division of Paid Reproductive Labor." *Signs* 18: 1–43.

Glennerster, Howard. 1995. *British Social Policy since 1945*. Oxford: Blackwell.

Goedicke, Anne and Heike Trappe. 2005. "Occupational Sex Segregation and Societal Change," pp. 84–116 in B. Peper, A. van Doorne-Huiskes and L. den Dulk (Eds.), *Flexible Working and Organisational Change: The Integration of Work and Personal Life*. Cheltenham, UK: Edward Elgar.

Goffman, Erving. 1977. "The Arrangement Between the Sexes." *Theory and Society* 4: 301–31.

Goldin, Claudia. 2001. "The Human Capital Century and American Leadership: Virtues of the Past." *Journal of Economic History* 61(2): 263–92.

—— 1990. *Understanding the Gender Gap: An Economic History of American Women*. New York: Oxford University Press.

Goldin, Claudia and Lawrence F. Katz. 2008. *The Race Between Education and Technology*. Cambridge, MA: Harvard University Press. See also NBER Working Paper 6144: "Why the United States Led in Education: Lessons from Secondary School Expansion, 1910–40." Washington, DC: National Bureau of Economic Research.

Goldscheider, Frances K. and Linda J. Waite. 1991. *New Families, No Families? The Transformation of the American Home*. Berkeley: University of California Press.

Goldthorpe, John H. 2006. *On Sociology. Second Edition Volume 2*. Stanford, CA: Stanford University Press.

Gonzalez, Maria J., Teresa Jurado and Manuela Naldini. 2000. "Introduction: Interpreting the Transformation of Gender Inequalities in Southern Europe." *Gender Inequalities in Southern Europe*. Essex, UK: Frank Cass.

Goodin, Robert, Bruce Heady, Ruud Muffels and Henk-Jan Dirven. 1999. *The Real Worlds of Welfare Capitalism*. Cambridge, UK: Cambridge University Press.

Goos, Maarten and Alan Manning. 2007. "Lousy and Lovely Jobs: The Rising Polarization of Work in Britain." *The Review of Economics and Statistics* 89: 118–33.

Gordon, Linda. 1994. *Pitied but Not Entitled: Single Mothers and the Origins of Welfare*. New York: Free Press.

—— 1990. *Women, the State, and Welfare*. Madison: University of Wisconsin Press.

—— 1976. *Woman's Body, Woman's Right: A Social History of Birth Control in America.* New York: Grossman.

Gornick, Janet C. and Jerry A. Jacobs. 1998. "Gender, the Welfare State, and Public Employment: A Comparative Study of Seven Industrialized Countries." *American Sociological Review* 63: 688–710.

Gornick, Janet C. and Markus Jäntti. 2009. "Child Poverty in Upper-Income Countries: Lessons from the Luxembourg Income Study." In Shelia B. Kamerman, Shelley Phipps and Asher Ben-Arieh (Eds.), *From Child Welfare to Child Wellbeing: An International Perspective on Knowledge in the Service of Making Policy.* New York: Springer.

Gornick, Janet C. and Marcia K. Meyers. 2003. *Families that Work: Policies for Reconciling Parenthood and Employment.* New York: Russell Sage Foundation.

Gornick, Janet C., Marcia K. Meyers and Katherin E. Ross. 1997. "Supporting the Employment of Mothers: Policy Variation Across Fourteen Welfare States." *Journal of European Social Policy* 7: 45–70.

Green, F. 1991. "Sex Discrimination in Job-Related Training." *British Journal of Industrial Relations* 29: 295–304.

Gregory, Jeanne. 1987. *Sex, Race and the Law: Legislating for Equality.* London: Sage.

Grief, A. 1994. "Cultural Beliefs and the Organization of Society: A Historical and Theoretical Reflection on Collectivist and Individualist Societies." *Journal of Political Economy* 102: 912–50.

Grimmett, Sadie and Aline M. Garrett. 1989. "A Review of Evaluations of Project Head Start." *The Journal of Negro Education* 58: 30–38.

Guest, Ross and Robyn Swift. 2008. "Fertility, Income Inequality, and Labour Productivity." *Oxford Economic Papers* 60: 597–618.

Guillén, Mauro F. 2001. "Is Globalization Civilizing, Destructive or Feeble? A Critique of Five Key Debates in the Social Science Literature." *Annual Review of Sociology* 27: 235–60.

Gupta, Sanjiv. 2007. "Autonomy, Dependence, or Display? The Relationship between Married Women's Earnings and Housework." *Journal of Marriage and Family* 69: 399–417.

—— 1999. "The Effects of Transitions in Marital Status on Men's Performance of Housework." *Journal of Marriage and Family* 61: 700–11.

Gupta, Sanjiv, Marie Evertsson, Daniela Grunow, Magnus Nermo and Liana C. Sayer. 2010. "Economic Inequality and Housework," pp. 105–23 in J. Treas and S. Drobnič (Eds.), *Dividing the Domestic: Men, Women, and Housework in Cross-National Perspective.* Stanford Series on Social Inequality. Palo Alto, CA: Stanford University Press.

Guruz, Kemal. 2008. *Higher Education and International Student Mobility in the Global Knowledge Economy.* Albany, NY: SUNY Press.

Hafner-Burton, Emilie M. and Mark A. Pollack. 2009. "Mainstreaming Gender in the European Union: Getting the Incentives Right." *Comparative European Politics* 7: 114–38.

Hagemann, Karen. 2006. "Between Ideology and Economy: The 'Time Politics' of Child Care and Public Education in the Two Germanys." *Social Politics* 13(2): 217–60.

Hakim, Catherine. 2000. *Work-Lifestyle Choices in the 21st Century: Preference Theory.* Oxford: Oxford University Press.

Hall, Matthew and George Farkas. 2008. "Does Human Capital Raise Earnings for Immigrants in the Low-Skill Labor Market?" *Demography* 45: 619–39.

Hall, Peter A. 1986. *Governing the Economy: The Politics of State Intervention in Britain and France.* Oxford: Oxford University Press.

Hall, Peter A. and David Soskice. 2001. *Varieties of Capitalism: The Institutional Foundations of Comparative Advantage.* New York: Oxford University Press.

Hancock, Ange-Marie. 2007. "When Multiplication Doesn't Equal Quick Addition: Examining Intersectionality as a Research Paradigm." *Perspectives on Politics* 5: 63–79.

Hank, Karsten, Katja Tillmann and Gert G. Wagner. 2001. "Außerhäusliche Kinderbetreuung in Ostdeutschland vor und nach der Wiedervereinigung. Ein Vergleich mit Westdeutschland in den Jahren 1990–99." Max Planck Institute for Demographic Research Working Paper 2001-3.

Hantrais, Linda. 1994. "Comparing Family Policy in Britain, France and Germany." *Journal of Social Policy* 23: 135–60.

Harkness, Susan. 1996. "The Gender Earnings Gap: Evidence from the UK." *Fiscal Studies* 17: 1–36.

Harkness, Susan and Jane Waldfogel. 1999. "The Family Gap in Pay: Evidence from Seven Industrialised Countries." Luxembourg Income Study Working Paper #219.

Harsch, Donna. 1997. "Society, the State, and Abortion in East Germany, 1950–72." *The American Historical Review* 102, 1: 53–84.

Hartmann, Heidi. 1981. "The Family as the Locus of Gender, Class, and Political Struggle: The Example of Housework." *Signs* 6: 366–94.

—— 1979. "Capitalism, Patriarchy and Job Segregation by Sex," pp. 206–47 in Zillah. R. Eisenstein (Ed.), *Capitalist Patriarchy*. New York: Monthly Review Press.

Heckman, James J. 1979. "Sample Selection Bias as a Specification Error." *Econometrica* 47: 153–61.

Heckman, James J. and Dimitriy V. Masterov. 2007. "The Productivity Argument for Investing in Young Children." National Bureau of Economic Research Working Paper W13016. Available at www.nber.org

Heineman, Elizabeth D. 1999. *What Difference Does a Husband Make?* Berkeley: University of California Press.

Henninger, A., C. Wimbauer and R. Dombrowski. 2008. "Demography as a Push Toward Gender Equality? Current Reforms of German Family Policy." *Social Politics* 15: 287–314.

Henshaw, Stanley K. 1986. "Induced Abortion: A Worldwide Perspective." *Family Planning Perspectives* 18: 250–54.

Henshaw, Stanley K., Susheela Singh and Taylor Haas. 1999. "The Incidence of Abortion Worldwide." *International Family Planning Perspectives* 25, Supplement: S30–S38.

Herdt, Gilbert. 1982. *Rituals of Manhood: Male Initiation in Papua New Guinea*. Berkeley: University of California Press.

Hernes, Helga M. 1987. "Women and the Welfare State: The Transition from Private to Public Dependence," pp. 72–92 in Anna Showstack Sassoon (Ed.), *Women and the State: The Shifting Boundaries of Public and Private*. London: Hutchinson.

Heuveline, Patrick and Jeffrey M. Timberlake. 2004. "The Role of Cohabitation in Family Formation: The United States in Comparative Perspective." *Journal of Marriage and Family* 66: 1214–30.

Heuveline, Patrick and Matthew Weinshenker. 2008. "The International Child Poverty Gap: Does Demography Matter?" *Demography* 45: 173–91.

Heuveline, Patrick, Jeffrey M. Timberlake and Frank F. Furstenberg. 2003. "Shifting Childrearing to Single Mothers: Results from 17 Western Countries." *Population and Development Review* 29: 47–71.

Hidalgo, Carlos Otero Andres Munoz Machado and Carlos J. Fernandez Rodriguez. 2002. *Vocational Education and Training in Spain*. Luxembourg: Office for Official Publications of the European Communities.

Hiilamo, Heikki and Olli E. Kangas. 2006. "Trap for Women or Freedom to Choose? Political Frames in the Making of Child Home Care Allowance in Finland and Sweden." Department of Social Policy 15/2006. Turku, Finland: University of Turku.

Hinrichs, Karl. 2001. "Elephants on the Move: Patterns of Public Pension Reform in OECD Countries," pp. 77–102 in Stephan Leibfried and Giuliano Bonoli (Eds.), *Welfare State Futures*. Cambridge: Cambridge University Press.

Hobson, Barbara. 2002. *Making Men Into Fathers: Men, Masculinities and the Social Politics of Fatherhood*. Cambridge, UK: Cambridge University Press.

—— 1993. "Feminist Strategies and Gendered Discourses in Welfare States: Married Women's Right to Work in the United States and Sweden," pp. 396–429 in Seth Koven and Sonya Michel (Eds.), *Mothers of a New World: Maternalist Politics and the Origins of Welfare States*. New York: Routledge.

—— 1990. "No Exit, No Voice: Women's Economic Dependence and the Welfare State." *Acta Sociologica* 33: 235–50.

Hochschild, Arlie, with A. Machung. 1989. *The Second Shift: Working Parents and the Revolution at Home*. London: Piatkus.

Hohn, C. 1990. "Country Report for the Federal Republic of Germany," pp. 79–102 in W. Dumon (Ed.), *Family Policy in EEC Countries*. Report prepared for the Commission of the European Communities, Directorate General for Employment, Social Affairs and Education.

Hook, Jennifer L. 2010. "Gender Inequality in the Welfare State: Sex Segregation in Housework, 1965–2003." *American Journal of Sociology* 115: 1480–523.

—— 2006. "Men's Unpaid Work in 20 Countries, 1965–1998." *American Sociological Review* 71: 639–60.

Hout, Michael and Thomas A. DiPrete. 2006. "What We Have Learned: RC28's Contributions to Knowledge About Stratification." *Research in Social Stratification and Mobility* 24: 1–20.

Howe, Renate. 1995. "A Paradise for Working Men But Not Working Women: Women's Wage Work and Protective Legislation in Australia, 1890–1914," pp. 318–37 in Ulla Wikander, Alice Kessler-Harris and Jane Lewis (Eds.), *Protecting Women: Labor Legislation in Europe, the United States, and Australia, 1880–1920*. Urbana: University of Illinois Press.

Immervoll, Herwig and David Barber. 2005. *Can Parents Afford to Work? Child care Costs, Tax-Benefit Policies and Work Incentives*. OECD Social, Employment and Migration Working Papers 31. Paris: OECD.

Jackson, Michelle, Robert Erikson, John H. Goldthorpe and Meir Yaish. 2007. "Primary and Secondary Effects in Class Differentials in Educational Attainment." *Acta Sociologica* 50: 211–29.

Jacobs, Jerry A. and Kathleen Gerson. 2004. *The Time Divide: Work, Family, and Gender Inequality*. Cambridge, MA: Harvard University Press.

Jaumotte, Florence. 2003. "Female Labour Force Participation: Past Trends and Main Determinants in OECD Countries." Economics Working Paper ECO/WKP 30. Paris: OECD.

Jenson, Jane. 2009. "Lost in Translation: The Social Investment Perspective and Gender Equality." *Social Politics* 16: 446–83.

—— 2004. "Changing the Paradigm: Family Responsibility or Investing in Children?" *Canadian Journal of Sociology* 10(2): 169–92.

—— 1987. "Changing Discourse, Changing Agendas: Political Rights and Reproductive Policies in France," pp. 64–88 in Mary F. Katzenstein and Carol M. Mueller (Eds.), *The Women's Movements of the United States and Western Europe*. Philadelphia, PA: Temple University Press.

Jenson, Jane and Denis Saint-Martin. 2006. "Building Blocks for a New Social Architecture: The LEGO Paradigm of an Active Society." *Policy and Politics* 34: 429–51.

Johansson, Matx, Katarina Katz and Håkan Nyman. 2005. "Wage Differentials and Gender Discrimination: Changes in Sweden 1981–98." *Acta Sociologica* 48(4): 341–64.

Jones, F. L. 1983. "Sources of Gender Inequality in Income: What the Australian Census Says." *Social Forces* 62(1): 134–52.

Jones, Helen. 1985. *Nothing Seemed Impossible: Women's Education and Social Change in South Australia 1875–1915*. St Lucia: Queensland University Press.

Joppke, Christian. 1996. "Multiculturalism and Immigration: A Comparison of the United States, Germany, and Great Britain." *Theory and Society* 25: 449–500.

Joshi, Heather, Pierella Paci and Jane Waldfogel. 1999. "The Wages of Motherhood: Better or Worse?" *Cambridge Journal of Economics* 23: 543–64.

Jurado Guerrero, Teresa and Manuela Naldini. 1996. "Is the South So Different? Italian and Spanish Families in Comparative Perspective." *Southern European Society and Politics* 1: 42–66.

Kagan, Richard L. 1974. *Students and Society in Early Modern Spain*. Baltimore, MD: Johns Hopkins University Press.

Kalleberg, Arne L., B. F. Reskin and K. Hudson. 2000. "Bad Jobs in America: Standard and Nonstandard Employment Relations and Job Quality in the United States." *American Sociological Review* 65: 256–78.

Kalleberg, Arne L. and Rachel Rosenfeld. 1990. "Work in the Family and in the Labor Market: A Cross-national, Reciprocal Analysis." *Journal of Marriage and Family* 52: 331–46.

Kamerman, Sheila B. 2000. "Early Childhood Education and Care: An Overview of Developments in the OECD Countries." *International Journal of Educational Research* 33: 7–29.

Kamerman, Sheila B. and A. J. Kahn 1997. *Family Change and Family Policies in Great Britain, Canada, New Zealand and the United States*. Oxford: Clarendon Press. Introduction.

Kamerman, Sheila B, Michelle Neuman, Jane Waldfogel and Jeanne Brooks-Gunn. 2003. "Social Policies, Family Types and Child Outcomes in Selected OECD Countries." Social, Employment and Migration Working Paper #6. Paris: OECD.

Kamo, Yoshinori. 2000. "He Said, She Said: Assessing Discrepancies in Husbands' and Wives' Reports on the Division of Household Labor." *Social Science Research* 29: 459–76.

Kangas, Olli and Joakim Palme. 2005. *Social Policy and Economic Development in the Nordic Countries*. Basingstoke, UK: Palgrave Macmillan.

Katz, Lawrence F. and Kevin M. Murphy. 1992. "Changes in Relative Wages, 1963–87: Supply and Demand Factors." *Quarterly Journal of Economics* 107: 35–78.

Kenworthy, Lane. 2010. "Labor Market Activation." Forthcoming in Herbert Obinger, Christopher Pierson, Francis G. Castles, Stephen Leibfried and Jane Lewis (Eds.), *The Oxford Handbook of Comparative Welfare States*. Oxford: Oxford University Press.

—— 2008. *Jobs with Equality*. New York: Oxford University Press.

Kessler-Harris, Alice. 1995. "The Paradox of Motherhood: Night Work Restrictions in the United States." Pp. 335–57 in Ulla Wikander, Alice Kessler-Harris and Jane Lewis (Eds.), *Protecting Women: Labor Legislation in Europe, the United States, and Australia, 1880–1920*. Urbana: University of Illinois Press.

Keynes, John Maynard. 1936. *A General Theory of Employment, Interest and Money*. London: Macmillan.

Kiernan, Kathleen. 2004a. "Cohabitation and Divorce across Nations and Generations," pp. 139–70 in P. L. Chase-Lansdale, K. Kiernan and R. J. Friedman (Eds.), *Human Development across Lives and Generations*. Cambridge: Cambridge University Press.

—— 2004b. "Unmarried Cohabitation and Parenthood in Britain and Europe." *Law and Policy* 26: 33–55.

Kilbourne, Barbara Stanek, George Farkas, Kurt Beron, Dorothea Weir and Paula England. 1994. "Returns to Skill, Compensating Differentials and Gender Bias: Effects of

Occupational Characteristics on the Wages of White Women and Men." *American Journal of Sociology* 100: 689–719.

Kimmel, Michael S. and Michael A. Messner. 2004. *Men's Lives, 6th Edition*. Boston: Pearson.

King, Desmond. 1995. *Separate and Unequal: African Americans and the US Federal Government*. Oxford: Oxford University Press.

Kingsley, Charles. 1850. *Cheap Clothes and Nasty*. London: W. Pickering. Restricted electronic access: http://galenet.galegroup.com/servlet/MOME?af=RN&ae=U106921651&srchtp=a&ste=14&locID=oxford

Knudsen, Knud and Kari Waerness. 2008. "National Context and Spouses' Housework in 34 Countries." *European Sociological Review* 24: 97–114.

Kofman, Eleonore. 2003. *Women Migrants and Refugees in the European Union*. Paris: Organisation for Economic Co-operation and Development.

Kofman, Eleonore, Annie Phizacklea, Parvati Raghuram and Rosemary Sales. 2000. *Gender and International Migration in Europe: Employment, Welfare and Politics*. London: Routledge.

Kohler, Hans-Peter, Francesco C. Billari and José Antonio Ortega. 2002. "The Emergence of Lowest-low Fertility in Europe During the 1990s." *Population and Development Review* 28: 641–80.

Kolbe, Wiebke. 1999. "Gender and Parenthood in West German Family Politics from the 1960s to the 1980s," pp. 133–67 in Rolf Torstendahl (Ed.), *State Policy and Gender System in the Two German States and Sweden 1945–1989*. Lund, Sweden: Bloms i Lund Tryckeri AB.

Kolinsky, Eva. 1989. *Women in West Germany: Life, Work, and Politics*. Worcester, UK: Billing and Sons.

Korn, Klaus, Günter Feierabend, G. Hersing and H.-D. Reuschel. 1984. *Education, Employment and Development in the German Democratic Republic*. Paris: UNESCO International Institute for Educational Planning.

Korpi, Walter. 1985. "Power Resources Approach vs. Action and Conflict: On Causal and Intentional Explanations in the Study of Power." *Sociological Theory* 3: 31–45.

—— 1983. *The Democratic Class Struggle*. London: Routledge.

Koven, Seth. 1993. "Borderlands: Women, Voluntary Action, and Child Welfare in Britain, 1840–1914," pp. 94–135 in Seth Koven and Sonya Michel (Eds.), *Mothers of a New World: Maternalist Politics and the Origins of Welfare States*. London: Routledge.

Koven, Seth and Sonya Michel (Eds.). 1993. *Mothers of a New World; Maternalist Politics and the Origins of Welfare States*. London: Routledge.

Koven, Seth and Sonya Michel. 1990. "Womanly Duties: Maternalist Politics and the Origins of Welfare States in France, Germany, Great Britain, and the United States, 1880–1920." *The American Historical Review* 95: 1076–108.

Kreyenfeld, Michaela. 2003. "Crisis or Adaptation-Reconsidered: A Comparison of East and West German Fertility Patterns in the First Six Years After the 'Wende.'" *European Journal of Population* 19: 303–29.

Krueger, Anne O. 1974. "The Political Economy of the Rent-Seeking Society." *American Economic Review* 64: 291–303.

Kunze, Astrid. 2008. "Gender Wage Gap Studies: Consistency and Decomposition." *Empirical Economics* 35: 63–76.

Kuznets, Simon. 1963. "Quantitative Aspects of the Economic Growth of Nations." *Economic Development and Cultural Change* 11(2): 1–80.

Kvist, Jon. 1999. "Welfare Reform in the Nordic Countries in the 1990s: Using Fuzzy-Set Theory to Assess Conformity to Ideal Types." *Journal of European Social Policy* 9: 231–52.

Labour Research Centre. 1990. *Pay Equity for Women in Australia*. Canberra: National Women's Consultative Council.

Ladd-Taylor, M. 1997. "Saving Babies and Sterilizing Mothers: Eugenics and Welfare Policies in the Interwar United States." *Social Politics* 4: 136–53.

Lake, Marilyn. 1993. "A Revolution in the Family: The Challenge and Contradictions of Maternal Citizenship in Australia," pp. 378–95 in Seth Koven and Sonya Michel (Eds.), *Mothers of a New World: Maternalist Politics and the Origins of Welfare States*. London: Routledge.

Land, Hilary. 1976. "Women: Supporters or Supported?" pp. 108–32 in Diana Leonard Barker and Sheila Allen (Eds.), *Sexual Divisions and Society: Process and Change*. London: Tavistock.

Lareau, Annette. 2000. *Home Advantage: Social Class and Parental Intervention in Elementary Education*. Lanham, MD: Rowman and Littlefield.

Lazerson, Marvin. 1998. "The Disappointments of Success: Higher Education after World War II." *Annals of the American Academy of Political and Social Science* 559: 64–76.

Le Grand, Julian. 1982. *The Strategy of Equality*. Boston: Allen & Unwin.

Legge, Jerome S., Jr. and John R. Alford. 1986. "Can Government Regulate Fertility? An Assessment of Pronatalist Policy in Eastern Europe." *The Western Political Quarterly* 39: 709–28.

Leibfried, Stephan and Giuliano Bonoli (Eds.), 2001. *Welfare State Futures*. Cambridge, UK: Cambridge University Press.

Leibfried, Stephan and Ilona Ostner. 1991. "The Particularism of West German Welfare Capitalism: The Case of Women's Social Security," pp. 164–86 in Michael Adler, Colin Bell, Jochen Clasen and Adrian Sinfield (Eds.), *The Sociology of Social Security*. Edinburgh: Edinburgh University Press.

León, Margarita. 2007. "Speeding Up or Holding Back? Institutional Factors in the Development of Childcare Provision in Spain." *European Societies* 9(3): 315–37.

—— 2005. "Welfare State Regimes and the Social Organization of Labour: Childcare Arrangements and the Work/Family Balance Dilemma." *Sociological Review* 53(s2): 204–18.

Leseman, Paul P. M. 2009. "The Impact of High Quality Education and Care on the Development of Young Children: A Review of the Literature," pp. 17–50 in *Early Childhood Education and Care in Europe: Tackling Social and Cultural Inequalities*. Brussels: Eurydice (European Commission).

Levanon, Asaf, Paula England and Paul Allison. 2009. "Occupational Feminization and Pay: Assessing Causal Dynamics Using 1950–2000 U.S. Census Data." *Social Forces* 88: 865–92.

Levi, Margaret. 1997. "A Model, a Method, and a Map: Rational Choice in Comparative and Historical Analysis," pp. 19–41 in Mark I. Lichbach and Alan S. Zuckerman (Eds.), *Comparative Politics: Rationality, Culture, and Structure*. Cambridge: Cambridge University Press.

Lewis, Jane. 2006. "Work/Family Reconciliation, Equal Opportunities, and Social Policies: The Interpretation of the Policy Trajectory at the EU Level and the Meaning of Gender Equality." *Journal of European Public Policy* 13: 420–37.

—— 1992a. "Gender and the Development of Welfare Regimes." *Journal of European Social Policy* 3: 159–73.

—— 1992b. *Women in Britain since 1945: Women, Family, Work and the State in the Post-War Years*. Oxford: Blackwell.

Lewis, Jane and Gertrud Astrom. 1992. "Equality, Difference, and State Welfare: Labor Market and Family Policies in Sweden." *Feminist Studies* 18: 59–87.

Lewis, Jane and Sonya Rose. 1995. "Let England Blush: Protective Labor Legislation, 1820–1914," pp. 91–124 in Ulla Wikander, Alice Kessler-Harris and Jane Lewis (Eds.), *Protecting Women: Labor Legislation in Europe, the United States, and Australia, 1880–1920*. Urbana: University of Illinois Press.

Liebert, Ulrike (Ed.). 2003. *Gendering Europeanisation*. Brussels: PIE-Peter Lang.

Liefbroer, Aart C. and Edith Dourleijn. 2006. "Unmarried Cohabitation and Union Stability: Testing the Role of Diffusion Using Data from 16 European Countries." *Demography* 43: 203–21.

Lipset, Seymour M. 1990. *Continental Divide: The Values and Institutions of the United States and Canada*. New York: Routledge.

Lister, Ruth. 2003. *Citizenship and Feminist Perspectives, 2nd edition*. New York: Palgrave Macmillan.

Lucifora, Claudio and Wiemer Salverda. 2009. "Low Pay," pp. 257–83 in Wiemer Salverda, Brian Nolan and Timothy M. Smeeding (Eds.), *The Oxford Handbook of Economic Inequality*. Oxford: Oxford University Press.

Luker, Kristin. 1984. *Abortion and the Politics of Motherhood*. Berkeley: University of California Press.

Luxembourg Income Study. 1999–2001. *LIS Database*, www.lisproject.org/techdoc.htm (multiple countries; microdata runs completed on 16 August 2009).

Lyon, Dawn and Miriam Glucksmann. 2008. "Comparative Configurations of Care Work across Europe." *Sociology* 42: 101–18.

Machin, Stephen. 2009. "Education and Inequality," pp. 406–31 in Wiemer Salverda, Brian Nolan and Timothy M. Smeeding (Eds.), *The Oxford Handbook of Economic Inequality*. Oxford: Oxford University Press.

Maddison, Angus. 2003. *The World Economy: Historical Statistics*. Paris: Organisation for Economic Co-operation and Development.

Magnusson, Lars, Lilja Mosesdottir and Amparo Serrano Pascual (Eds.). 2003. *Equal Pay and Gender Mainstreaming in the European Employment Strategy*. Brussels: European Trade Union Institute.

Mahony, David. 1993. "The Construction and Challenges of Australia's Post-Binary System of Higher Education." *Oxford Review of Education* 19: 465–83.

Mahoney, James and Dietrich Rueschemeyer. 2003. *Comparative Historical Analyses in the Social Sciences*. Cambridge: Cambridge University Press.

Malthus, Thomas R. 1806 [1798]. *An Essay on the Principle of Population, 3rd Edition*. London: Johnson.

Mandel, Hadas and Moshe Semyonov. 2005. "Family Policies, Wage Structures, and Gender Gaps: Sources of Earnings Inequality in 20 Countries." *American Sociological Review* 70: 949–68.

—— 2006. "A Welfare State Paradox: State Interventions and Women's Employment Opportunities in 22 Countries." *American Journal of Sociology* 111: 1910–49.

Mann, Horace. 1850. *Lectures on Education*. Boston: Ide. Available on-line at www.archive. org/stream/lecturesoneduide00mannuoft/lecturesoneduide00mannuoft_djvu.txt, accessed 30 June 2009.

March, James G. and Johan P. Olsen. 1984. "The New Institutionalism: Organizational Factors in Political Life." *The American Political Science Review* 78: 734–49.

Mare, Robert D. 1991. "Five Decades of Assortative Mating." *American Sociological Review* 56: 15–32.

Marshall, T. H. 1950. *Citizenship and Social Class*. Cambridge: Cambridge University Press.

Marx, Karl. 1967 [1848]. *The Manifesto of the Communist Party*. Harmondsworth, UK: Penguin.

—— 1966 [1875]. *Critique of the Gotha Programme.* New York: International Publishers.
—— 1930. *Das Kapital.* London: Dent.
Mason, Karen Oppenheim. 2001. "Gender and Family Systems in the Fertility Transition." *Population and Development Review* 27: 160–76.
Massey, Douglas S. and Nancy A. Denton. 1993. *American Apartheid: Segregation and the Making of the Underclass.* Cambridge, MA: Harvard University Press.
Matysiak, Anna and Stephanie Steinmetz. 2008. "Finding Their Way? Female Employment Patterns in West Germany, East Germany, and Poland." *European Sociological Review* 24(3): 331–46.
May, Martha 1991. "Bread Before Roses: American Working Men, Labor Unions and the Family Wage," pp. 1–21 in Milkman, Ruth (Ed.), *Women, Work and Protests: A Century of US Women's Labor History.* London: Routledge.
Mazon, Patricia M. 2003. *Gender and the Modern Research University: The Admission of Women to German Higher Education, 1865–1914.* Stanford, CA: Stanford University Press.
McBride, Dorothy E. 2007. *Abortion in the United States: A Reference Handbook.* Santa Barbara, CA: ABC-CLIO.
McCall, Leslie. 2005. "The Complexity of Inequality." *Signs* 30: 1771–800.
—— 2001. *Complex Inequality: Gender, Class and Race in the New Economy.* New York: Routledge.
McCall, Leslie and Christine Percheski. 2010. "Income Inequality: New Trends and Research Directions." *Annual Review of Sociology* 36: 329–47.
McDonald, Peter. 2000. "Gender Equity, Social Institutions and the Future of Fertility." *Journal of Population Research* 17: 1–16.
McGinnity, Frances and Patricia McManus. 2007. "Paying the Price for Reconciling Work and Family Life: Comparing the Wage Penalty for Women's Part-time Work in Britain, Germany and the United States." *Journal of Comparative Policy Analysis* 9: 115–34.
McGlynn, Clare. 2006. *Families and the European Union: Law, Politics and Pluralism.* Cambridge, UK: Cambridge University Press.
—— 2001. "European Union Family Values: Ideologies of 'Family' and 'Motherhood' in European Union Law." *Social Politics* 8: 325–50.
McKnight, A., P. Elias and R. Wilson. 1998. "Low Pay and the National Insurance System: A Statistical Picture." Equal Opportunities Commission, Research Discussion Series, July 1998.
McLanahan, Sarah. 2004. "Diverging Destinies: How Children Are Faring Under the Second Demographic Transition." *Demography* 41: 607–27.
McNicoll, Geoffrey. 1976. "The Borrie Report: Issues of Population Policy in Australia." *Population and Development Review* 2: 79–89.
Medalia, C. and Jerry A. Jacobs. 2008. "Working Time for Married Couples in 28 Countries." In C. L. Cooper (Ed.), *Working Hours and Work Addictions.* Amsterdam: Elsevier. pp. 137–58 in Ronald J. Burke and Cary L. Cooper (Eds.), *The Long Work Hours Culture.* Bingley, UK: Emerald.
Meers, Sharon and Joanna Strober. 2009. *Getting to 50–50: How Working Couples Can Have It All by Sharing It All.* New York: Bantam.
Messina, Anthony M. 2001. "The Impacts of Post-WWII Migration to Britain: Policy Constraints, Political Opportunism and the Alternation of Representational Politics." *The Review of Politics* 63: 259–85.
Meyer, John, Francisco O. Ramirez, Richard Rubinson and John Boli-Bennett. 1977. "The World Education Revolution 1950–70." *Sociology of Education* 50: 242–58.
Michalopoulos, Charles, Philip K. Robins and Irwin Garfinkel. 1992. "A Structural Model of Labor Supply and Child Care Demand." *Journal of Human Resources* 27: 166–203.

Michel, Sonya. 1993. "The Limits of Maternalism: Policies Toward American Wage-Earning Mothers During the Progressive Era," pp. 277–320 in Seth Koven and Sonya Michel (Eds.), *Mothers of a New World: Maternalist Politics and the Origins of Welfare States*. New York: Routledge.

Millar, Jane and Karen Rowlingson. 2001. *Lone Parents, Employment and Social Policy: Cross-National Comparisons*. Bristol, UK: Policy Press.

Miller, Trevor. 1970. "Changes in Secondary Education in Australia," pp. 38–53 in Frederick M. Katz and Ronald K. Browne (Eds.), *Sociology of Education: A Book of Readings Pertinent to the Australian Education System*. Sydney: Macmillan.

Mills, Melinda, Letizia Mencarini, Maria L. Tanturri and Katia Begall. 2008. "Gender Equity and Fertility Intentions in Italy and the Netherlands." *Demographic Research* 18: 1–26.

Mincer, Jacob. 1974. *Schooling, Experience, and Earnings*. New York: National Bureau of Economic Research.

Ministerio de Educacion y Ciencia. 1990. *The White Paper for the Reform of Educational System*. Deposito legal: M-31090–990. Madrid.

Mink, Gwendolyn. 1986. *Old Labor and New Immigrants in American Political Development. Union, Party, and State, 1875–1920*. Ithaca, NY: Cornell University Press.

Misra, Joya, Jonathan Woodring and Sabine N. Merz. 2006. "The Globalization of Care Work: Neoliberal Economic Restructuring and Migration Policy." *Globalizations* 3: 317–32.

Mitchell, Brian R. (Ed.). 2000. *International Historical Statistics, Europe, 1750–1993, 4th edition*. New York: Palgrave Macmillan.

Moeller, Robert G. 1997. *West Germany Under Construction: Politics, Society, and Culture in the Adenauer Era*. Ann Arbor: University of Michigan Press.

—— 1993. *Protecting Motherhood: Women and the Family in the Politics of Postwar West Germany*. Berkeley: University of California Press.

Moffitt, Robert A. 2000. "Female Wages, Male Wages, and the Economic Model of Marriage," pp. 302–19 in Linda J. Waite (Ed.), *The Ties That Bind: Perspectives on Marriage and Cohabitation*. New York: Aldine de Gruyter.

Monnier, Alain. 1990. "The Effects of Family Policies in the German Democratic Republic: A Re-Evaluation." *Population: An English Selection* 2: 127–40.

Moraga, Cherríe and Gloria Anzaldúa. 1983. *This Bridge Called My Back*. New York: Kitchen Table, Women of Color Press.

Morgan, Kimberly J. 2006. *Working Women and the Welfare State: Religion and the Politics of Work-Family Policies in Western Europe and the United States*. Stanford, CA: Stanford University Press.

—— 2005. "The 'Production' of Child Care: How Labor Markets Shape Social Policy and Vice Versa." *Social Politics* 12(2): 243–63.

Müller, Detlef K., Fritz Ringer and Brian Simon (Eds.). 1987. *The Rise of the Modern Educational System: Structural Change and Social Reproduction, 1870–1920*. New York: Cambridge University Press.

Münch, Joachim. 1991. *Vocational Training in the Federal Republic of Germany*. Berlin: European Centre for the Development of Vocational Training (CEDEFOP).

Münz, Rainer and Ralf E. Ulrich. 1995. "Depopulation After Unification? Population Prospects for East Germany, 1990–2010." *German Politics and Society* 13: 1–49.

Myles, John. 2002. "A New Social Contract for the Elderly?" pp. 130–72 in Gøsta Esping-Andersen, Duncan Gallie, Anton Hemerijck, and John Myles (Eds.), *Why We Need a New Welfare State*. Oxford: Oxford University Press.

Nash, Mary. 1991. "Pronatalism and Motherhood in Franco's Spain," pp. 160–77 in Gisela Bock and Pat Thane (Eds.), *Maternity and Gender Policies: Women and the Rise of the European Welfare States 1880s–1950s*. London: Routledge.

Nazio, Tiziana. 2008. *Cohabitation, Family and Society*. New York: Routledge.

NCES (National Center for Education Statistics). 2008. *The Condition of Education 2008* (NCES 2008–31). Washington, DC: US Department of Education.

Neumark, David, Mark Schweitzer and William Wascher. 2004. "Minimum Wage Effects Throughout the Wage Distribution." *Journal of Human Resources* 39: 425–250.

Nickel, Hildegard Maria. 2000. "Employment, Gender and the Dual Transformation in Germany," pp. 106–22 in Chris Flockton, Eva Kolinsky and Rosalind Pritchard (Eds.), *The New Germany in the East*. London: Frank Cass.

—— 1992. "Women in the German Democratic Republic and in the New Federal States: Looking Backwards and Forwards." *German Politics and Society* 24 and 25: 34–52.

Nicholson, Linda J. (Ed.). 1997. *The Second Wave: A Reader in Feminist Theory*. New York: Routledge.

Noguera, Carles Simo, Teresa Castro Martin and Asuncion Soro Bonmati. 2005. "The Spanish Case: The Effects of the Globalization Process on the Transition to Adulthood," pp. 376–402 in Hans-Peter Blossfeld, Melinda Mills, Erik Klijzing and Karin Kurz (Eds.), *Globalization, Uncertainty and Youth in Society*. London: Routledge.

North, David. 1984. "Down Under Amnesties: Background, Programs and Comparative Insights." *International Migration Review* 18: 524–40.

North, Douglass C. 1990. *Institutions, Institutional Change and Economic Performance*. Cambridge, UK: Cambridge University Press.

Nugent, Walter T. K. 1992. *Crossings: The Great Transatlantic Migrations 1870–1914*. Bloomington: Indiana University Press.

Oaxaca, Ronald L. 1973. "Male-Female Wage Differentials in Urban Labor Markets." *International Economics Review* 14: 693–709.

O'Brien, Margaret, Berit Brandth and Elin Kvande. 2007. "Fathers, Work and Family Life." *Community, Work and Family* 10: 375–86.

O'Connor, James. 1973. *The Fiscal Crisis of the State*. New York: St. Martin's Press.

O'Connor, Julia. 1996. "Special Issue: From Women in the Welfare State to Gender Welfare State Regimes." *Current Sociology* 44(2).

—— 1993. "Gender, Class and Citizenship in the Comparative Analysis of Welfare State Regimes: Theoretical and Methodological Issues." *British Journal of Sociology* 44: 501–18.

O'Connor, Julia, Ann Shola Orloff and Sheila Shaver. 1999. *States, Markets, Families: Gender, Liberalism and Social Policy in Australia, Canada, Great Britain and the United States*. Cambridge, UK: Cambridge University Press.

Offe, Claus. 1972. "Advanced Capitalism and the Welfare State." *Politics and Society* 4: 479–88.

Office of the Status of Women. 2003. *Women 2003*. Canberra: Department of the Prime Minister and Cabinet, Commonwealth of Australia.

Oláh, Livia. 2003. "Gendering Fertility: Second Births in Sweden and Hungary." *Population Research and Policy Review* 22: 171–200.

Oppenheimer, Valerie Kincade. 1997. "Women's Employment and the Gain to Marriage: The Specialization and Trading Model." *Annual Review of Sociology* 23: 431–53.

Organisation for Economic Co-operation and Development (OECD). 2010. *Going for Growth*. Paris: Organisation for Economic Co-operation and Development.

—— 2009a. *OECD Reviews of Tertiary Education: Spain*. Paris: Organisation for Economic Co-operation and Development.

—— 2009b. *Doing Better for Children*. Paris: Organisation for Economic Co-operation and Development.

—— 2008a. *A Profile of Immigrant Populations in the 21st Century*. Paris: Organisation for Economic Co-operation and Development.

—— 2008b. *Education at a Glance: OECD Indicators 2008*. Paris: Organisation for Economic Co-operation and Development.

—— 2008c. *Employment Outlook 2008*. Paris: Organisation for Economic Co-operation and Development.

—— 2007. *Education at a Glance 2007*. Paris: Organisation for Economic Co-operation and Development.

—— 2004. *Education at a Glance 2004*. Paris: Organisation for Economic Co-operation and Development. Country briefing notes for Germany, Spain, the United Kingdom, and the United States.

—— 2002. *Employment Outlook*. Paris: Organisation for Economic Co-operation and Development.

—— 2001. *Employment Outlook*. Paris: Organisation for Economic Co-operation and Development.

—— 1992. *OECD Education Statistics 1985–1992*. Paris: Organisation for Economic Co-operation and Development.

—— 1965. *The Mediterranean Regional Project: Spain*. Paris: Organisation for Economic Co-operation and Development.

Orloff, Ann Shola. 1996. "Gender in the Welfare State." *Annual Review of Sociology* 22: 51–78.

—— 1993a. *The Politics of Pensions: A Comparative Analysis of Britain, Canada and the United States, 1880–1940*. Madison: University of Wisconsin Press.

—— 1993b. "Gender and the Social Rights of Citizenship: The Comparative Analysis of Gender Relations and Welfare States." *American Sociological Review* 58: 303–28.

Orloff, Ann Shola and Theda Skocpol. 1984. "Why Not Equal Protection? Explaining the Politics of Public Social Spending in Britain, 1900–1911, and the United States, 1880s–1920." *American Sociological Review* 49: 726–50.

Ostner, Ilona. 1993. "Slow Motion: Women, Work and the Family in Germany," pp. 92–115 in Jane Lewis (Ed.), *Women and Social Policies in Europe: Work, Family and the State*. Aldershot, UK: Edward Elgar.

—— 1992. "Ideas, Institutions, Traditions: The Experience of West German Women, 1945–90." *German Politics and Society* 24 and 25: 87–99.

Palier, Bruno and Kathleen Thelen. 2009. "Institutionalizing Dualism: Complementarities and Change in France and Germany." Paper presented at the annual meeting of the Society for the Advancement of Socio-Economics, Paris, July 18–19, 2009.

Palme, Joakim. 1990. *Pension Rights in Welfare Capitalism: The Development of Old-Age Pension in 18 OECD Countries 1930 to 1985*. Stockholm: Swedish Institute for Social Research Dissertation Series, no. 14.

Parreñas, R. S. 2005. *Children of Global Immigration*. Stanford, CA: Stanford University Press.

Parsons, Talcott. 1942. "Age and Sex in the Social Structure of the United States." *American Sociological Review* 7: 604–16.

Pascall, Gillian. 1997. *Social Policy: A New Feminist Analysis*. London: Routledge.

Pateman, Carole. 1988. *The Disorder of Women*. Cambridge, UK: Polity Press.

Paz-Fuchs, Amir. 2008. *Welfare to Work: Conditional Rights in Social Policy*. Oxford: Oxford University Press.

Pedersen, Susan. 1993. *Family, Dependence, and the Origins of the Welfare State: Britain and France, 1914–1945*. Cambridge, UK: Cambridge University Press.

Petchesky, Rosalind Pollak. 1990. *Abortion and Woman's Choice: The State, Sexuality, and Reproductive Freedom*. Boston: Northeastern University Press.

Peters, B. Guy, Jon Pierre and Desmond S. King. 2005. "The Politics of Path Dependency: Political Conflict in Historical Institutionalism. *The Journal of Politics* 67(4): 1275–300.

Pettit, Becky and Stephanie Ewert. 2009. "Employment Gains and Wage Declines: The Erosion of Black Women's Relative Wages since 1980." *Demography* 46: 469–492.

Pettit, Becky and Jennifer L. Hook. 2009. *Gendered Tradeoffs: Family, Social Policy, and Economic Inequality*. New York: Russell Sage Foundation.

Pfau-Effinger, Birgit. 2010. "Household Work in Cultural and Institutional Context," pp. 125–146 in Judith Treas and Sonja Drobnič (Eds.), *Dividing the Domestic: Men, Women, and Housework in Cross-national Perspective*. Stanford Series on Social Inequality. Palo Alto, CA: Stanford University Press.

—— 1998. "Gender Cultures and the Gender Arrangement: A Theoretical Framework for Cross-national Gender Research," *Innovation: The European Journal of Social Sciences* 11: 147–66.

Pierson, Christopher. 1998. *Beyond the Welfare State? The New Political Economy of Welfare, Second Edition*. Cambridge, UK: Polity Press.

Pierson, Paul. 2000. "Increasing Returns, Path Dependence, and the Study of Politics." *The American Political Science Review* 94: 251–67.

Piven, Francis Fox and Richard A. Cloward. 1971. *Regulating the Poor: The Function of Public Welfare*. New York: Pantheon.

Plantenga, Janneke and Chantal Remery. 2005. *Reconciliation of Work and Private Life: A Comparative Review of Thirty European Countries*. Directorate-General for Employment, Social Affairs and Equal Opportunities. Luxembourg: The European Commission.

Pocock, Barbara. 1995. "Women's Work and Wages," pp. 95–120 in Anne Edwards and Susan Magarey (Eds.), *Women in a Restructuring Australia: Work and Welfare*. Sydney: Allen and Unwin.

Polanyi, Karl. 1944. *The Great Transformation*. Boston: Beacon Hill Press.

Polavieja, Javier G. 2006. "The Incidence of Temporary Employment in Advanced Economies: Why is Spain Different?" *European Sociological Review* 22: 61–78.

Pong, Suet-Ling, Jaap Dronkers and Gillian Hampden-Thompson. 2003. "Family Policies and Children's School Achievement in Single-versus Two-parent Families." *Journal of Marriage and Family* 65: 681–99.

Pratt, J. J. 1970. "The General Pattern of Development in Australian Education since World War II," pp. 3–20 in Frederick M. Katz and Ronald K. Browne (Eds.), *Sociology of Education: A Book of Readings Pertinent to the Australian Education System*. Sydney: Macmillan.

Preston, Alison C. and Geoffrey V. Crockett. 1999. "Equal Pay: Is the Pendulum Swinging Back?" *The Journal of Industrial Relations* 41(4): 561–74.

Ragin, Charles C. 1987. *The Comparative Method*. Berkeley: University of California Press.

Rahman, Anika, Laura Katzive, and Stanley K. Henshaw. 1998. "A Global Review of Laws on Induced Abortion, 1985–97." *International Family Planning Perspectives* 24: 56–64.

Rainwater, Lee and Timothy M. Smeeding. 2004. "Single-Parent Poverty, Inequality, and the Welfare State," pp. 96–155 in Daniel P. Moynihan, Timothy M. Smeeding and Lee Rainwater (Eds.), *The Future of the Family*. New York: Russell Sage Foundation.

—— 2003. *Poor Kids in a Rich Country: America's Children in Comparative Perspective*. New York: Russell Sage Foundation.

Raley, Kelly. 2000. "Recent Trends and Differentials in Marriage and Cohabitation: The United States," pp. 18–39 in Linda J. Waite, Christine Bachrach, Michelle Hindin, Elizabeth Thomson and Arland Thornton (Eds.), *The Ties that Bind: Perspectives on Marriage and Cohabitation*. New York: Aldine de Gruyter.

Ramirez, Francisco O. and John Boli. 1987. "The Political Construction of Mass Schooling: European Origins and Worldwide Institutionalization." *Sociology of Education* 60: 2–17.

Rees, Teresa. 1998. *Mainstreaming Equality in the European Union: Education, Training, and Labor Market Policies.* New York: Routledge.

Reskin, Barbara and Irene Padavic. 1994. *Women and Men at Work.* Thousand Oaks, CA: Pine Forge Press.

Reskin, Barbara and Patricia Roos. 1990. *Job Queues, Gender Queues: Explaining Women's Inroads into Male Occupations.* Philadelphia, PA: Temple University Press.

Riley, James C. 2001. *Rising Life Expectancy: A Global History.* Cambridge, UK: Cambridge University Press.

Ringer, Fritz K. 2000. *Toward a Social History of Knowledge.* New York: Berghahn Books.

—— 1979. *Education and Society in Modern Europe.* Bloomington: Indiana University Press.

Rosenfeld, Rachel A., Heike Trappe and Janet C. Gornick. 2004. "Gender and Work in Germany: Before and After Reunification." *Annual Review of Sociology* 30: 103–24.

Rosholm, Michael and Nina Smith. 1996. "The Danish Gender Wage Gap in the 1980s: A Panel Data Study." *Oxford Economic Papers, New Series,* 48(2): 254–79.

Rowley, Charles K. and Friedrich Schneider. 2005. *Encyclopedia of Public Choice, Volume 2.* New York: Kluwer Academic Publishers.

Royo, Sebastien. 2007. "Varieties of Capitalism in Spain: Business and the Politics of Coordination." *European Journal of Industrial Relations* 13: 47–65.

Rueschemeyer, Marilyn. 1989. "The Private Side of State Socialism: Observations on Social Change in the GDR." *German Politics and Society* 17: 50–60.

Rumberger, Russell W. and Stephen P. Lamb. 1998. "The Early Employment and Further Education Experiences of High School Dropouts: A Comparative Study of the United States and Australia." Paris: OECD. www.oecd.org/dataoecd/40/37/1925643.pdf, accessed 13 September 2009.

Ryan, Edna and Anne Conlon. 1989. *Gentle Invaders: Australian Women at Work. 2nd Edition.* Ringwood, VIC: Penguin.

Sainsbury, Diane. 2006. "Immigrants' Social Rights in Comparative Perspective: Welfare Regimes, Forms of Immigration and Immigration Policy Regimes." *Journal of European Social Policy* 16: 229–44.

—— 2001. "Gender and the Making of Welfare States: Norway and Sweden." *Social Politics* 8: 113–43.

—— 1994. "Women's and Men's Social Rights: Gendering Dimensions of Welfare States," pp. 150–69 in Diane Sainsbury (Ed.), *Gendering Welfare States.* London: Sage.

Sapiro, Virginia. 1990. "The Gender Bias of American Social Policy," pp. 36–54 in Linda Gordon (Ed.), *Women, the State and Welfare.* Madison: University of Wisconsin Press.

Sayer, Liana. 2005."Gender, Time and Inequality: Trends in Women's and Men's Paid Work, Unpaid Work and Free Time." *Social Forces* 84: 285–303.

Sayer, Liana, Anne Gauthier and Frank Furstenberg. 2004. "Educational Differences in Parents' Time with Children: Cross-national Variations." *Journal of Marriage and Family* 66: 1152–169.

Scarr, Sandra and Marlene Eisenberg. 1993. "Child Care Research: Issues, Perspectives, and Results." *Annual Review of Psychology* 44: 613–44.

Scharpf, Fritz W. and Vivian A. Schmidt. (Eds.). 2000. *Welfare and Work in the Open Economy: From Vulnerability to Competitiveness* (Volume 1). Oxford: Oxford University Press.

Seccombe, Wally. 1993. *Weathering the Storm.* London: Verso.

Sedgh, Gilda, Stanley K. Henshaw, Susheela Singh, Akinrinola Bnakole and Joanna Drescher. 2007. "Legal Abortion Worldwide: Incidence and Recent Trends." *International Family Planning Perspectives* 33: 106–16.

Sen, Amartya. 1981. "Ingredients of Famine Analysis: Availability and Entitlements." *The Quarterly Journal of Economics* 96: 433–64.

Serrano Pascual, Amparo (Ed.). 2004. *Are Activation Policies Converging in Europe? The European Employment Strategy for Young People.* Brussels: European Trade Union Institute.

Shannon, Richard. 1992. *The Age of Disraeli, 1868–1881: The Rise of Tory Democracy.* London: Longman.

Shavit, Yossi, Richard Arum and Adam Gamoran. 2007. *Stratification in Higher Education: A Comparative Study.* Stanford Series in Social Inequality. Stanford, CA: Stanford University Press.

Shavit, Yossi and Hans-Peter Blossfeld. 1993. *Persistent Inequality: Changing Educational Attainment in Thirteen Countries.* Boulder, CO: Westview Press.

Shelton, Beth A. and Daphne John. 1996. "The Division of Household Labor." *Annual Review of Sociology* 22: 299–322.

Sigle-Rushton, Wendy. 2010. "Men's Unpaid Work and Divorce: Reassessing Specialization and Trade in British Families." *Feminist Economics* 16: 1–26.

Sigle-Rushton, Wendy and Jane Waldfogel. 2007. "Motherhood and Women's Earnings in Anglo-American, Continental European and Nordic Countries." *Feminist Economics* 13: 55–91.

Simpson, Ida Harper and Paula England. 1981. "Conjugal Work Roles and Marital Solidarity." *Journal of Family Issues* 2: 180–201.

Sklar, Kathryn Kish. 1993. "The Historical Foundations of Women's Power in the Creation of the American Welfare State, 1830–1930," pp. 43–93 in Seth Koven and Sonya Michel (Eds.), *Mothers of a New World: Maternalist Politics and the Origins of Welfare States.* New York: Routledge.

Skocpol, Theda. 1992. *Protecting Soldiers and Mothers.* Cambridge, MA: Harvard University Press.

—— 1979. *States and Social Revolutions: A Comparative Analysis of France, Russia and China.* New York and Cambridge: Cambridge University Press.

Sleebos, Joëlle. 2003. "Low Fertility Rates in OECD Countries: Facts and Policy Responses." OECD Social, Employment and Migration Working Papers no. 13, Paris.

Sleifer, Jaap. 2006. *Planning Ahead and Falling Behind. The East German Economy in Comparison with West Germany 1936–2002.* Berlin: Akademie Verlag GmbH.

Smith, Adam. 1970 [1776]. *The Wealth of Nations.* Harmondsworth, UK: Penguin.

Smith, Alison J. and Donald R. Williams. 2007. "Father-friendly Legislation and Paternal Time across Western Europe." *Journal of Comparative Policy Analysis* 9: 175–92.

Smith, Dorothy E. 1987. *The Everyday World as Problematic: A Feminist Sociology.* Milton Keynes, UK: Open University Press.

Sobotka, Tomas. 2008. "The Diverse Faces of the Second Demographic Transition in Europe." *Demographic Research* 19: 171–224.

—— 2005. "Childless Societies? Trends and Projections of Childlessness in Europe and the United States." Paper presented at the 2005 Population Association of America annual meeting, Philadelphia, PA, April 1–3, 2005.

Solomon, Barbara. 1986. *In the Company of Educated Women: History of Women and Higher Education in America.* New Haven, CT: Yale University Press.

Sorensen, Annemette and Sarah McLanahan. 1987. "Married Women's Economic Dependency, 1940–80." *American Journal of Sociology* 93: 659–87.

Sorensen, Annemette and Heike Trappe. 1995. "The Persistence of Gender Inequality in Earnings in the German Democratic Republic." *American Sociological Review* 60: 398–406.

Sorokin, Pitirim A. 1927, 2nd edition 1959. *Social Mobility*. Glencoe, IL: Free Press.

Soskice, David. 2005. "Varieties of Capitalism and Cross-National Gender Differences." *Social Politics* 12: 170–79.

South, Scott and Glenna Spitze. 1994. "Housework in Marital and Nonmarital Households." *American Sociological Review* 59: 327–47.

Spencer, Geraldine M. 1971. "Fertility Trends in Australia." *Demography* 8: 247–59.

Standing, Guy. 1999. *Global Labor Flexibility: Seeking Redistributive Justice*. Basingstoke, UK: Macmillan.

Stanley, T. D. and Stephen B. Jarrell. 1998. "Gender Wage Discrimination Bias? A Meta Regression Analysis." *Journal of Human Resources* 33: 947–73.

Stephens, John D. 1979. *The Transition from Capitalism to Socialism*. London: Macmillan.

Stetson, Dorothy McBride. 2001. "US Abortion Debates 1959–98: The Women's Movement Holds On," pp. 247–66 in Dorothy McBride Stetson (Ed.), *Abortion Politics, Women's Movements, and the Democratic State*. Oxford: Oxford University Press.

—— 1995. "The Oldest Women's Policy Agency: The Women's Bureau of the United States," pp. 254–71 in Dorothy McBride Stetson and Amy Mazur (Eds.), *Comparative State Feminism*. Thousand Oaks, CA: Sage.

Stier, Haya and Noah Lewin-Epstein. 2007. "Policy Effects on the Division of Housework." *Journal of Comparative Analysis: Research and Practice* 9: 235–59.

Stinchcombe, Arthur L. 1997. "On the Virtues of the Old Institutionalism." *Annual Review of Sociology* 23: 1–18.

Stites, Richard. 1978. *The Women's Liberation Movement in Russia: Feminism, Nihilism, and Bolshevism 1860–1930*. Princeton, NJ: Princeton University Press.

Stoehr, Irene. 1991. "Housework and Motherhood: Debates and Policies in the Women's Movement in Imperial Germany and the Weimar Republic," pp. 213–32 in Gisela Bock and Pat Thane (Eds.), *Maternity and Gender Policy: Women and the Rise of the European Welfare States, 1880s–1950s*. London: Routledge.

Sutcliffe, James T. 1967[1921]. *A History of Trade Unionism in Australia*. Melbourne: Macmillan of Australia.

Szelewa, D. and M. P. Polakowski. 2008. "Who Cares? Changing Patterns of Childcare in Central and Eastern Europe." *Journal of European Social Policy* 18: 115–31.

Tataki, Ronald. 1990. *Strangers from a Different Shore: A History of Asian Americans*. New York: Penguin.

Taylor Cole, R. 1973. "Federalism and the Universities in West Germany: Recent Trends." *The American Journal of Comparative Law* 21: 45–68.

Taylor-Gooby, Peter (Ed.). 2004. *New Risks, New Welfare*. Oxford: Oxford University Press.

Teese, Richard. 1998. "Curriculum Hierarchy, Private Schooling, and the Segmentation of Australian Secondary Education, 1947–85." *British Journal of Sociology of Education* 19: 401–17.

Thelen, Kathleen. 2004. *How Institutions Evolve: The Political Economy of Skills in Germany, Britain, the United States, and Japan*. New York: Cambridge University Press.

—— 1999. "Historical Institutionalism in Comparative Politics." *Annual Review of Political Science* 2: 369–404.

Tilly, Charles. 1984. *Big Structures, Large Processes, Huge Comparisons*. New York: Russell Sage Foundation.

Timmer, Ashley S. and Jeffrey G. Williamson. 1998. "Immigration Policy Prior to the 1930s: Labor Markets, Policy Interactions, and Globalization Backlash." *Population and Development Review* 24: 739–71.

Thane, Pat. 1996. *Foundations of the Welfare State, 2nd Edition.* Harlow, UK: Pearson/ Longman.

Thompson, E. B. 1991 [1963]. *The Making of the English Working Class.* London: Penguin.

Thompson, Warren S. 1929. "Population." *American Journal of Sociology* 34: 959–75.

Timmins, Nicholas. 1995. *The Five Giants: A Biography of the Welfare State.* London: HarperCollins.

Tinkler, Penny. 2001. "Girlhood and Growing Up," pp. 35–50 in Ina Zweiniger-Bargielowska (Ed.), *Women in Twentieth-Century Britain.* Harlow, UK: Longman.

Titmuss, Richard M. 1958. *Essays on the Welfare State.* London: Allen and Unwin.

Tobio, Constanza. 2001. "Working and Mothering: Women's Strategies in Spain." *European Societies* 3: 339–72.

Tomaskovic-Devey, Donald, Melvin Thomas and Kecia Johnson. 2005. "Race and the Accumulation of Human Capital across the Career: A Theoretical Model and Fixed-Effects Application." *American Journal of Sociology* 111: 58–89.

Töns, Katrin and Brigitte Young. 2001. "The Case of Germany," pp. 129–56 in Ute Behning and Amparo Serrano Pascual (Eds.), *Gender Mainstreaming in the European Employment Strategy.* Brussels: European Trade Union Institute.

Torr, Berna M. and Susan E. Short. 2004. "Second Births and the Second Shift: A Research Note on Gender Equity and Fertility." *Population and Development Review* 30: 109–30.

Trappe, Heike. 2000. "Work and Family in Women's Lives in the German Democratic Republic," pp. 5–29 in Toby L. Parcel and Daniel B. Cornfield (Eds.), *Work and Family: Research Informing Policy.* Thousand Oaks, CA: Sage.

Tronto, Joan C. 1993. *Moral Boundaries: Political Argument for an Ethic of Care.* New York: Routledge.

Trow, Martin A. 1973. *Problems in the Transition from Elite to Mass Higher Education.* Berkeley, CA: Carnegie Commission on Higher Education.

UNESCO. 2008. *Global Education Digest.* Paris. Accessed February 27, 2009: www.uis. unesco.org/template/pdf/ged/2008/GED%202008_EN.pdf.

United Nations Population Division. 2000a. *Replacement Migration: Is It a Solution to Declining and Ageing Populations?* New York: United Nations.

—— 2000b. *World Population Monitoring 2000.* New York: United Nations.

US Census Bureau. 2000. *Child Support for Custodial Mothers and Fathers. Current Population Reports* P60–212 (October 2000). Washington, DC.

Valiente, Celia. 2003. "Central State Child Care Policies in Postauthoritarian Spain: Implications for Gender and Carework Arrangements." *Gender and Society* 17(2): 287–92.

—— 2002. "An Overview of Research on Gender in Spanish Society." *Gender and Society* 16: 767–92.

—— 2001. "Gendering Abortion Debates: State Feminism in Spain," pp. 229–45 in Dorothy McBride Stetson (Ed.), *Abortion Politics, Women's Movements, and the Democratic State.* Oxford: Oxford University Press.

Van de Kaa, D. 1987. "Europe's Second Demographic Transition." *Population Bulletin* 42(1). Washington: The Population Reference Bureau.

Vanek, Joann. 1974. "Time Spent in Housework." *Scientific American* 231: 116–20.

Verloo, Mieke. 2006. "Multiple Inequalities, Intersectionality and the European Union." *European Journal of Women's Studies* 13: 211–28.

Villagómez Morales, Elizabeth. 2007. "Gender Mainstreaming in Spain." Paper presented at the First European Union Gender Conference for the New Member States, April 19–21, 2007, Berlin.

Voitchovsky, Sarah. 2009. "Inequality and Economic Growth," pp. 549–74 in Wiemer Salverda, Brian Nolan and Timothy M. Smeeding (Eds.), *The Oxford Handbook of Economic Inequality.* Oxford: Oxford University Press.

von Oertzen, Christine. 1999. "Women, Work and the State: Lobbying for Part-Time Work and 'Practical Equality' in the West German Civil Service 1958–69," pp. 79–104 in Rolf Torstendahl (Ed.), *State Policy and Gender System in the Two German States and Sweden 1945–1989*. Lund, Sweden: Bloms i Lund Tryckeri AB.

Walby, Sylvia. 2010. "The Implications of Gender in the Financial Crisis for Theorizing Gender and the Economy." Paper presented at the International Sociological Association XVII World Congress, Gothenburg, Sweden, July 11–17.

—— 2009. *Globalization and Inequalities: Complexity and Contested Modernity*. London: Sage.

—— 2001. "The Case of the United Kingdom," pp. 221–50 in Ute Behning and Amparo Serrano Pascual (Eds.), *Gender Mainstreaming in the European Employment Stragegy*. Brussels: European Trade Union Institute.

—— 1990. *Theorizing Patriarchy*. Oxford: Blackwell.

Waldfogel, Jane. 1998. "Understanding the 'Family Gap' in Pay for Women with Children." *Journal of Economic Perspectives* 12: 137–56.

Wallerstein, Immanuel. 1976. *The Modern World-System: Capitalist Agriculture and the Origins of the European World-Economy in the Sixteenth Century*. New York: Academic Press.

Wanger, S. 2006. "Erwerbstätigkeit, Arbeitszeit und Arbeitsvolumen nach Geschlecht und Altersgruppen." Working Paper 2/2006. Nuremberg: Instituts für Arbeitsmarkt-und Berufsforschung.

Warren, Tracey. 2004. "Working Part-time: Achieving a Successful 'Work—Life' Balance?" *British Journal of Sociology* 55: 99–122.

Weber, Max. 2009 [1905]. *The Protestant Ethic and the Spirit of Capitalism*. Trans. Talcott Parsons. New York: Norton.

—— 1968. *Economy and Society: An Outline of Interpretive Sociology*. Ed. Guenther Roth and Claus Wittich. New York: Bedminster Press.

Wedderburn, Dorothy. 1965. "Facts and Theories of the Welfare State." *Socialist Register* 2: 127–46.

Weichselbaumer, Doris and Rudolf Winter-Ebmer. 2005. "A Meta-Analysis of the International Gender Wage Gap." *Journal of Economic Surveys* 19: 479–511.

West, Candace and Don H. Zimmerman. 1987. "Doing Gender." *Gender and Society* 1: 125–51.

Western, Bruce, Deirdre Bloome and Christine Percheski. 2008. "Inequality among American Families with Children, 1975 to 2005." *American Sociological Review* 73: 903–20.

Wikander, Ulla, Alice Kessler-Harris and Jane Lewis (Eds.). 1995. *Protecting Women: Labor Legislation in Europe, the United States, and Australia, 1880–1920*. Urbana: University of Illinois Press.

Wilde, Oscar. 1950. *Plays, Prose Writing, and Poems by Oscar Wilde*. London: J. M. Dent & Sons.

Wilensky, Harold. 1981. "Leftism, Catholicism and Democratic Corporatism," pp. 345–82 in Peter Flora and Arnold J. Heidenheimer (Eds.), *The Development of Welfare States in Europe and America*. London: Transaction Books.

—— 1975. *The Welfare State and Equality: Structural and Ideological Roots of Public Expenditures*. Berkeley: University of California Press.

Williams, Fiona. 2004. "Trends in Women's Employment, Domestic Service, and Female Migration: Changing and Competing Patterns of Solidarity," pp. 201–18 in T. Knijn and A. Komter (Eds.), *Solidarity between the Sexes and the Generations*. Cheltenham, UK: Edward Elgar.

—— 1989. *Social Policy: A Critical Introduction* 1989. Cambridge: Polity Press.

Williamson, John and Barry J. Fraser. 1991. "Elementary Education in Australia." *The Elementary School Journal* 92: 5–21.

Wilson, William J. 1987. *The Truly Disadvantaged*. Chicago: University of Chicago Press.

Wincott, Daniel. 2006. "Paradoxes of New Labour Social Policy: Toward Universal Child Care in Europe's 'Most Liberal' Welfare Regimes?" *Social Politics* 13(2): 286–312.

Witte, James C. and Arne L. Kalleberg. 1995. "Matching Training and Jobs: The Fit Between Vocational Education and Employment in the German Labour Market." *European Sociological Review* 11: 293–317.

Women's Equality Unit. 2005. "Key Indicators of Women's Position in Britain." London: DTI. www.womenandequalityunit.gov.uk

Woodward, C. Vann and William S. McFeely. 2001. *The Strange Career of Jim Crow*. New York: Oxford University Press.

Wright, Erik Olin. 2005. *Approaches to Class Analysis*. Cambridge: Cambridge University Press.

Wrohlich, Katharina. 2005. "The Excess Demand for Subsidized Child Care in Germany." Institute for the Study of Labor (IZA) Discussion Paper 1515.

Yuval-Davis, Nira. 2006. "Intersectionality and Feminist Politics." *European Journal of Women's Studies* 13: 193–209.

Zimmerman, Klaus. 1993. "Labour Responses to Taxes and Benefits in Germany," pp. 192–240 in A. B. Atkinson and Gunnar Viby Mogensen (Eds.), *Welfare and Work Incentives: A Northern European Perspective*. Oxford: Clarendon Press.

Zimmerman, Mary K., Jacquelyn S. Litt and Christine E. Bose. 2006. *Global Dimensions of Gender and Carework*. Stanford, CA: Stanford University Press.

Zinn, Howard. 2005 [1980]. *A People's History of the United States: 1492 to Present*. New York: Harper.

Zweiniger-Bargielowska, Ina. 2001. *Women in Twentieth-Century Britain*. Harlow, UK: Longman.

INDEX

Page numbers in *italics* denote a table

abortion 15, 46, 47, 50–1, 61–4, *64*
Abortion Act (1967) (Britain) 61–2
Act of Uniformity (1662) (England) 77
active labor market policies *see* labor activation policies
adult education 99–100, *99*, 101–2
affirmative action policies 4, 12, 13, 198–9, 211
ageing population 105
American Federation of Labor (AFL) 108
American Medical Association 50, 53
Amsterdam Treaty (1997) 121
Andersen, Robert 213
'Anti-Coolie' Act (1862) (US) 53
Arrow, Kenneth 26
Australia 2, 6, 7, 29, 33, 213–14;

Aboriginals 76; abortion and contraception 50, 61, 62, 64, *64*; adult educational attainment 99–100, *99*, 101; educational system 6, 75–6, 80, 210; effects of education, partnership and children on employment probability 134, *135*, 137, *137*, 138, 139–40, 142; effects of education, partnership and children on weekly work hours *144*, 145–7, 149, 158, *161*; employment equality policies 105, 113, 114–15, 117; family policies 56, *56*, 58; gender employment gap *8*, 10; gender-class equalities 40; and Harvester Judgement (1907) 7, 10, 29, 106–7, 108; hourly wages 150, 151, *151*, 152,

163, *164*; housework and gendered division of unpaid labor 172–3, *174*, *177*, 179, 181, *182*, 184, 187–8; immigration policies 54, 59, 68; preschool education 83, 102; secondary education 87, 89, 94; student performance 90–1, *91*; universities and colleges 97, 99; wage inequality and gender wage gap 7, *8*, 114–15, 117, 126, 152, 154, 155, *156*, 159–60; welfare costs 121, *122*; work-family reconciliation policies 125–6; worker mobilization and trade unions 12, 40, 104, 106–7, 125–6, 127

Baby Boom 47
bargaining model 35, 168, 171, 172, 173, 176, 186, 205
Basic Law (1949) (West Germany) 110
Beauvoir, Simone de 25
Becker, Gary 31; *The New Home Economics* 206
Berlin Wall: fall of (1989) 67
Beveridge, William 56
Bianchi, Suzanne 178, 214
Bigge, Commissioner 75
birth control 15, 46, 47, 49–51, 64
birth rates *52*, 58, *58*; nonmarital 65–6, *66*, 105
Black, Dan 26
blacks (US): and educational system 74; and employment *137*, 141
Blair, Tony 97
Blank, Rebecca 126
Blau, Francine 150, 158

Blinder, Alan S. 149
Bradlaugh-Beant trial (1876) (England) 50
Bretton Woods Accord 55, 61
Britain 7, 33, 35, 198; abortion and contraception 50, 61–2, 64, *64*; adult educational attainment *99*, 100, 101; educational system 76–8, 80; effects of education, partnership and children on employment probability 134, *135*, *137*, 138, 139, 140; effects of education, partnership and children on weekly work hours 145–7, *145*, 149, 158, *161*; employment equality policies 105, 111–12, 113, 118–19; family policies 56, *56*, 58; gender-class equalities 39; hourly wages 150, 151, *151*, *163*, *164*; housework and gendered division of unpaid labor 174–5, *174*, 175–6, 178, *182*, 183–4, 187, 188; immigration policies 59–60, 68–9; part-time work 39; preschool education 84, 102; secondary education 87, 89, 94; student performance 91, *91*; trade unions 106; universities and colleges 97; wage inequality 7, *8*, 152, 154; welfare state and costs 39, 121, *122*; work-family reconciliation policies 124
British Nationality Act (1948) 59
Brown v. Board of Education of Topeka (1954) (US) 88

Cambridge University 77
care work, unpaid 9, 13, 15, 32, 33,

40, 42, 45–6, 49, 55, 57–8, 69, 72, 82, 84, 100, 127, 135, 140
Catholic Church 3, 30, 50, 51, 79
Charles III, King of Spain 78
Charles, Maria 25
child allowance *56*, 56–58
child care 1, 33, 35, 38, 48, 211; private 85–6, *86*, 102
Child Care Act (1972) (Australia) 83
child poverty 19, 66, 102, *122*, 123, 208, 212; maternal employment and reduction in 67, 209
children: effect of having on employment probability *137*, 140–1, 142, 205; effect of having on weekly work hours 143, *144–5*, 147, 148, 158, *161*; and mothers' educational attainment 38–9; and social investment strategies 19, 209–10
Chinese Exclusion Act: (1882) (US) 53; (1943) 59
Chinese immigrants 53, 54, 59, 220.
Civil Rights Act (1964) (US) 12, 115
civil rights movement 36
class equality policies: and gender wage gap 151–5, *153*, 158, 159, 195
class-gender equality: and paid/ unpaid work in countries *129*, *200–1*
cohabitation: increase in 65
collective bargaining agreements 120
Commonwealth Conciliation and Arbitration Court (Australia) 107
Commonwealth Immigrants Act: (1962) (Australia) 60; (1968) 60
Commonwealth Women's Employment Board (Australia) 114
comprehensive schools (Germany, England) 89
compulsory schooling systems 15, 28, 33, 72, 132, 196, 203
Comstock Law (1873) (US) 50
Conciliation and Arbitration Commission (Australia) 114–15
contraception *see* birth control
Council of Action for Equal Pay (Australia) 114
couple households 55, 180–6, *182–3*, 186, 205 *see also* partnership
Crenshaw, Kimberlé 4
Currie, Janet 210
Czech Republic 199, *201*

day schools (Britain) 77
disability benefits 111
discrimination 12, 23, 59, 108, 115, 118; sex 118, 119; statistical 26
division of labor, gendered 1, 3, 9–10, 14–15, 180–6, 187–8, 189, 197–8, 205–6, 208, 212; and state policies 31–5, *34*
divorce 105, 187, 207–8, 213
domestic servants 171, 184, 186, 188
domestic work: and immigrant workers 37, 39, 43, 46, 48, 67, 68, 69, 70, 187, 199
Dourleijn, Edith 207
dual-earner model/households 18, 34, *34*, 172, 180, 181, 190, 198, 206, 213

East Germany 18, 35, 198, 212; abortion 63–4, 64, *64*; childhood

care provision 132; and dual-
earner model 34; educational
system 203–4; effects of education,
partnership and children on
employment probability 133, *135*,
136, *137*, 139, 140, 142; effects of
education, partnership and
children on weekly work hours
145, 147–8, *161*; employment
equality policies 105, 109, 113,
120; family policies 40, *56*, 57–8;
gender employment gap *8*, 10;
gender-class equalities 40–1;
hourly wages 150, 151, *151*, *164*,
165; housework and gendered
division of unpaid labor 172, *174*,
175, *177*, 179, *183*, 185, 188, 189;
preschool education 81, 85, 86, 87,
102; vocational training 95; wage
inequality 152, 156–7, *156*; work-
family reconciliation policies 125
economic growth: and inequality
203, 211
Economic Opportunity Act (1964)
(Britain) 82
Economy Act (1932) (US) 108
education 1, 15–16, 23–4, 28, 42,
71–102, 196, 197, 203–4; adult
99–100, *99*, 101–2; care void
created by systems of 72, 102, 196;
compulsory schooling system 15,
28, 33, 72, 132, 196, 203; country
comparisons *see* individual
countries; and economic
competiveness 80; effect on
employment probability 132–4,
135, 197, 212; effect on weekly
work hours 143–4, *144–5*, 145–6,

147–9, 157, 160–1, *161*, 197; equal
opportunity policies 15–16, 36–7;
GDP spent on 211; and
housework and gendered division
of unpaid labor 175–6, 180, 181,
182–3, 184–5, 188, *193*, 196–7,
198; impact of mothers'
educational attainment on child
outcomes 38–9; post-secondary
95–100, 101; preschool provision
16, 80–7, 102, 204, 210, 211; and
rural-urban divide 83, 90–1, *92*,
101; secondary 87–95; and social
investment strategies 210–11;
student performance 90–3, *91*, *92*,
93; subject differences 23–4,
universities 77, 95–9, 101 *see also*
university degree; and wages 23,
103, 152, *163*; and weekly work
hours 143–4, *144–5*, 145–6,
147–9, 157
Education Act (1902) (England) 77
EEOC (Equal Employment
Opportunities Commission) (US)
115, 116
Ehrenreich, Barbara 48
employment 1, 104, 131–65, 204;
and divorce 207; effect of
education on probability of 132–4,
135, 197, 212; effect of individual
characteristics on probability of
134–42, *137*; effect of parenthood
on *137*, 140–1, 142, 205; effect of
partnership on *137*, 138, 141–2,
204–5; equal opportunity policies
16–17, 118; and fertility 141, 206,
208; and having a university
degree 136–7, *137*, 142, 157, 173,

197, 204; and housework *174*, 175, 186; and immigrants *137*, 141; and other household income effect *137*, 138–40, 142; reduction of child poverty by female 67, 209; trajectories 24; wage inequalities 149–57; and weekly work hours 17–18, 142–9, 160–1, *161–2*; *see also* labor supply and demand
employment equality policies 103–29; Australian versus US post-war initiatives 114–17; country differences 128, *129*; and European Union 117–21; post-war policies 109–14; in twenty-first century 127–9; and work-family reconciliation policies 19, 48, 121–7; and worker mobilization during nineteenth century 104, 106–9
England *see* Britain
Equal Employment Opportunity Commission *see* EEOC
Equal Opportunities Commission (Britain) 118
equal opportunity policies 4, 12, 117, 121, 131, 198–9; and education 15–16, 36–7; and employment 16–17, 118
equal pay: Australia 114–15; Britain 118, 119; Spain 120; United States 115; West Germany 119
Equal Pay Act (1963) (US) 115
Equal Pay Act (1970) (Britain) 118
Equal Value Amendment (1984) (Britain) 119
Equality Act (1957) (West Germany) 110

equality directives 105
Esping-Andersen, Gøsta 19, 29, 103, 104, 195, 212

ethnic minorities 4, 9 *see also* immigration/immigrants
European Commission 118, 119, 121
European Court of Justice 13, 119, 127
European Economic Community 105, 117
European Employment Strategy 123
European Structural Funds 118
European Union 84, 113–14, 210; and employment gender equality 117–21; work-family reconciliation policies 127
EU's Directive on Equal Treatment 119
Executive Order 11246 (1965) (US) 12

Factory Act (1833) (Britain) 2, 76
Fair Labor Standards Act (1938) (US) 108
families 2, 3, 21–2; shrinking of size of 105
family allowances *see* child allowance
family characteristics 17; effect on employment hours 142–9, 160–1, *161–2*; effect on employment probability 134–42, *137*
Family Law Code (1965) (East Germany) 81, 109
Family and Medical Leave Act (1993) (US) 116
family policies 40, 42, 55–8, *56*
fascism 46

Federal Ministry for Family, Senior
    Citizens, Women and Youth
    (Germany) 124
feminists/feminism 36–7, 170;
    second-wave 61, 113
fertility: decline in rates 45, 47, 49,
    52, *52*, 58, *58*, 69, 105; and
    employment 141, 206, 208
fetus: civil rights of 46, 54
Franco 51, 79, 84, 112
Frederick II of Prussia 71–2, 73
free markets 9, 109, 122, 202, 203,
    208, 213, 214
Fuero del Trabajo (1938) (Spain)
    112

gender category 26
gender employment gap *8*, 10–11,
    13, 17, 41, 199
gender essentialism 25
gender identity 26
gender mainstreaming 121, 124
gender revolution 35
gender wage gap 17, 25, 26, 38, 128,
    129, 136, 149–51, 155–7, *156*,
    197, 205; Australia 114–15, 117,
    126; and class equality policies
    151–5, *153*, 158, 159, 195;
    Germany 109, 125, 156–7; Spain
    113; US 116–17, 128, 149–50; and
    wage compression 150
gendered division of labor *see*
    division of labor, gendered
General Law on Education (1970)
    (Spain) 84
Germany 2; abortion and
    contraception 51, 63–4, *64*; adult
    educational attainment *99*, 100,

101; educational system 73–4, 80,
    210; effects of education,
    partnership and children on
    weekly work hours *145*, 147–9,
    161; employment equality policies
    119–20; gender employment gap
    10–11; hourly wages 152;
    housework 172, 187, 188–9;
    immigration 68, 69; pre-school
    education 81–2; reunification 67;
    secondary education 87, 89, 94;
    universities 98; vocational training
    148; wage inequality and gender
    wage gap 109, 125, 156–7; 154,
    156–7, *156*, 197; welfare costs 121,
    122; *see also* East Germany; West
    Germany
Gershuny, Jonathan 35
GI Bill (US) 96
Gini coefficient 7, *8*, 9
globalization 61
grammar schools 77, 84, 89
Great Depression 108
Grusky, David 25
Gupta, Sanjiv 171

Hartmann, Heidi 3
Harvester Judgement (1907)
    (Australia) 7, 10, 29, 106–7, 108
Head Start (US) 82–3, 210
Heagney, Muriel 114
higher education 95–100, 101 *see also*
    universities
Higher Education Act (2004)
    (Britain) 97
Hobson, Barbara 32, 109
Hochschild, Arlie 35, 48, 170, 178,
    180, 189, 198

Hook, Jennifer L. 170, 196, 211
horizontal segregation 24, 25
household income effect: and
    employment *137*, 138–9, 142
household labor: gendered division
    of *see* division of labor, gendered
housework 1, 168–80, *200–1*, 205–6,
    207–8, 212–13; and couple
    households 180–6, *182–3*, 186;
    and education 175–6, 180, 181,
    182–3, 184–5, 188, *193*, 196–7,
    198; effects of education,
    partnership and parenthood on
    173–6, *174*; and employment *174*,
    175, 186; and fertility intentions
    207; and gendered division of
    labor 9–10, 18, 31–5, *34*, 180–6,
    187–8, 189, 197–8, 205, 205–6,
    208, 212; ISSP study appendix
    190–3, *192–3*; market substitution
    for 39, 171–2, 186–7, 188–9, 206,
    212; and men 170, 189, 207;
    predicting hours spent on 176–80,
    177, 191, *192*
human capital model 17, 18, 21, 22,
    25, 149, 157, 205
Human Fertilisation and
    Embryology Act (1990) (Britain)
    62
human rights 109
Hyde Amendment (1976) (US) 62

immigration/immigrants 4, 15, 46–7,
    58; domestic work and women 37,
    39, 43, 46, 48, 67, 68, 69, 70, 187,
    199; and employment *137*, 141;
    foreign- born populations *68*, 69;
    in the 'new' global economy 67–9;

nineteenth/early twentieth century
    52–4; and post-war economic
    recovery 59–61; and student
    performance 92–3, *93*, 94
Immigration Act (1990) (US) 67
Immigration and Nationality Act
    (1952) (US) 59
Immigration Restriction Act (1901)
    (Australia) 54
income inequality/equality 2, 7–8, *8*,
    9, 23, 152, 202–3; and economic
    growth 203; and education 23,
    103, 152
industrialization 9–10, 23, 27, 28, 31,
    48, 71
insider-outsider distinction 30, 196
Institute of Women's Affairs (Spain)
    120
International Labour Organization
    113–14
International Monetary Fund (IMF)
    55, 61
International Social Survey Program
    (ISSP) 18, 168, 173, 190
'invisible hand' 10, 12
Irish: migration to United States
    53
Italy 199, *201*

Kahn, Lawrence M. 150, 158
Kenworthy, Lane 104, 214
Keynes, John Maynard 55
Kuznets, Simon 202

labor activation policies 48, 66–7,
    106, 123, 127
labor market: and state 27–31
labor market model 22

Labor Party (Australia) 114
labor supply and demand: gender
    differences in 22–7; *see also*
    employment
laissez-faire policy 203
Levi, Margaret 11–12
Lewis, Jane 32
liberal markets 7, 9, 29, 30, 38–9,
    42–3, 151, 172
Liefbroer, Aart 207
life expectancy 45
Lisbon Treaty (2000) 123, 209
Lochner v. New York (1905) 107
Luxembourg Income Study (LIS) 17,
    131, 136, 160–5

Maastricht Treaty (1993) 67
McGlynn, Clare 127
McLanahan, Sarah 38, 209
male breadwinner model 16, 32,
    33, 34, *34*, 36, 55, 70, 86, 112,
    136, 139, 142; challenges to and
    partial erosion of 65, 140, 158,
    181; reinforcement of gendered
    division of paid and unpaid work
    167
Malthus, Thomas 49
Mandel, Hadas 159
Mann, Horace 74
Marcos, Borra 85
market inequalities: inefficiency of
    202–8
market substitution: housework 39,
    171–2, 186–7, 188–9, 206, 212
marriage rates 47, 65, *65*
*Marschall v. Land Nordrhein-
    Westfalen* 119
Marx, Karl 195

maternity leave 33, 55, 57, 127
migrant women: and domestic work
    37, 39, 46, 48, 67, 68, 69, 187, 199;
    see also immigration
Mills, Melinda 207
minimum wage laws 104, 124, 155
modernization theory 42
Mother and Child Care Act (1950)
    (East Germany) 57, 63
Moyano Law (1857) (Spain) 78–9
Muller v. Oregon 107–8

National Action Plan (1999)
    (Britain) 124
National Action Plans (EU) 121
National Child Care Strategy
    (Britain) 84
National Education Act (Britain):
    (1944) 77–8; (1946) 111
National Labor Relations Act (1935)
    (US) 108
Naturalization Act: (1790) 52;
    (1870) 53
Nazis 47, 51
Neumark, David 104
New Deal 108
New Labour 84
nonmarital births 65–6, *66*, 105

Oaxaca, Ronald L. 149
occupational ghettos 25
occupations: gender differences 24
O'Connor, Julia 27
Offences Against the Persons Act
    (1861) 50
oil shocks (1973–4) 61
on-the-job training 3, 22, 26, 109,
    204

Organization for Economic Co-operation and Development (OECD) 113–14
Orloff, Ann Shola 6
Oxford University 77

parental leave 33, 48, 67, 109, 116, 207
Parental Leave Directive (EU) (1996) 127
parenthood: effect of on employment probability 142, 205; effect of on weekly work hours 143, *144–5*, 147, 148, 158, *161*; and housework *174*, 175, 178; and wages *163*
part-time work 17, 24–5, 37, 111, 112, 116, 125, 126, 128, 157
partnership: effect of on employment probability *137*, 138, 141–2, 204–5; effect of on weekly work hours 143, *144–5*, 146–7, 148, 157–8, *161*; and housework *174*, 176, 178, 179, 185, 188; and wages *163*
pensions 103
Personal Responsibility and Work Opportunity Reconciliation Act (1996) (US) 126
Pettit, Becky 196, 211
PISA (Program for International Student Assessment) 89–90, *91*
Poland 199, *201*
Polanyi, Karl 27–8, 195
Polish migrants 69
population policies 3, 14–15, 45–70, 196; and abortion 15, 46, 47, 50–1, 61–4, *64*; and birth control 15, 46, 47, 49–51; family policies 40, 42, 55–8, *56*; and immigration 4, 15, 46–7, 52–4, 58, 59–61, 67–9; institutionalization of gender and ethnic hierarchies 46–7; reproductive policies 48–52, 61–7
post-industrial economies: gender-class equality in 36–42
post-secondary education 95–100, 101 *see also* universities
Potsdam Agreement (1945) 60
poverty 19, 209 *see also* child poverty
pregnancy: categorization as an employment-related disability in US 116
Pregnancy Discrimination Act (1978) (US) 116
Pregnancy and Maternity Leave Directive (EU) (1992) 127
preschool education 16, 80–7, 102, 204, 210, 211
private child care 85–6, *86*, 102
private schooling 77, 89, *90*
Program for International Student Assessment *see* PISA

Quota Law (1921) (US) 53

racial differences: and US secondary education 88–9; and Australian Compulsory Schooling 76
rational choice models 14
reproductive policies: in 'new' global economy 61–7; in nineteenth/early twentieth century 48–52; *see also* abortion; birth control
Rivera, General Primo de 79
Robbins Report (1963) (England) 89
Roe v. Wade (1973) (US) 62

Rome, Treaty of (1957) 12, 84, 117
rural-urban divide: and education 83,
90–1, *92*, 101

Schröder, Chancellor Gerhard 98
Second Act on Equality for Men and
  Women (1994) (Germany) 119
'second shift' 178, 189, 198
secondary education 87–95, 101;
  enrolment ratios *88*; gender and
  student performance *93*, 94;
  immigrants and student
  performance 92–3, *93*; public-
  private division 89, *90*; rural-urban
  divide and student performance
  90–1, *92*
Semyonov, Moshe 158, 159
service sector: shift from
  manufacturing to 22, 37
Servicemen's Readjustment Act
  (1944) (US) 96
sex discrimination 119
Sex Discrimination Act (1975)
  (Britain) 118
single European market 67
single-parent households 47, 66, 123,
  126–7, 208
Skocpol, Theda 6
Smith, Adam 10, 23
Smith, Alison 179
social investment strategies 19,
  208–12, 212, 214, 215
social work 37
socialist states 16, 28–9
Soviet Union 67, 109
Spain 3, 6, 33, 35; abortion 50–1, 63,
  64, *64*; adult educational
  attainment 99–100, *99*, 101; black

market 41, 112; Constitution
  (1978) 120; educational system
  78–9, 80; effects of education,
  partnership and children on
  employment probability 134, *135*,
  136, 137, *137*, 138, 140–1; effects
  of education, partnership and
  children on weekly work hours
  143–4, *144*, 149, 158, *161*;
  employment equality policies 105,
  112–13, 120; family policies 56–7,
  56, 58; gender employment gap *8*,
  11; gender-class equalities 41–2;
  hourly wages 150, 151, *151*, *164*,
  165; housework and gendered
  division of unpaid labor 174, *174*,
  175–6, *177*, 179, *183*, 184–5, 188;
  insider-outsider divides 113, 152;
  preschool education 84–5, 86, 102;
  secondary education 87, 88, 89,
  94; student performance 90–1, *91*;
  universities 97, 98, 99; wage
  inequality and gender wage gap 9,
  113, 152, 154, 155–6, *156*, 159,
  197; work-family reconciliation
  policies 125
state: and gendered division of
  household labor 31–5; and
  institutional equality frames 5–7;
  and labour market 27–31
state-market nexus 103
statistical discrimination 26
sterilization: and Nazis 51
Stopes, Marie 50
sustainable policy 195–215
Sweden *200*, 202

tax credits 55, 124

taxation 214
Teachers Federation of New South
    Wales 114
Teaching and Higher Education Act
    (1988) (Britain) 97
technology: growth in 22
Temporary Assistance for Needy
    Families (TANF) (US) 126
temporary contracts 120
Thatcher, Margaret 84, 118
Thomas, Duncan 210
time allocation model 3, 160, 169,
    171, 181, 189, 193, 196, 205; *see
    also* time availability model
time availability model 168, 171,
    173, 176, 180, 186, 187
time poverty 18, 19, 41, 172, 181,
    189, 198
trade unions 106–7; Australia 12, 40,
    127; Britain 106
Tronto, Joan 45
tuition fees 97–8

UK *see* Britain
Unabhaengiger Frauenverband 82
unemployment 105, 120, 139
United States 6, 7, 29, 34, 35;
    abortion and contraception 50,
    62–3, 64, *64*; adult educational
    attainment *99*, 100, 102; blacks
    and employment *137*, 141;
    educational system 74–5, 80,
    210–11; effects of education,
    partnership and children on
    employment probability 133–4,
    135, *137*, 138, 139, 140, 141;
    effects of education, partnership
    and children on weekly work

hours 143, *144*, 158; employment
    equality policies 114, 115–17;
    family policies 55–6, *56*, 58;
    fertility rates 206; gender-class
    equalities 39; hourly wages 150,
    151, *151*, *163*, *164*; housework and
    gendered division of unpaid labor
    174, 175, *177*, 178, *182*,185, 187;
    immigration 52–3, 59, 67–8;
    preschool education 82–3, 102;
    racial disparities in education
    88–9; secondary education 87,
    88–9, *88*, 89, 94; student
    performance 91, *91*;universities
    and colleges 95–7, 98, 101; wage
    inequality and gender wage gap 7,
    8, 116–17, 128, 149–50, 154;
    welfare costs 121, *122*; work-
    family reconciliation policies
    126–7; worker mobilization and
    trade unions 104, 106
United Steelworkers Union (US) 115
university degree, having a 197;
    effect on employment probability
    136–7, *137*, 142, 157, 173, 197,
    204; effect on hourly wages 152,
    153, 154, *163–5*; effect on weekly
    work hours 143, *144–5*, 146,
    147–8, 157, 160–1, *161*, 173; and
    housework 173, *174*, 175, 178,
    180, 181, *182–3*, 185
university education 77, 95–9, 101
unpaid time: policy and sustainable
    212–15
unpaid work 2, 9, 167–93;
    components of 3; gendered
    division of 1, 3, 9–10, 14–15,
    167–8, 170, 180–6, 187–8, 189,

197–8, 205–6, 208, 212; shifting of to public sphere 36; state and gendered division of 31–5, *34*; *see also* housework
urbanization 48

vertical segregation 24, 25
vocational training 30, 90
voting 32

wage compression 150
wage inequalities/equality 7–8, *8*, 38, 103, 104, 149–57, 197
wages 18, 162–3, *163–5*; average hourly 150–2, *151*; and education 23, 103, 152, *163*; LIS technical appendix 162–3, *163–4*; and university degrees 152, *153*, 154, *163–5*; *see also* gender wage gap
Wallerstein, Immanuel 61
Wedderburn, Dorothy 195
weekly work hours *see* work hours, weekly
welfare costs 121, *122*
welfare state 37, 212
West Germany 3, 34–5; abortion 63, *64*; effect of education, partnership and children on employment probability 134, *135*, 136, 137–8, *137*, 139, 140, 141, 142; effect of education, partnership and children on weekly work hours *145*, 147–8, 158, *161*; employment equality policies 105, 110–11, 113, 119; family policies *56*, 57, 58; gender employment gap *8*, 10; gender- class equalities 41; hourly wages 150, 151, *151*, *164*, *165*;

housework and gendered division of labor 172, *174*, 175, *177*, 179, *183*, 184, 207–8; immigration 60; male breadwinner model 33; preschool education 81–2, 86, 87, 102; secondary education 89; universities 97, 98; vocational training 95; wage inequality 156–7, *156*, 159; work-family reconciliation policies 124–5
Wilensky, Harold 28, 29, 80, 98
Williams, Donald R. 179
women's groups 28
Women's Rights Act (1950) (East Germany) 57, 63
work experience 3, 22, 23, 25, 26, 32, 33, 38, 104, 131, 136, 142, 149, 157, 163, 196, 204
work-family balance 106, 213
work-family reconciliation policies 19, 48, 67, 121–7
work hours, weekly 17–18, 142–9, 160–1, *161–2*; effect of education on 143–4, *144–5*, 145–6, 147–9, 157, 160–1, *161*, 197; effect of parenthood on 143, *144–5*, 147, 148, 158, *161*; effect of partnership on 143, *144–5*, 146–7, 148, 157–8, *161*; LIS technical appendix 160–1, *161–2*
worker mobilization 104; Australian vs US nineteenth century 106–9; *see also* trade unions
Workers' Statute (1980) (Spain) 120
Workplace Relations Act (1996) (Australia) 125
World Bank 61
World War II 12, 54